Arve Hansen

URBAN PROTEST

A Spatial Perspective on Kyiv, Minsk, and Moscow

With a foreword by Julie Wilhelmsen

Bibliografische Information der Deutschen Nationalbibliothek
Die Deutsche Nationalbibliothek verzeichnet diese Publikation in der Deutschen Nationalbibliografie; detaillierte bibliografische Daten sind im Internet über http://dnb.d-nb.de abrufbar.

Bibliographic information published by the Deutsche Nationalbibliothek
Die Deutsche Nationalbibliothek lists this publication in the Deutsche Nationalbibliografie; detailed bibliographic data are available in the Internet at http://dnb.d-nb.de.

Cover image: ID 36146045 © Sergiy Palamarchuk | Dreamstime.com

ISBN-13: 978-3-8382-1495-5
© *ibidem*-Verlag, Stuttgart 2021
Alle Rechte vorbehalten

Das Werk einschließlich aller seiner Teile ist urheberrechtlich geschützt. Jede Verwertung außerhalb der engen Grenzen des Urheberrechtsgesetzes ist ohne Zustimmung des Verlages unzulässig und strafbar. Dies gilt insbesondere für Vervielfältigungen, Übersetzungen, Mikroverfilmungen und elektronische Speicherformen sowie die Einspeicherung und Verarbeitung in elektronischen Systemen.

All rights reserved. No part of this publication may be reproduced, stored in or introduced into a retrieval system, or transmitted, in any form, or by any means (electronical, mechanical, photocopying, recording or otherwise) without the prior written permission of the publisher. Any person who does any unauthorized act in relation to this publication may be liable to criminal prosecution and civil claims for damages.

Printed in the EU

Soviet and Post-Soviet Politics and Society (SPPS) Vol. 234
ISSN 1614-3515

General Editor: Andreas Umland,
Swedish Institute of International Affairs, umland@stanfordalumni.org

Commissioning Editor: Max Jakob Horstmann,
London, mjh@ibidem.eu

EDITORIAL COMMITTEE*

DOMESTIC & COMPARATIVE POLITICS
Prof. **Ellen Bos**, *Andrássy University of Budapest*
Dr. **Gergana Dimova**, *University of Winchester*
Dr. **Andrey Kazantsev**, *MGIMO (U) MID RF, Moscow*
Prof. **Heiko Pleines**, *University of Bremen*
Prof. **Richard Sakwa**, *University of Kent at Canterbury*
Dr. **Sarah Whitmore**, *Oxford Brookes University*
Dr. **Harald Wydra**, *University of Cambridge*

SOCIETY, CLASS & ETHNICITY
Col. **David Glantz**, *"Journal of Slavic Military Studies"*
Dr. **Marlène Laruelle**, *George Washington University*
Dr. **Stephen Shulman**, *Southern Illinois University*
Prof. **Stefan Troebst**, *University of Leipzig*

POLITICAL ECONOMY & PUBLIC POLICY
Dr. **Andreas Goldthau**, *Central European University*
Dr. **Robert Kravchuk**, *University of North Carolina*
Dr. **David Lane**, *University of Cambridge*
Dr. **Carol Leonard**, *Higher School of Economics, Moscow*
Dr. **Maria Popova**, *McGill University, Montreal*

FOREIGN POLICY & INTERNATIONAL AFFAIRS
Dr. **Peter Duncan**, *University College London*
Prof. **Andreas Heinemann-Grüder**, *University of Bonn*
Prof. **Gerhard Mangott**, *University of Innsbruck*
Dr. **Diana Schmidt-Pfister**, *University of Konstanz*
Dr. **Lisbeth Tarlow**, *Harvard University, Cambridge*
Dr. **Christian Wipperfürth**, *N-Ost Network, Berlin*
Dr. **William Zimmerman**, *University of Michigan*

HISTORY, CULTURE & THOUGHT
Dr. **Catherine Andreyev**, *University of Oxford*
Prof. **Mark Bassin**, *Södertörn University*
Prof. **Karsten Brüggemann**, *Tallinn University*
Dr. **Alexander Etkind**, *University of Cambridge*
Dr. **Gasan Gusejnov**, *Moscow State University*
Prof. **Leonid Luks**, *Catholic University of Eichstaett*
Dr. **Olga Malinova**, *Russian Academy of Sciences*
Dr. **Richard Mole**, *University College London*
Prof. **Andrei Rogatchevski**, *University of Tromsø*
Dr. **Mark Tauger**, *West Virginia University*

ADVISORY BOARD*

Prof. **Dominique Arel**, *University of Ottawa*
Prof. **Jörg Baberowski**, *Humboldt University of Berlin*
Prof. **Margarita Balmaceda**, *Seton Hall University*
Dr. **John Barber**, *University of Cambridge*
Prof. **Timm Beichelt**, *European University Viadrina*
Dr. **Katrin Boeckh**, *University of Munich*
Prof. em. **Archie Brown**, *University of Oxford*
Dr. **Vyacheslav Bryukhovetsky**, *Kyiv-Mohyla Academy*
Prof. **Timothy Colton**, *Harvard University, Cambridge*
Prof. **Paul D'Anieri**, *University of Florida*
Dr. **Heike Dörrenbächer**, *Friedrich Naumann Foundation*
Dr. **John Dunlop**, *Hoover Institution, Stanford, California*
Dr. **Sabine Fischer**, *SWP, Berlin*
Dr. **Geir Flikke**, *NUPI, Oslo*
Prof. **David Galbreath**, *University of Aberdeen*
Prof. **Alexander Galkin**, *Russian Academy of Sciences*
Prof. **Frank Golczewski**, *University of Hamburg*
Dr. **Nikolas Gvosdev**, *Naval War College, Newport, RI*
Prof. **Mark von Hagen**, *Arizona State University*
Dr. **Guido Hausmann**, *University of Munich*
Prof. **Dale Herspring**, *Kansas State University*
Dr. **Stefani Hoffman**, *Hebrew University of Jerusalem*
Prof. **Mikhail Ilyin**, *MGIMO (U) MID RF, Moscow*
Prof. **Vladimir Kantor**, *Higher School of Economics*
Dr. **Ivan Katchanovski**, *University of Ottawa*
Prof. em. **Andrzej Korbonski**, *University of California*
Dr. **Iris Kempe**, *"Caucasus Analytical Digest"*
Prof. **Herbert Küpper**, *Institut für Ostrecht Regensburg*
Dr. **Rainer Lindner**, *CEEER, Berlin*
Dr. **Vladimir Malakhov**, *Russian Academy of Sciences*

Dr. **Luke March**, *University of Edinburgh*
Prof. **Michael McFaul**, *Stanford University, Palo Alto*
Prof. **Birgit Menzel**, *University of Mainz-Germersheim*
Prof. **Valery Mikhailenko**, *The Urals State University*
Prof. **Emil Pain**, *Higher School of Economics, Moscow*
Dr. **Oleg Podvintsev**, *Russian Academy of Sciences*
Prof. **Olga Popova**, *St. Petersburg State University*
Dr. **Alex Pravda**, *University of Oxford*
Dr. **Erik van Ree**, *University of Amsterdam*
Dr. **Joachim Rogall**, *Robert Bosch Foundation Stuttgart*
Prof. **Peter Rutland**, *Wesleyan University, Middletown*
Prof. **Marat Salikov**, *The Urals State Law Academy*
Dr. **Gwendolyn Sasse**, *University of Oxford*
Prof. **Jutta Scherrer**, *EHESS, Paris*
Prof. **Robert Service**, *University of Oxford*
Mr. **James Sherr**, *RIIA Chatham House London*
Dr. **Oxana Shevel**, *Tufts University, Medford*
Prof. **Eberhard Schneider**, *University of Siegen*
Prof. **Olexander Shnyrkov**, *Shevchenko University, Kyiv*
Prof. **Hans-Henning Schröder**, *SWP, Berlin*
Prof. **Yuri Shapoval**, *Ukrainian Academy of Sciences*
Prof. **Viktor Shnirelman**, *Russian Academy of Sciences*
Dr. **Lisa Sundstrom**, *University of British Columbia*
Dr. **Philip Walters**, *"Religion, State and Society"*, *Oxford*
Prof. **Zenon Wasyliw**, *Ithaca College, New York State*
Dr. **Lucan Way**, *University of Toronto*
Dr. **Markus Wehner**, *"Frankfurter Allgemeine Zeitung"*
Dr. **Andrew Wilson**, *University College London*
Prof. **Jan Zielonka**, *University of Oxford*
Prof. **Andrei Zorin**, *University of Oxford*

* While the Editorial Committee and Advisory Board support the General Editor in the choice and improvement of manuscripts for publication, responsibility for remaining errors and misinterpretations in the series' volumes lies with the books' authors.

Soviet and Post-Soviet Politics and Society (SPPS)
ISSN 1614-3515

Founded in 2004 and refereed since 2007, SPPS makes available affordable English-, German-, and Russian-language studies on the history of the countries of the former Soviet bloc from the late Tsarist period to today. It publishes between 5 and 20 volumes per year and focuses on issues in transitions to and from democracy such as economic crisis, identity formation, civil society development, and constitutional reform in CEE and the NIS. SPPS also aims to highlight so far understudied themes in East European studies such as right-wing radicalism, religious life, higher education, or human rights protection. The authors and titles of all previously published volumes are listed at the end of this book. For a full description of the series and reviews of its books, see www.ibidem-verlag.de/red/spps.

Editorial correspondence & manuscripts should be sent to: Dr. Andreas Umland, Department of Political Science, Kyiv-Mohyla Academy, vul. Voloska 8/5, UA-04070 Kyiv, UKRAINE; andreas.umland@cantab.net

Business correspondence & review copy requests should be sent to: *ibidem* Press, Leuschnerstr. 40, 30457 Hannover, Germany; tel.: +49 511 2622200; fax: +49 511 2622201; spps@ibidem.eu.

Authors, reviewers, referees, and editors for (as well as all other persons sympathetic to) SPPS are invited to join its networks at www.facebook.com/group.php?gid=52638198614 www.linkedin.com/groups?about=&gid=103012 www.xing.com/net/spps-ibidem-verlag/

Recent Volumes

225 David Mandel
"Optimizing" Higher Education in Russia
University Teachers and Their Union "Universitetskaya solidarnost'"
ISBN 978-3-8382-1519-8

226 Daria Isachenko, Mykhailo Minakov, Gwendolyn Sasse (Eds.)
Post-Soviet Secessionism
Nation-Building and State-Failure after Communism
ISBN 978-3-8382-1538-9

227 Jakob Hauter (Ed.)
Civil War? Interstate War? Hybrid War?
Dimensions and Interpretations of the Donbas Conflict in 2014–2020
With a foreword by Andrew Wilson
ISBN 978-3-8382-1383-5

228 Tima T. Moldogaziev, Gene A. Brewer, J. Edward Kellough, (Eds.)
Public Policy and Politics in Georgia
Lessons from Post-Soviet Transition
ISBN 978-3-8382-1535-8

229 Oxana Schmies (Ed.)
NATO's Enlargement and Russia
A Strategic Challenge in the Past and Future
With a foreword by Vladimir Kara-Murza
ISBN 978-3-8382-1478-8

230 Christopher Ford
UKAPISME—Une Gauche Perude
Le marxisme anti-colonial dans la révolution ukrainienne 1917 - 1925
Avec une preface de Vincent Présumey
ISBN 978-3-8382-0899-2

231 Anna Kutkina
Between Lenin and Bandera
Decommunization and Multivocality in Post-Euromaidan Ukraine
With a foreword by Juri Mykkänen
ISBN 978-3-8382-1506-8

232 Lincoln E. Flake
Defending the Faith
The Russian Orthodox Church and the Demise of Religious Pluralism
With a foreword by Peter Martland
ISBN 978-3-8382-1378-1

233 Nikoloz Samkharadze
Russia's Recognition of the Independence of Abkhazia and South Ossetia
Analysis of a Deviant Case in Moscow's Foreign Policy Behavior
With a foreword by Neil MacFarlane
ISBN 978-3-8382-1414-6

Contents

Figures 11
Abbreviations 13
A Note on Language 15

Foreword by *Julie Wilhelmsen* 17
Preface 19

1 Starting Point 25

Part I

2 Space in Context 31
    2.1   Complexities of Urban Contention 34
           2.1.1   Form 34
           2.1.2   Motivation 35
           2.1.3   Waves 36
    2.2   Ukraine, Belarus, and Russia 40
    2.3   Relevance 43

3 Mapping the Field 45
    3.1   Protests 45
           3.1.1   Repertoires 47
           3.1.2   Nonviolent Contention 50
           3.1.3   Colour Revolutions 52
           3.1.4   Non-spatial Factors 59
    3.2   Space 60
           3.2.1   Public Space 61

	3.2.2	Physical Space 65
	3.2.3	Contested Spaces 69
3.3	The Gap 71

4 Definitions and Research Questions 75
4.1 What Is a Mass Protest? 75
4.2 What Is Urban Public Space? 77
4.3 Research Questions 79

5 Theorising and Development 81
5.1 Approaches to Theorising 81
    5.1.1 Field Work 84
    5.1.2 Respondents 88
    5.1.3 Mapping 92
5.2 Ethical Considerations 93
    5.2.1 Interview Ethics 94
    5.2.2 Practical Utility 96
5.3 Geographical Determinism 97
5.4 Conception 98
    5.4.1 M.A. Thesis 99
    5.4.2 PhD Proposal 100
5.5 Theorising 101
    5.5.1 Prestudy 101
    5.5.2 Formulating a Theory 103
    5.5.3 Transitional Study 104
5.6 Causal Chains 107
5.7 Main Study 110
5.8 Post-test Theorising 112

6 Variables and Methodology 113
6.1 Independent Variables 113
6.1.1 Perceived Elements 114
6.1.2 Physical Elements 116
6.1.3 Social Elements 118
6.2 Intermediary Variables 120
6.2.1 Spatial Qualities 120
6.2.2 The Political Environment 123
6.3 Dependent Variables 124
6.3.1 Emergence 124
6.3.2 Realisation 125
6.3.3 Impact 125

Part II

7 Prestudy 129
7.1 Physical Space 133
7.1.1 Spatial and Urban History 134
7.1.2 Daily Use 141
7.1.3 Protest Space 142
7.2 Symbolic Value 144
7.2.1 25 Years of Protest 145
7.3 Function 149
7.4 Conclusions 152

8 Transitional Study 155
8.1 A Spatial Perspective 157
8.2 Belarusian Protests from Glasnost' to Lukashenka 160
8.3 Perceived elements 164
8.3.1 October Square 168

		8.3.2	Independence Square..170
	8.4	Social Elements 174	
		8.4.1	The Political Centre 174
		8.4.2	The People's Centre 176
		8.4.3	Independence Square..177
		8.4.4	October Square 178
	8.5	Physical Elements 180	
		8.5.1	October Square and Ploshcha 2006 180
		8.5.2	Independence Square and Ploshcha 2010....................184
	8.6	Conclusions..187	

9 Main Study...189			
	9.1	Towards a Spatial Perspective..193	
		9.1.1	Spatial Elements 195
		9.1.2	Spatial Qualities and the Political Environment........196
		9.1.3	Protest Areas 199
	9.2	Moscow, Swamp Square and *the March of Millions*.................201	
		9.2.1	The Political Environment of Moscow 204
		9.2.2	Public Spaces in Moscow 206
		9.2.3	The Elements 208
		9.2.4	Spatial Qualities 214
		9.2.5	Emergence, Realization, Impact................................218
	9.3	Conclusions..222	

Part III

10 To Paris and Beyond 227		
	10.1 Republic Square and the Yellow Vests 229	
		10.1.1 Applying the Model..230
	10.2 Summary and Conclusions 239	

    10.2.1 "So what?" 241

    10.2.2 Limitations 243

  10.3 Moving On 244

References 247

Index 271

Figures

1	Post-electoral protest, Minsk, August 2020	23
2	Maidan, Kyiv, February 2014a	26
3	Maidan, Kyiv, December 2013	29
4	Althing, Iceland	34
5	Notable protests and colour revolutions	39
6	The Slavic Triangle (map)	41
7	Micro, meso, and macro factors	60
8	The political environment	60
9	Swedberg's basic rules	82
10	Great Assembly Square, Chișinău, August 2016	86
11	Elements of the city, first version	104
12	Causality diagram, second version	110
13	Methodology	113
14	Elements of the city, second version	114
15	Maidan, Kyiv, January 2014	122
16	Tverskaia Street, Moscow, June 2017	127
17	Maidan, Kyiv, August 2016	131
18	Maidan and the surrounding area (map)	136
19	The Independence Monument, Kyiv, May 2019	138
20	Kyiv within the Ring Road (map)	140
21	Maidan, Kyiv, November 2013	144
22	Maidan, Kyiv, March 2014	149
23	Maidan, Kyiv, February 2014b	154

24	Elements of the city, first version	159
25	The Belarusian Great Patriotic War Museum	164
26	Minsk City Centre (map)	167
27	The Palace of the Republic, Minsk	169
28	Independence Square, Minsk	171
29	The Red Church, Minsk	173
30	October Square, Minsk (map)	181
31	The Wall on Aliaksandrawski, Minsk	182
32	Independence Square, Minsk (map)	184
33	House of Government, Minsk	187
34	Causality diagram, first version	195
35	Elements of the city, second version	196
36	Public spaces in Moscow (map)	207
37	Swamp Square, Moscow (map)	209
38	Swamp Square, Moscow, June 2017a	210
39	Swamp Square, Moscow, 2017b	216
40	Swamp Square Road, Moscow, June 2017	218
41	March of Millions, Agreed upon rally (map)	221
42	Actual rally (map)	221
43	Khreshchatyk Avenue, Kyiv, November 2013	225
44	Republic Square, Paris (map)	233
45	The pink van, Paris	235
46	Yellow Vests, Paris	245

Abbreviations

CAT	Collective Action Theory
DOC	Dynamics Of Contention
NESH	National Committee for Research Ethics in the Social Sciences and the Humanities (Norway)
OWS	Occupy Wall Street
POS	Political Opportunity Structure theory
PRT	Prospect-Refuge Theory
PT	Process Tracing
RCT	Rational Choice Theory
RMP	Resource Mobilisation Perspective
ROC	Repertoire Of Contention
RSCPR	Russian Space: Concepts, Practices, Representations
SCM	Structure-Cognitive Model

A Note on Language

This book describes events, people, and places mainly from three Eastern Slavic countries: Ukraine, Belarus, and Russia. Each of these countries uses the Cyrillic script and has its own national language, as well as linguistic variations encompassing proper nouns: yet, for historical reasons, Russian has become the lingua franca of the region. The long history of Russian hegemony and long periods of russification have also led to the widespread international adoption of Russian forms for Ukrainian and Belarusian proper nouns. For these reasons, the Ukrainian capital is usually known as *Kiev* (from Rus. *Киев*), rather than *Kyiv* (from Ukr. *Київ*). Likewise, the Belarusian president is known as *Lukashenko* (Rus.: *Лукашенко*), not *Lukashenka* (Bel.: *Лукашенка*); while the conflict region in Eastern Ukraine is known as *Donbass* (Russian: *Донбасс*), not *Donbas* (Ukrainian: *Донбас*). Conversely, some proper nouns are known by their national variants, as is the case with the current Ukrainian president Volodymyr Zelenskyi (Ukr.: *Володимир Зеленський*), not *Vladimir Zelenskii* (Rus.: *Владимир Зеленский*), and *Hrodna* for the town in Western Belarus (Bel.: *Гродна*), rather than *Grodno* (Rus.: *Гродно*).

Scholars are often advised to use the transliterations most predominant in English, as these are most recognisable to the majority of readers. Yet such a language policy often leads to inconsistencies, and readers asking why some proper nouns are based on the Russian forms while others are not. As far as I can see, there are only two solutions to this problem. Either the scholar consistently and exclusively transliterates from the relevant Russian forms; or, conversely, they transliterate all proper nouns from the local languages. The former solution is often used because it is more consistent with the predominant name forms in English. (Another reason might be that most scholars within the field have a level of proficiency in Russian, but limited knowledge of the other two languages). The choice of Russian could additionally be justified by the large prevalence of Russophone speakers in all three countries. Although there is a precedent for the former solution in East Slavic area studies, the latter is not unheard-of, and scholars such as the Canadian historian David R. Marples (2004) and the British political scientist Taras Kuzio (2005) use the national variants of proper nouns.

I have chosen the latter option. Thus, the transliterations of proper nouns found in this book reflect their national origins. The reader will also encounter proper nouns that are less frequently used, such as *Kyiv* and *Lukashenka* (rather than *Kiev* and *Lukashenko*). However, I have retained the familiar variants of some terms and proper nouns in order to avoid confusion (e.g. *Kievan Rus'*, not *Kievskaia Rus'* from Rus. *Киевская Русь*; or *Kyivs'ka Rus'* from Ukr. *Київська Русь*).

I have used the ALA-LC Romanisation tables from The Library of Congress for all Ukrainian, Belarusian, and Russian words, with some exceptions. I have avoided confusing typographic ligatures and diacritical marks, such as *i͡e* for the Russian *е*; and *ï* for the Ukrainian *ї*. Similarly, I have kept some internationally recognised variants that are too omnipresent to change: for example, the former Russian president is *Boris Yeltsin* rather than *Ieltsin* (or, with ligatures, *IEltsin*).

To complicate the matter further, in Belarus, there are three written languages: Russian and Belarusian, both of which are official languages, and the classic Belarusian Tarashkevitsa. The name of the president could be transliterated as *Aleksandr Lukashenko* (Russian); *Aliaksandr Lukashenka* (Belarusian); and *Aliaksandar Lukashenka* (Belarusian Tarashkevitsa). I use the official Belarusian (*Aliaksandr*) for proper nouns. Please note that the Belarusian letter *ў* is transliterated as *w*, not *u*.

For consistency's sake, I use the translated forms of place names in this book (i.e. October Square, not *Kastrychnitskaia*). A notable exception is Maidan (Ukr.: *square*), which is used both instead of the longer original (*Maidan Nezalezhnosti*) and the translation (Independence Square), the reason being that Maidan has become a widely recognised word in the West, even among non-Slavists.

All translations are my own unless stated otherwise.

Foreword

What impact does the physical space in which protesters raise their grievances have on their success or failure in achieving their goals? This is the intriguing question that Arve Hansen raises, and to which this book provides a theoretically, methodologically, and empirically sophisticated answer. It elaborates a theoretical model to explore the causal connections between urban public space and mass protests. As such, it is not only a valuable but also a major contribution to the growing research on mass protests and urban space.

This book also presents and analyses three of the most acute cases of urban protest today, namely those of Kyiv, Minsk, and Moscow. The combination of thematic focus and empirical case studies can, therefore, hardly be more timely. A wave of protest movements is rolling across what we refer to as the 'former Soviet space'. Judging by recent events, it is not going to stop any time soon; even in Russia, where enormous and costly efforts have been made to create 'stability' under President Putin. The intense, at times highly simplistic public debate around these events makes this distinctly scholarly contribution particularly welcome. The book gives us details and specifics about the very different social and physical spaces of Kyiv, Minsk, and Moscow, despite their common Soviet heritage.

This analysis is built on the results of the author's extensive field work: interviews as well as personal observations, all based in Hansen's thorough knowledge of all three East Slavic languages and cultures and his experience of living in Belarus, Russia, and Ukraine. Careful attention is paid to the history and symbolic value of the urban spaces under analysis. The meticulous circuit of observing, noting, mapping, and interviewing is particularly commendable, resulting as it does in clear visual and textual presentations of the protest spaces in Kyiv, Minsk, and Moscow.

Hansen's approach to the theoretical debate on protest, and the core terms within it, is also nuanced and attentive to detail. He crafts his definitions of *mass protest* and *urban public space*, as well as his theoretical model, using the cases at hand and in close consultation with the extant literature. The outcome is an excellent piece of academic handiwork. The process of developing the theoretical model over time, guided by empirical findings in the individual case studies, is presented clearly and well. Reading this book will prove highly instructive for students who wish to learn how to combine in-depth empirical work with theory development.

Examining the theoretical debate on protest, Hansen identifies a lack of attention in the literature to the connection between space and protest. Rightly pointing out the dangers of geographical determinism, he sets himself the ambitious aim of providing the systematic and generalised approach to space and protest that is missing. A comprehensive explanation of urban protest will have to include a wider set of social variables beyond those investigated in this book, which is clearly part of a broader, evolving research agenda under development. However, by the end of the book, Hansen has convincingly demonstrated the importance of geographical space and how it contributes to the emergence, realisation, and impact of protests. The spatial perspective also promises a fruitful application to cases beyond the former Soviet space.

Julie Wilhelmsen
Senior Research Fellow
Norwegian Institute of International Affairs

Preface

This book is based on my doctoral thesis, *Mass Protests from a Spatial Perspective: Discontent and Urban Public Space in Kyiv, Minsk, and Moscow* (Hansen 2020), which I defended and published in March 2020 at UiT: the Arctic University of Norway.

The question that spurred me to write my thesis—and, subsequently, this book—was how mass protests are affected by urban public space.

Based on field work in Eastern Europe spanning several years and interviews with demonstrators, protest organisers, and observers, I gradually developed an approach to assess the enabling and constraining effects of urban public spaces on public protest. I call this model *the spatial perspective on mass protests*; or *the spatial perspective*, for short.

The model was tested and refined by looking closely at three case studies, each of which served as the basis for an academic article. These case studies investigate protest spaces in three different cities—Kyiv, Minsk, and Moscow—and reflect three stages in the development of the spatial perspective. My thesis originally consisted of the three articles mentioned here, framed by seven introductory chapters.

The main difference between the thesis and the book you are now reading is that the three articles have here been integrated as chapters in their own right, for improved readability.

In addition, feedback from the doctoral committee has been incorporated where required, and some additional minor tweaks have been made to the case studies. However, the arguments and structure of the original articles have been kept largely unchanged. The main advantage of this approach is that it more clearly shows how the spatial perspective was developed.

One possible drawback of keeping the article-based chapters intact is that it has prevented me from updating some key information: The president of Ukraine, for instance, is no longer Petro Poroshenko, as stated in the first case study from 2016. The opposition in Minsk of 2020 is no longer coloured by its geopolitical views to the extent it was at the time of publishing the second case study in 2017. And Moscow, described in the third case study from 2019, is no longer as cluttered by fences and building projects as it was when I conducted field work in the city.

The purpose of these chapters is not, however, to describe current events—such information may be found elsewhere—but to illuminate the importance of urban protest, and to help researchers across a range of academic disciplines to understand this largely neglected element of societal contention. I believe the minor issues I have mentioned here will not distract the reader from the main subject and message of the book. In any case, it is necessary to summarise in brief the key events that have taken place since I wrote my original thesis.

Since the publication of *Mass Protests from a Spatial Perspective*, several important things have happened in the post-Soviet part of the world, demonstrating that a spatial perspective is relevant and important for our understanding of protest.

In the far eastern region of Russia, Khabarovsk Krai, for example, thousands of people have regularly gathered on Lenin Square since July 2020 to demonstrate against the Russian regime and the imprisonment of former governor Sergei Frugal (Flikke 2020, 16–18). The contestation between demonstrators and police over who controls Lenin Square shows that this particular space is symbolically important, at least for the parties involved.

Lenin Square has also contributed to producing powerful imagery for the national and regional opposition. A movement against the Russian leadership, able to fill one of the largest urban squares in Russia with people (the square's size is second only to Red Square in Moscow), has the potential to reduce Kremlin influence over the Far East.

The protests have now spread from Khabarovsk to other Siberian cities, including Novosibirsk, Irkutsk, Krasnoyarsk, Vladivostok, and Omsk (Gladkikh and Ievstafieva 2020; Taiga.info 2020), and there have even been demonstrations of support for the Siberian dissenters in St. Petersburg and Moscow (BBC Russian Service 2020a). Increasingly, the authorities have begun resorting to violence in order to supress the movement (BBC Russian Service 2020b), but the protesters show few signs of stopping.

Another mass movement for change is currently underway in Belarus, on the borderland between Russia and the EU. Here, a wave of urban contention has struck every major city and most towns across the republic, beginning well before the presidential elections of 9 August 2020. Angered by election fraud and spurred on by the relentless brutality of government agencies, hundreds of thousands of Belarusians have aimed at—and in many cases succeeded in—occupying and appropriating urban spaces that have long been associated with President Aliaksandr Lukashenka. This has happened in spite of presidential control over a powerful army of law enforcement agencies, ready to use violence to suppress dissent.

In the capital, Minsk, protesters are marking "their" territories with the white-red-white flag of the opposition and tying ribbons wherever they can. An open space on Charviakova Street, outside the city centre, has even been turned into the Square of Changes (Bel.: *Ploshcha peramen*), complete with opposition flags, a mural to "the DJs of change", and regular evening concerts (Boguslavskaia 2020). The struggle over the Belarusian presidency is an urban conflict in more than one sense.

Finally, in Kyrgyzstan, mass protests erupted on Ala-Too Square in the capital Bishkek in early October 2020, triggered by fraudulent parliamentary elections (Pikulicka-Wilczewska 2020). Here, too, the protesters' choice of square was no coincidence. Two previous revolutions began on Ala-Too Square, and it seems likely that the protests of October 2020 will result in a third Kyrgyz Revolution in the space of little over 15 years.

These three events show how social and political protests continue to utilise and interact with urban public space and its possibilities. The spatial perspective presented in this book offers an additional dimension for understanding their complex dynamics.

I would like to thank the many people who have read and commented on this project during its development, especially my examiners Julie Wilhelmsen, Andrii Portnov, and Bjarge Schwenke Fors and my two closest colleagues at UiT, Yngvar Steinholt and Andrei Rogatchevski.

Thanks are also due to Kirsty Jane Falconer for her thorough language editing, Valerie Lange and Jana Dävers at *ibidem* Press, and to the Soviet and Post-Soviet Politics and Society series editor Andreas Umland.

I would further like to thank all respondents and interviewees for contributing to this book. Their accounts have been invaluable.

Finally, I wish to thank my family—especially my wife and friend Marina Dyshlovska—for loving support while writing this book.

Arve Hansen, Oslo, January 2021

Figure 1: Post-electoral protest, Minsk, August 2020

Photo: Artem Podrez / Pexels. https://www.pexels.com/photo/protesters-in-belarus-5119461/

1 Starting Point

> Went to Kyiv [...] metro still closed [...] Got around the police blockades easily. [...] I returned to the Maidan. Still felt like a safe place.
>
> Kyiv, 20th February 2014

This excerpt is from one of the numerous field notes I made during the final days of the Ukrainian revolution (2013–2014). I was studying the events in Kyiv for a research project in East Slavic area studies (Hansen 2015), and went to the iconic site of the protests, Maidan (Independence Square), to observe the scene after the latest clashes between police and protesters. The contention in Kyiv had started three months earlier in response to the government's sudden U-turn away from EU integration, and it had rapidly changed into a broad movement against the incumbent president Ianukovych. The conflict escalated into violence and, by this point, many people had been killed.

I arrived at Maidan for the second time that day at approximately four or five o'clock in the afternoon. At the time, rumour had it that 780 protesters had been killed over the previous 24 hours.[1] The city was in a state of shock, and there was much uncertainty as to what would happen next. Yet, for some reason, I felt quite safe where I was standing.

I knew Maidan well: the entrances and exits, the many tunnels underneath, the seemingly random monuments mixed with intrusive advertising boards, kiosks, and architecture from all periods of Ukraine's Soviet and post-Soviet past. Many times over the previous three months, I had wondered why this particular space had become the symbol of protest in Ukraine. Now, during these final days of the revolution, it was evident that the authorities had been unable to clear the square and stop protesters (or curious people like me) from entering it, despite numerous road blocks and a heavy riot police presence. Strangely, I also noticed that, even though everything was uncertain and no one knew whether the authorities would

---

[1] The Ukrainian Ministry of Health later announced that the actual number of those killed was 82 (Ukrainian Ministry of Health 2014).

launch another attack, it didn't feel particularly frightening to be where I was standing. If anything, I figured, I could always find a way out.

It became apparent to me then that Maidan was a very suitable place for protest, although I could not define precisely why.

Maidan is merely one of several examples of a town square that has turned into a location of great political significance. Actions and events spring immediately to mind at the mere mention of the Bastille, Red Square, Taksim, or Tahrir. We associate these places with the making of history: places where revolutions have been started, dictators ousted, or rebellions crushed.

Central urban spaces can thus create powerful imagery, and we intuitively understand that space has importance. Yet how are massive collective actions, such as the latest Ukrainian revolution, affected by urban public space? Or, to put it another way, how does urban space facilitate and/or inhibit public protests? These questions led me to the current study.

Figure 2: Maidan, Kyiv, February 2014a

Photo: Arve Hansen

Structure

This book describes the development of a spatial perspective on mass protests, a model which has been applied to three case studies: Kyiv, Minsk, and Moscow. It consists of ten chapters, divided into three main parts, one theoretical, one practical, and one concluding.

Part *I* opens in chapter 2 with a contextualisation of space and its central position in human society since the prehistoric era. It outlines a history of contention in urban public spaces, and explains why public spaces in the East Slavic region form the topic of this book.

Having established that urban public space has both a historic and a contemporary relevance, chapter 3 provides a systematic review, in two sections, of the existing research on protests and space. The first section (3.1) includes general theories within sociology and political science, and research on the specific conditions necessary for a collective action or revolution to occur. The second (3.2) looks at the various research on public (philosophy), physical (architecture, urban planning, geography), and contested space (urbanism). In the third section (3.3), an existing gap in the available research is identified. Even if connections between space and protest are discovered in the research literature, and from a variety of perspectives, none of the publications surveyed provide a systematic and generalised approach to the analysis of this causal relationship.

Chapter 4 continues the discussion of chapter 3 by providing two key definitions of mass protests (4.1) and urban public space (4.2), before stating the primary and secondary research questions of this book in full (4.3).

The theorising and development of the spatial perspective, from the conception of an idea to a complete theoretical model, are described in chapter 5. This includes the theory and approaches to theorising applied during the various stages of the model's development (5.1), and some of the ethical considerations taken into account during the process (5.2), as well as my main reservation about developing a theory with a focus on geography. From this starting point, the development of the model is traced from its beginnings (5.4) through different stages of theorising and testing (5.5) to a description of the causal chains between urban space and mass protests employed in the final model (5.6). The project's three case studies were written in parallel with the model's development, and thus also reflect the various stages of the process. The first case is described as a prestudy (5.5.1), the second as a transitional study (5.5.3), and the third as the main study, demonstrating how the spatial perspective can be applied in its current form (5.7).

The causal mechanisms described in chapter five are explicated in chapter 6, including the model's independent (6.1), intermediary (6.2), and dependent variables (6.3).

Part II consists of three chapters, each based to a large extent on the cases described in chapter 5: The prestudy of Maidan in Kyiv (chapter 7); the transitional study of October Square and Independence Square in Minsk (chapter 8); and the main study of Swamp Square in Moscow (chapter 9).

The single chapter of *Part III*—chapter 10—provides a final demonstration of the spatial perspective as applied to Republic Square (*Place de la République*), Paris, during a demonstration there on 6 January 2019 by the Yellow Vests (Fr.: *Mouvement des gilets jaunes*). The case study is used to demonstrate how the research questions outlined in chapter 4 have been answered, and forms the basis for arguing that the model can be used as a tool and a language to discuss spaces of contention and to provide new insights into the study of social movements and mass protests. Following a brief review of the contents, findings, and utility of this book, I then suggest a few ways in which the spatial perspective can be developed further.

Part I

Figure 3:   Maidan, Kyiv, December 2013

Photo: Arve Hansen

2 Space in Context

Human beings are cognitive creatures. We experience the world around us through our external sensory input, such as touch, smell, and sight, which our brains interpret based on our experiences, memory, and thoughts. One fundamental aspect of the experienced world is space and, consciously or subconsciously, we never stop interpreting the physical environment around us. This does not imply that we are necessarily aware of how this analysis is done, or even that it is being done in the first place. We often are unable to appreciate the full extent and impact of it or to explain how it works to a third party. Nevertheless, we are instinctively aware of our surroundings, sense their uses, opportunities, dangers, and risks, and adapt our behaviour accordingly.[2]

This keen sense of place has probably played a vital part in the survival of our species. When our early hominid ancestors, millions of years ago, entered new ground, instincts would be activated to provide information about the possibilities and dangers that particular space might provide. Exploring a new location, an individual would be sensitive to whether the space made them feel relaxed and safe, or alert and uneasy.

Over time, as the human capacity for social interaction evolved, space would come to be perceived not just as a place that might provide food and a chance to eat (or, conversely, a threat of being attacked and eaten), but also as a location for the increasingly complex social interactions between individuals within a group. Thus, the instinctive human perception of space would come to include information about other people and about the social interactions and relations occurring in that space. A newly arrived individual would, for example, soon sense whether this was

---

2   This way of thinking about human nature has its roots back in the *cognitive turn* of the mid 1950s. At this time, sciences such as psychology, linguistics, and anthropology began distancing themselves from the traditional way of looking at the mind and body as separate entities; and the new *cognitive sciences* moved towards a more integrated interpretation of the human mind, which sees most aspects of the human body (and possibly the environment in which it moves) as interrelated (Miller 2003; Núñez and Cooperrider 2013; Thagard 2018).

a place to eat, relax, converse, and mate, or to be on its guard against other individuals in the group. It would know—with little conscious effort—where its allies and friends were, find the possible exits, sense whether it belonged in the group, and locate itself strategically according to its position in the social hierarchy: whether funny, loud, and boastful at the centre of the group, or reserved, quiet, and humble near one of the exits. Individuals who were oblivious to such social space would probably end up as outcasts, or worse, killed.

According to the Australian anthropologist Terrence Twomey (2014), our discovery and domestication of fire hundreds of thousands, perhaps even over a million years ago (Gowlett 2016) probably facilitated the evolution of human cooperation. Twomey explains how making a fire and keeping it going was a costly endeavour, yet the result was a good from which all the individuals in a group could greatly benefit. Hence, the domestication of fire would stimulate cooperation (Twomey 2014). We could therefore imagine that, for groups of hunter-gatherers in prehistoric times, the campfire would become one of the first dedicated spaces for social interaction. Here, people would flock together not only to eat and sleep in the relative safety from predators, insects, and cold weather, but also to process past events, discuss gains and risks, and make a plan of action for the day to come.

After the Neolithic Revolution of approximately 10 000 BCE, humans gradually started to live in fixed settlements and the new agricultural technology laid the foundation for explosive population growth (Bellwood and Oxenham 2008). In the new and increasingly urban setting, the locations of social interaction and planning would probably move from the campfire into urban spaces, such as marketplaces, town squares, or other focal points of growing villages and cities. We can find archaeological evidence from the Bronze and Iron ages, for instance, which indicate that social and deliberative spaces were valued to such an extent that they were formalised as various forms of political institutions. Popular assemblies in urban space could be found in the Ancient Greek *Agora* (Anc. Greek.: ἀγορά), the Roman *Forum Romanum*, and the Slavic *Veche* (Rus.: вече);

or, conversely, in the outskirts of settlements, such as the Scandinavian *Thing* (Icel.: þing).

However, urban spaces have some significant limitations as formal places of deliberation and public administration. Notably, the central plaza of a large city may not have enough physical space available for all people to attend, and large groups of people are often at risk of being affected by demagoguery. For these and other reasons, in most societies, public organisation moved into the remit of formal political institutions. Yet the cities' urban spaces have remained as necessary parts of the landscape, needed in order for people to move from one place to another. Additionally, they function as places for trade, recreation, and social interaction. Urban spaces are often the location of joyful activities such as festivals and public entertainments, but also, sometimes, of floggings and executions. Some rulers might use the city's focal point to display their might, too—for instance, in the form of army drills and parades. Moreover, although the majority of formal decisions now occur in buildings, the potential use value of urban space for people to discuss, deliberate, and decide on a course of action has not gone away.

Throughout human history, people have tended to congregate in central places in times of trouble. Such gatherings sometimes occur on the initiative of rulers to collectively find a solution to a shared problem (such as how to respond to an imminent invasion or the death of a prince). Yet, every so often, the ruling elites are themselves perceived as the problem, and the urban squares and marketplaces might be seized by the people and turned into arenas of opposition.

Figure 4: Althing, Iceland

Iceland's form of popular assembly (Icel.: Alþingi) was first located on Thingvellir (the Assembly Fields, Icel.: Þingvellir)/Lögberg in the tenth century CE. Photo: Andrei Rogatchevski

2.1 Complexities of Urban Contention

Urban contention has a large number of aspects, and several of these are discussed in the next chapter. But there are three ways to look at and categorise urban collective actions that should be mentioned here to provide the reader with a sense of the complexity of the phenomenon: 1) the various forms of urban contention, 2) the motivations people have for action: and, 3) the local, regional, and global tendencies or waves of contention of which the collective action is part.

2.1.1 Form

One form of urban contention is the violent mob, wholly or partially controlled by powerful individuals such as politicians, religious leaders, and oligarchs. The mob has often been used as a tool to incite violence in cities against political opponents and so change the political landscape. In the Ancient Roman Republic, for example, groups of discontented plebeians often became an important force in the frequent (and often violent) transitions of power (Brunt 1966). Another example might be the *veche* (popular assembly) of the Medieval East Slavic Novgorod Republic (1136–1478), where the crowd were often more powerful than their prince. Historical chronicles recount how the Novgorodians, under heavy influence from wealthy boyars, sometimes removed ineffective leaders by force (Paul 2008; Evtuhov, Goldfrank, Hughes, and Stites 2004, 88–89).

Urban contention can also be seen in the uncontrolled violent crowd which, under pressure, stands up to the ruling elites and overthrows them in violent riots, uprisings, and revolutions. The French Revolution (1789–1799) is a particularly prominent example because it shows how space can both foster discontent and provide a suitable environment for insurgencies.[3]

Conversely, urban discontent can manifest as nonviolent protests, such as the 1913 Women's Suffrage Parade on Pennsylvania Avenue in Washington, D.C. (Lumsden 2000), or the 1919 May Fourth Movement at Tiananmen Square in Beijing (Wasserstrom 2005).

2.1.2 Motivation

Another way to look at urban contention is by considering the motivation for the action. The US is a fitting example to illustrate that urban contention can have a wide range of different motives, ranging from a wish to improve living conditions, e.g. the Great Railroad Strike of 1877 (DeMichele 2008), to the many movements against wars and military interventions (see for example the protests against the war in Vietnam [History.com 2019], and in Iraq [Chan 2003]). Cities in the US have also seen multiple protests for the equal rights of oppressed groups in society, such as the 1969 Stonewall Riots and the birth of the Gay Rights Movement (Kuhn 2011), the feminist movements of the 1970s (Spain 2016), and the more recent Black Lives Matter protests (Karduni 2017); collective actions aimed at causing harm, such as racially motivated violence in Southern US

---

3   The revolution erupted in 1789 with the storming of the Bastille, a symbol of monarchical oppression, and was fuelled by the poverty and sickness created in the overcrowded and unsanitary districts of Paris. Moreover, the insurgency was possible in no small part due to barricades raised in the city's narrow and easily defendable streets and alleys (Doyle 1989, 178-191; Traugott 1993; Wilde 2018).

cities (Olzak 1990); religiously inspired protests, such as the Washington for Jesus rally in 1980 (Flippen 2011, 1–23), and social movements against economic inequality, such as the 2011 Occupy Wall Street protest movement (Gillham, Edwards, and Noakes 2013).

2.1.3 Waves

A third approach to urban discontent is to see it as waves that come and go, sweeping through periods in history, changing power structures and the layout of societies. A large number of such waves of contention have occurred throughout history in cities across the globe. In Eastern Europe, for example, we can identify at least four waves, shown here together with their political aftermath:

1917

Eastern Europe did not become part of the three European waves of revolution of the 1820s, 1830s and 1840s that followed in the aftermath of the French Revolution. But the radical new ideas of European thinkers, combined with the grievances of war and deep inequality in society, turned into a series of urban uprisings in the Russian Empire and eventually into the October Revolution of 1917. The Soviet Union was created in the aftermath of this revolution.[4]

1950s and 1960s

The second wave of urban discontent in Eastern Europe started during the period of thaw introduced by Nikita Khrushchev in the aftermath of Stalin's death in 1953. A series of mass protests against poor standards of living and political repressions broke out in the streets and squares of major cities in the Eastern Bloc. Notably, uprisings and demonstrations occurred

---

4   At its peak, in the 1960s and 70s, the Soviet Union covered a sixth of the planet's landmass, controlled the world's largest nuclear arsenal, and dominated the Warsaw Pact military alliance. This alliance was created as a counterweight to NATO in May 1955 and consisted of the 15 Soviet Republics in the USSR as well as Albania (until 1968), Bulgaria, Czechoslovakia, East Germany, Hungary, Poland, and Romania. This group of republics and countries is referred to as the Eastern Bloc.

in 1953 on Leipziger Straße in Berlin (Ostermann and Byrne 2001, 163–165), in 1956 on Adam Mickiewicz Square in Poznań (Grzelczak n.d., 98–101) and on Kossuth Lajos Square in Budapest, also in 1956.[5] The public spaces of cities in several of the Warsaw Pact countries also featured in the worldwide protest movements of 1968, four years after the thaw ended.[6]

1985 to 1991

From the second half of the 1980s, triggered by the 1986 *glasnost* (transparency/openness) and *perestroika* (restructuring) reform policies, urban protests started to appear in the Eastern Bloc. In the Baltics, for example, protesters actively used music in what would later be known as the Singing Revolution of 1987–1991 (Smidchens 2014). Opponents of the Soviet regime organised numerous concerts in city centres and formed a human chain between the three capitals, Tallinn, Riga, and Vilnius, to demonstrate their unity in their discontent with the USSR (2014, 249). These actions inspired similar protests, notably in Ukraine (Hansen, Rogatchevski, Steinholt and Wickström 2019, 36–37). Between 1989 and 1991, the Warsaw Pact gradually fell apart as series of both nonviolent and violent anticommunist revolutions occurred in capital cities across the Eastern Bloc. Notable events include masses of East Germans tearing down the Berlin Wall in November 1989, and the failed military coup of August 1991,

---

5   The Hungarian student protests turned into a revolution and triggered a Soviet military intervention the same year, resulting in "more than 3,000 dead and 13,000 injured as well as over 4,000 destroyed buildings. Actual losses were probably higher" (Hoensch 1984, 219).

6   1968 is a year famous for the amount of urban protests worldwide. In the West, public spaces were occupied by demonstrators in London, Madrid, Mexico, Paris, Rome, West Berlin and numerous other cities; and the social movements of that year showed that even seemingly stable democracies can burst into protests, riots, and even revolutions (see Kurlansky 2005.). While people in the West were largely protesting in the name of equality and socialism, the protests in the East demanded political freedoms and increased autonomy from the Soviet Union. When the Kremlin ordered the invasion of Czechoslovakia in 1968 to stop the Prague government's new reform programme, thousands of Prague-dwellers took to the streets to protest. A number of demonstrations in support of the Czechoslovaks appeared in cities across the Soviet Union, too, including at Red Square in Moscow (Wojnowski 2018, 85; Bichof, Karner, and Ruggenthaler 2010; Kondrashova 2018).

which was partly stopped by the masses of people who went out into the public spaces of Moscow and other Russian cities (Marples 2004, 84). The Soviet Union was dissolved later that same year.

2000s

Following a somewhat chaotic decade in the 1990s,[7] a new wave of social movements and mass protests hit the Balkans, Eastern Europe, and Central Asia in the 2000s (see fig. 5). Inspired by the Eastern European protests of the late 1980s, the demonstrators used nonviolent means to occupy central public squares in capital cities. The protests were often triggered by election fraud, and they demanded (and often achieved) the resignation of the elites that had managed to hold on to power after the breakup of the Eastern Bloc. The social movements of the 2000s are usually known as colour revolutions, with reference to the bright colours and symbols employed by the protesters. Although not in the former Soviet Union, the Yugoslavian Bulldozer Revolution, which overthrew President Slobodan Milošević in 2000, is often regarded as the first of the colour revolutions (e.g. by Tucker 2005).

---

7   In Eastern Europe, the 1990s are often known by the Russian term *Likhie devianostye*, which can be translated into English as the Wild Nineties. The period got this label due to the chaos that followed the Soviet Union's collapse. The 15 newly born post-Soviet states had to reorient their economic models towards a new reality and create new political systems while struggling with severe scarcity of consumer goods and social security, explosive crime rates, rampant corruption, and uncontrolled privatisation. At the same time, wars and uprisings for independence broke out frequently in the Caucasus (notably in Abkhazia, Chechnya, Dagestan, Ingushetia, Nagorno-Karabakh, and South-Ossetia) and in the Transnistria Region of Moldova, triggering several, often unpopular, military interventions by Russia and other countries. Just when the economic situation started to recover, the 1997 financial crisis in Asia hit the former Soviet Union hard, particularly Russia and its trade partners Ukraine and Belarus. It should be noted that the Russian authorities support the use of the term *Likhie devianostye*, as it focuses on the negative aspects of the unstable decade between the Soviet Union (stability) and Putin (new stability), although for many Eastern Europeans, the decade was seen as one of freedom and possibilities rather than anarchy (see for example Rusin 2016; Boldyrev 2018; Osipov-Gipsh 2019).

Figure 5: Notable protests and colour revolutions in post-Soviet states in the 2000s

Year	Country	Focal point	Name(s)	Result
2003	Georgia	In front of the Parliament (Tbilisi)	Rose Revolution	Resignation of President Shevardnadze, new parliamentary elections.
2003–2004	Armenia	Freedom Square (Yerevan)	2003–2004 Armenian Protests	Forceful removal of protesters, legal retributions against protesters and protest organisers.
2004–2005	Ukraine	Maidan (Kyiv)	Orange Revolution	New presidential elections.
2005	Kyrgyzstan	Ala-Too Square (Bishkek)	Tulip Revolution	Resignation of President Akayev, new presidential elections.
2005	Azerbaijan	Gelebe/Galaba Square (Baku)	2005 Azerbaijani Protests	Some concessions. "[O]fficial results for 7 or 8 of 125 parliamentary seats [were] annulled." (Chivers 2005)
2006	Belarus	October Square (Minsk)	Kalinowskyi Square/Jeans Revolution	Forceful removal of the protest camp, legal retributions against protesters and protest organisers.
2008	Armenia	Freedom Square (Yerevan)	2008 Armenian Protests	Forceful removal of the protest camp, protesters killed, legal retributions against protesters and protest organisers.
2009	Moldova	Great National Assembly Square (Chișinău)	Twitter Revolution	New parliamentary elections, resignation of President Voronin.

The above three categories (form, motivation, waves) are not intended to be exhaustive, but to illustrate that "urban contention" is a multifaceted term with historic and contemporary relevance to most regions in the world. The following section serves two purposes: 1) to provide a justification for choosing Kyiv, Minsk, and Moscow as case studies for the three articles in this study; and 2) to show that space and protests are important factors which have affected, and continue to affect, the political situation in the East Slavic area.

2.2 Ukraine, Belarus, and Russia

Since this study is limited by a number of factors, such as time, funding, and space available, the project has been narrowed down geographically. The case studies are limited to the capital cities of Ukraine, Belarus, and Russia for three main reasons. Firstly, the three countries have many similarities. Secondly, despite these similarities, there are some interesting differences between the respective national opposition movements. Finally, two outside factors have pushed me to select these cases. I shall return to these shortly.

Furthermore, each case study has also been geographically limited to one or two urban public spaces, as the word limitations provided by the journal article format rarely allow for more. The choices and delimitations for each case study are discussed more thoroughly in each of the three chapters.

Similarities

Kyiv, Minsk, and Moscow are the capital cities of the countries often referred to as the *Slavic Triangle* (see e.g. Godin 2014), a term originating from the countries' shared history. The territories of Ukraine, Belarus, and Russia each cover parts of Kievan Rus' (approx. 882–1240), the Tsardom of Russia (1547–1722), and the Russian Empire (1722–1917), and they were all signatories to the Treaty of the Creation of the USSR in 1922, which was dissolved in 1991 by the collective decision of the three heads of state. In post-Soviet times, the three countries have struggled with many of the same obstacles: a brutal transition from planned to market economy, widespread corruption, autocratic leadership, popular discontent, etc. Moreover, there are strong ethnic, linguistic, cultural, political, architectural, economic, and criminal similarities and bonds between the three countries.

Figure 6: The Slavic Triangle (map)

Map: Júlio Reis/<u>Wikimedia Commons</u>. Licensed under CC-BY-SA 3.0 (https://creativecommons.org/licenses/by-sa/3.0/deed.en) (edited by Arve Hansen)

Differences

However, the differences between the three countries are significant, too. Ukraine was one of the countries upended by a revolution in the 2000s, as the Orange Revolution of 2004–2005 resulted in regime change. Conversely, Belarus and Russia avoided becoming part of the wave of colour revolutions.[8] This tendency repeated itself in the 2010s, as protests in Minsk and Moscow at the start of the decade all ended badly for the protesters,[9] whilst the latest Ukrainian revolution of 2013–2014, centred on Maidan in downtown Kyiv, led to regime change for the second time in nine years.[10] Today, protests continue to exert an influence on local and regional politics.[11]

Moreover, whereas the opposition in Kyiv has Maidan as an urban space designated for protest, the opposition in Minsk has very limited

---

8   In Russia in 2000, the presidency changed from the unpopular, ageing and sickly Boris Yeltsin to the comparatively young, reasonably sober and physically very fit Vladimir Putin, who for several reasons enjoyed high levels of popularity well into the mid-to-late 2000s (9.2). In Belarus, too, the economy had been growing since the early 2000s, and mass protests were mostly ideological (driven by Belarusian nationalists) or constitutional (against the policies of President Aliaksandr Lukashėnka). Yet none of these protests resulted in a colour revolution (8.2).

9   The 2006 protests in Minsk and the 2011–2012 protest movement in Moscow were suppressed so harshly that the opposition of both countries was effectively disabled for several years to come (8.3.2, 9). In both cases, the protesters were met with violence, hundreds of demonstrators were arrested, and the leaders of the opposition received long prison sentences.

10   The revolution has greatly affected both regional and global power politics. Russia has accused the EU and US of orchestrating what they perceive to be a coup d'état, and the Ukrainian revolution became Russia's pretext for occupying the Crimean Peninsula and supporting the separatist movements in the Donbas region in Eastern Ukraine. Thus, the revolution indirectly became one of the triggering events for the deteriorating relations between Russia and the West today.

11   Since 2014, protests in Ukraine have for the most part been aimed at the policies of President Petro Poroshenko (2013–2019) and President Volodymyr Zelenskyi (since 2019). In Belarus, little has changed, and protests are usually suppressed in much the same manner as before. In Russia, following the annexation of Crimea, a surge in patriotic sentiment led to members of the opposition being labelled traitors, and discontent has remained at low levels. Since 2016, there has been an upswing in public protests in the country. A variety of economic and social problems have motivated hundreds of thousands of Russians to participate in numerous collective actions in cities across the country (9.2.1).

access to the city's urban spaces; and in Moscow, although the authorities do allow protests, they carefully select which spaces to sanction for such actions, most probably to restrict the impact of the protests.

Outside factors

This study forms part of a research group studying Russian space (broadly understood to include Belarus and Ukraine).[12] I have also lived in each country for an extended period of time (in Belarus, 2006–2010; in Ukraine, the first half of 2011 and 2013–2017; in Russia, 2011–2013). I thus have first-hand knowledge of, and a network of friends and acquaintances in, each of the three cities.

2.3 Relevance

Since prehistoric times, people have related by necessity to the intricacies of physical and social space, to the associations and emotions such spaces evoke, as well as to the possibilities and obstacles they provide. Even though our environment has changed, our basic human instincts are still active and, as in the prehistoric era, people congregate to discuss, deliberate, interact, and—in times of trouble—struggle together to find a solution to the problem.

The small selection of collective actions mentioned in this chapter demonstrates that urban mass protest can be a means of changing society, used by people across the world. With the spread of social media, waves of protest can expand with increased speed, and the Internet has facilitated the extension of protest movements, such as the colour revolutions, the Arab Spring, the Occupy movement, and the Yellow Vests. However, although the Internet is available in and used by the majority of the world's population, people still use physical space in order to protest. This is

---

12 The research group RSCPR (Russian Space: Concepts, Practices, Representations) "is engaged in a multidisciplinary study of Russian attitudes to their own and other people's/nations' spaces […] which can provide insights into the interdependence of Russian space and Russian identity, both at an individual and a state policy level" (UiT n.d.). Ukraine and Belarus are often (and especially in Russia) perceived as integral parts of a "Russian" world.

because the presence of a group of people assembled at a focal point of the city serves a number of purposes that are rarely served by collective online action. A physical protest shows that there is discontent in the city, and that people are willing to sacrifice time and effort to come out in support of their cause.

I do not wish to undermine the power of the Internet as a tool for mobilising people to protest. Social media outlets clearly have several qualities suitable for facilitating and/or organising mass protest (see for example Herasimenka 2016). Yet, for a collective action to be effective, it more often than not needs some form of physical manifestation. Urban protests occur where people are concentrated, and so are often hard to ignore. On one hand, citizens are forced to react to the protests as they obstruct movement and demand attention, and some might be inspired to join in. On the other, the authorities are also forced to react, and their reaction (whether by way of official statements, violence, or both) might further spread the news of discontent. Mass protest also represents a form of threat to the authorities. It might mean that people expect the authorities to change their ways, or else they will not vote for those in power again; and it might discourage others from doing so, too. It can also be a threat of violence, as a large group of discontented people has the potential of turning into a mob and removing the authorities by force.

Consequently, urban public space has both a historic and a contemporary relevance, and the ways in which people perceive and use space, especially at times of contention, still have an impact on local, regional, and global politics and society today.

How are mass protests affected by geographical urban space in modern cities? To answer this question, it is first of all necessary to consult the research literature to see whether such a spatial perspective exists. If not, how should such a model be structured?

3 Mapping the Field

The previous chapter outlined some key aspects of space and contention. Historical and contemporary examples were cited to illustrate the important psychological and practical effects of urban space on mass actions.

The aim of the current chapter is to provide a more detailed overview of academic publications concerned with space and/or protests. Starting from this proposition, two key questions may be asked: 1) What academic literature recognises and/or relates to the links between space and protests?; and 2) What approaches and concepts can be integrated into a theoretical model which examines the causal relationship between space and protest? To facilitate reading, the body of research literature is split into three main sections: literature on protests (3.1), literature on various types of space (3.2), and then a section that sums up the findings of this chapter and outlines a gap in the research literature (3.3).

3.1 Protests

Protest is a broad subject that has been approached by scholars from a range of academic disciplines. If theories on social movements are included, the amount of literature on protests becomes even greater. A good starting point to make sense of these broad categories is sociology, which is naturally concerned with the act of protest.

In *Theories of Political Protest and Social Movements* by the German sociologist Karl-Dieter Opp (2009), six major theoretical perspectives on protests and social movements are defined and criticised. These are collective action theory (CAT), resource mobilisation perspective (RMP), political opportunity structure theory (POS), identity theory, framing perspective, and dynamics of contention approach (DOC). Opp describes these theories particularly with a view to the degree in which they present macro (i.e. structural) and micro (i.e. psychological) perspectives on social movements and protests, and how these are interlinked. His main point of critique is that the existing theoretical frameworks do not properly combine macro and micro factors in their attempts to explain protests (2009, 349). Opp's proposed solution is a synthesis of the major theoretical approaches, which he calls the structure-cognitive model (SCM).[13]

Opp analyses these models in detail, but not one of them is shown by his analysis to give specific consideration to the spatial element of protest. I would argue that all seven models, for various reasons, would benefit from applying a spatial perspective of this type.[14] The model that comes closest in nature to a such a perspective is POS theory.

The aim of POS theory, as it was first developed by the US political scientist Peter Eisinger (1973), is to understand the behaviour of protests and to calculate the chance of success of protests and social movements. To do this, the theoretical model relies on the thorough examination of the political environment (i.e. the context within which politics take place). If significant changes occur to the POS (i.e. to the factors and conditions of the political environment), reasons and opportunities for political action are created. POS theory thus strives to identify various factors in the political environment and to prove each factor's causal effect on the chances of a given action occurring and/or succeeding. What constitutes "success" needs to be defined empirically by the researcher (Opp 2009, 162).

One part of Opp's (2009) extensive critique of this theory is that it is virtually impossible to identify all factors in the political environment (or find the 'correct' ones), and thus hard to calculate the "chances of success". Opp also argues that the theory is poorly defined and not clearly distinct from RMP and rational choice theory (RCT), and he questions why POS theory emphasises changes in the political environment rather than just opportunities (167–171; 177–178). However, in his view, the utility of the model is that it demonstrates how the political environment may affect

---

13 Opp's structure-cognitive model has itself been criticised for being too theoretical, to the point that it is hard to put into use in practice (DeCesare 2013, 521).

14 CAT, for example, emphasises the expected number of participants in a collective action as important for people's willingness to protest (Opp 2009, 62). Thus it is natural that a square where protests have been successful in the past will produce more incentives to protest than another, less successful square. Space is also relevant to *identity theory*, which highlights negotiations and in-group interactions (Opp 2009, 207–208)—aspects which can be affected by the protesters' physical location.

protest behaviour. POS could also be used to identify factors in the political environment that inhibit and/or facilitate protests, even if the causal effect of each factor is difficult to assess. (200–201.)

The political environment is relevant to a theoretical model on space and protest for two reasons: 1) As I argue throughout this book, geographical space can significantly contribute to the emergence, realisation, and impact of protests, and it should thus be considered as one of the factors in the political environment. 2) In order to understand the causal relationship between space and protests, it is necessary to identify not only the effects of space, but also the other factors and conditions that have an effect on protests (the importance of mapping such rival theories is explained more thoroughly in chapter 5, 5.6). The following three subsections survey research literature that contributes to our understanding of protest, with a particular view to spatial and non-spatial factors in the political environment that make contentious politics successful or unsuccessful.

3.1.1 Repertoires

The term *repertoire of contention* (ROC) was initially coined by the US sociologist Charles Tilly. The concept is used as an analytical tool by sociologists and political scientists to identify tendencies in contentious politics and to explain why people choose to act the way they do. Strategies utilised during contentious collective actions are often repeated, and social groups develop traditions for methods of protest over time, affected by social, political, and cultural factors. Such repertoires include oft-repeated forms of contentious action (e.g. sit-ins, riots, and protests), and the participants' preferred tools of choice, which develop and change over time (Tarrow 1993).[15] The activists' choice of urban space often becomes a part of such repertoires, and an analysis of a given space should therefore also consider whether or not it is included in any ROCs (see history of protest as a spatial element, 6.1.1).

---

15   For example the pragmatic use of music in social movements (see Hansen et al. 2019, 36–38, on music in Ukrainian repertoires of contention).

The Italian scholars Donatella della Porta and Mario Diani have written extensively on the ROCs of social movements. In one of their books, *Social Movements: An Introduction* (della Porta and Diani 2006), the two authors use various theoretical approaches, such as ROC, RMP, and POS, to approach social movements[16] on three levels of analysis—micro levels (e.g. feelings, identity, beliefs, values, etc.), meso levels (the organisation, and the social networks the movements are comprised of), and macro levels (i.e. structural factors, such as economy, political system, etc.)—and the relationship between these three levels (see figure 7 for a graphical representation). Particularly relevant to this book is the authors' overview of the literature on the policing of protests (see policeability/defensibility as a spatial quality, 6.2.1), to which della Porta has made significant contributions (della Porta and Reiter 1998; della Porta 2013; della Porta, Peterson, and Reiter 2006).

Della Porta and Diani (2006, 197) elaborate on the act of policing protests and identify three prevailing policing strategies: coercive strategies (i.e. the use of physical force); persuasive strategies (attempts to control events through contact with activists and organisers); and informative strategies (which consist of "widespread information-gathering as a preventive feature in protest control"). While choice of strategy on the part of the police has a great impact on the outcome of protests, it is not clear which of the two first strategies is most efficient in controlling events. The authors do note a tendency of coercive (repressive) strategies increasing the risk of escalation, and thus also the proportion of radical protesters.[17]

In addition to the police, della Porta and Diani (2006) identify other actors in opposition to or allied with the social movements, and whose

---

16 Diani defines social movements as "a distinct social process, consisting of the mechanisms through which actors engaged in collective action: are involved in conflictual relations with clearly identified opponents; are linked by dense informal networks; [and] share a distinct collective identity." (della Porta and Diani 2006, 20–22). This definition may include protests.

17 Other factors, such as the nature of the police's use of force (soft or brutal); whether the police's actions are perceived by activists as legal or illegal; the police's attitude to the protesters (often either "good" or "bad"); and their level of tolerance towards activists' conduct, are also discussed.

structural makeup, strength, weaknesses, and other characteristics also function as POSs. These might be institutional, such as government agencies, political parties, trade unions, foundations, religious institutions, etc. Other important actors are provocateurs, used to incite violence and legitimate coercive strategies, and social countermovements that arise "as a reaction to the successes obtained by social movements", develop in parallel to the social movements, and often use similar strategies to those of the movements they oppose (2006, 2011).[18]

Containment and Kettling

Some of the literature on the policing of protest is particularly concerned with the strategic aspects that space provides, both for protesters and police (e.g. Whelan and Molnar 2018, 123–153; Noakes and Gillham 2006; McCarthy and McPhail 2006). Gillham, Edwards, and Noakes (2013), for example, have analysed the mass contentious actions during the 2011 Occupy Wall Street protests (OWS) in New York City, and argue that OWS created a transition to a new form of police ROC, marked by a decrease in persuasive and increase in coercive strategies. During the contestations over public space in New York (notably over Zuccotti Park in Lower Manhattan), the authors argue, the police started using 'strategic incapacitation'. This is a multi-method approach to the policing of protest, which includes informative strategies to survey and infiltrate the movement beforehand and the creation of zones in which different groups are contained and kept apart from each other (e.g. different protest and no-protest zones; zones for the media; and a separate zone for the financial elite).

A more confrontational form of containing people that should be mentioned specifically is *kettling*. The British sociologist Hilary Pilkington defines kettling as

---

18 An example of this is the counterrevolutionary, pro-governmental protests, known as Antimaidan, which appeared in Ukraine as a reaction to the Euromaidan protests against president Viktor Ianukovych (2013–2014). The two movements were opposed to one another, and both movements adopted elements of the other's ROCs. See for example Antimaidan's use of music (Hansen et al. 2019, 47–50, 52–53) and urban space (Hansen 2015, 62–64).

> [...] a police strategy of surrounding demonstrators at a protest in order to contain them in a particular place. The police argue it is necessary as a preventative measure to avoid violence or disorder during demonstrations, [...] protest groups have argued that it is deployed to deliberately frustrate demonstrators or as a means of ascertaining personal details and photographs of protestors. (Pilkington, 2012)

Kettling should thus be defined as a coercive strategy that could be used to suppress demonstrations with physical force, escalate the conflict (by bringing the "kettle" to a boil), and/or arrest a maximum number of demonstrators.

The police's ability to carry out such containment and/or 'kettling' is to a large extent affected by the urban space. See, for example, the difficulties Ukrainian police had in containing Maidan in 2014 (Hansen 2015, 36), or how easy it was for the Russian police to kettle the March of Millions gathered on Swamp Square in 2012 (chapter 9).

3.1.2 Nonviolent Contention

Thus far, the topic of this chapter has been two general approaches to understanding a broad spectrum of activities defined as social movements and protests, as well as their counteractivities. The next two subsections examine research literature aiming to identify more specific conditions and factors that determine whether or not protests occur and what makes them successful. The topic of this subsection is literature on nonviolent contentious actions, whilst the topic of the next is works about what are usually called colour revolutions (3.1.3), including the Western, Russian, Belarusian, and Ukrainian perspectives on the phenomenon. Despite their nonviolent methods, the colour revolutions are kept as a separate category from nonviolent contention. This is because colour revolutions are perceived by some scholars and governments as covert warfare, and as a deliberate pretext to violence (see 3.1.3, below).

In research literature on nonviolent resistance and social movements, one of the earliest attempts to provide a systematic overview and analysis of nonviolent was the US political scientist Gene Sharp's frequently cited 1973 book *The Politics of Nonviolent Action*. The three-volume book provides the reader with a theory of political power (vol. 1);

descriptions of 198 methods of nonviolent protest and persuasion (such as 'fraternising' and 'student strike') (vol. 2); and a practical guide for developing, employing, and defending nonviolent campaigns (vol. 3). (Sharp 1973). Sharp's three volumes have formed the basis of many theories of contentious action. For instance, Ackerman and Kruegler (1994) condensed Sharp's 198 methods into 12 principles of strategic nonviolent action. More recently, the key player behind the *Resistance!* (Scb.: 'Otpor!') student movement in Serbia (1998–2000), Srdja Popovic, together with Andrej Milivojevic and Slobodan Djinovic—two other prominent members of the opposition to Slobodan Milošević—published the book *Nonviolent Struggle: 50 Crucial Points* (2006), based on Sharp's 1973 work.

Popovic, Milivojevic and Djinovic (2006) is a practical step-by-step guide for protesters, divided into three parts: "Before You Start", "Starting Out", and "Running the Nonviolent Campaign." Presented as an easy-to-read and richly illustrated textbook, it provides potential protest organisers with practical exercises, suggestions, and case study examples to analyse (mainly from the Yugoslavian Bulldozer Revolution of 2000). In 2015, Popovic wrote *Blueprint for Revolution*, another book on the same topic (Popovic and Miller 2015). Both books emphasise strength in numbers and diversity among protesters as decisive for the outcome of protests.

One of the most systematic analyses of nonviolent actions to date is provided by the US political scientists Erica Chenoweth and Maria J. Stephan (2011). The authors build on statistical analysis of 323 major violent and nonviolent resistance campaigns between 1900 and 2006 and four qualitative case studies, in addition to the works of other scholars, such as Sharp (1973) and Ackerman and Kruegler (1994), who are discussed above. The authors argue that nonviolent campaigns are nearly twice as likely to be successful than violent campaigns, and they emphasise the ability of campaign organisers to mobilise large and diverse segments of the population as a key condition for success (Chenoweth and Stephan 2011). In a TEDx talk, Chenoweth states that the critical mass of any resistance campaign, violent or nonviolent, is as little as 3.5 % of the total population (whichever the country), stressing that nonviolent actions are much more likely to mobilise a sufficient proportion of the population (Chenoweth 2013).

A key element in virtually all existing studies on nonviolent collective actions is emphasis on the number of participants. What is surprising is that, although the majority of the research also underline the importance of planning and of developing strategies, tactics, and methods, there are almost no references to physical space, which is often of major importance to these practical aspects of collective action.

3.1.3 Colour Revolutions

We now turn to publications concerned with the colour revolutions. As described in the previous chapter, a wave of colour revolutions ousted autocratic leaders and changed the political landscape of Eastern Europe and Central Asia in the 2000s (2.1.3).[19] The often unforeseen protest movements and their influence on protests in other parts of the world gave rise to a host of explanations of why colour revolutions intermittently occur, and under which conditions they achieve regime change. This literature is particularly relevant to this book, since a majority of the colour revolutions were carried out as static occupations of central urban spaces, and it should therefore be possible to assess whether space is considered a factor by leading scholars within the field. Moreover, because the factors identified in the literature are based on collective actions in the post-Soviet region, they should be particularly suitable as a tool for describing the political environment of the case studies in this book.

Among the more influential publications on the subject is the US political scientist Michael McFaul's article "Transitions from Postcommunism" (2005). Basing his argument on similarities between colour revolutions in Serbia (2000), Georgia (2003), and Ukraine (2004), McFaul

---

19 In political sciences, *waves of democracy* is a term coined by Samuel Huntington in 1991. The term covers those periods in history during which a large number of countries become more democratic. Huntington writes of three such waves: the nineteenth century, post-Second World War, and from the mid-1970s (Huntington 1991). Colour revolutions are often perceived as a fourth wave of democratisation (e.g. by McFaul 2002).

presents seven basic factors he deems necessary for a colour revolution to occur:

> 1) a semi-autocratic rather than fully autocratic regime; 2) an unpopular incumbent; 3) a united and organized opposition; 4) an ability quickly to drive home the point that voting results were falsified, 5) enough independent media to inform citizens about the falsified vote, 6) a political opposition capable of mobilizing tens of thousands or more demonstrators to protest electoral fraud, and 7) divisions among the regime's coercive forces. (McFaul 2005, 7)

McFaul thus emphasises internal macro and meso factors more than micro factors such as the motivation and psychology of the protesters. Space is also left out of the equation, although one could imagine that the protesters' choice of space affects the sixth factor. Furthermore, McFaul discusses and eventually downplays other macro factors, such as economic trauma, ethnic tension, and Western support for democratisation and/or the protesters.

Several political scientists have followed McFaul's approach in order to explain the absence or presence of colour revolutions (e.g. Marples 2006, on Belarus), which shows that there is room for such an approach. Others have strived to nuance or change McFaul's factors, among them the British political scientist Taras Kuzio (2008), who has increased the overall number of factors to nine and included micro and macro factors:

> [1] [A] competitive- (i.e. semi-) authoritarian state facilitating space for the democratic opposition; [2] "return to Europe" civic nationalism that assists in mobilizing civil society; [3] a preceding political crisis that weakened the regime's legitimacy; [4] a pro-democratic capital city; [5] unpopular ruling elites; [6] a charismatic candidate; [7] a united opposition; [8] mobilized youths; and [9] regionalism and foreign intervention (Russia or the EU). (Kuzio 2008, 98)

Contrary to McFaul (2005) and Kuzio (2008), the US political scientist Scott Radnitz identifies the level of economic disparity as the vital condition. Drawing on successful (Georgia, Ukraine, Kyrgyzstan) and unsuccessful colour revolutions (Azerbaijan, Belarus, Kazakhstan), he argues that colour revolutions only occur in countries where cooperation exists between activists and capitalists (i.e. financial supporters of the protests) (Radnitz 2010).

The problem of McFaul (2005), Kuzio (2008), Radnitz (2010), and others who create lists of such "minimum requirements" for colour revolutions to occur is that collective actions of a large magnitude—which colour revolutions surely are—are immensely complex events. They comprise a large number of aspects, and any attempt to generalise such events to a set number of factors will inevitably exclude important aspects. See for example Tucker (2007), where the author criticises the existing literature on colour revolutions (among them McFaul) for being overly elite-based and downplaying the role of the masses who participated in the colour revolutions. Tucker uses CAT to explain how major electoral fraud provides people with a focal point and a window of opportunity for mass collective action, arguing that, from the moment the falsified results are announced to the moment they are implemented, people have an extra incentive to protest.[20]

Tucker's (2007) emphasis on the masses of people is corroborated by the book *The Colour Revolutions in the Former Soviet Republics: Successes and Failures*, edited by the Irish political scientists Donnacha Ó Beacháin and Abel Polese (2010). In this book, 12 post-Soviet countries (Georgia, Ukraine, Kyrgyzstan, Moldova, Armenia, Azerbaijan, Belarus, Russia, Uzbekistan, Tajikistan, Kazakhstan, and Turkmenistan) are compared in order to identify reasons for the occurrence of colour revolutions. In each of the 12 case studies, five factors are examined: 1) regime type; 2) the degree of unity in the opposition; 3) external influences; 4) the strength of civil society; and 5) the people (i.e. how they organise and act, and how they

---

20 The article reviews the existing literature on colour revolutions and identifies two main approaches to their origin. The first approach emphasises "the lure of the West", either as a political goal of the protesters or (as it is often portrayed in Russia) as Western attempts to weaken Russian influence in the region by provoking upheavals in its Near Abroad (Rus.: *blizhnee zarubezh'e*, a term used in Russia for post-Soviet countries). The second approach examines the nature of the opposition movements (i.e. their ability to organise, mobilise people, access resources, etc.) (Tucker 2007, 539). The observation that elections are used as focal points for democratic opposition in authoritarian regimes is further developed and nuanced in a statistical analysis of regime transitions in the post-communist region by Bunce and Wolchik (2010).

relate to the other actors in society). The latter two factors are highlighted as particularly important (2010, 9).

Beacháin and Polese (2010) contradict the view of Canadian political scientist Lucan Way (2008), who mainly highlights macro factors such as the protesters' geopolitical connections with the West and the structural makeup of the state, rather than internal micro factors such as the motivation and innovations of the protest movements. Way argues that scholars tend to put too much weight on the number of protesters in collective actions, illustrating this point by referring to the relatively small numbers of protesters in the Georgian (2003) and Kyrgyz (2005) revolutions. He asserts that the protesters' external connections often are of greater importance. Just as McFaul and Kuzio, Way uses macro-level explanations for the fall of autocratic regimes:

> Authoritarian stability is most affected by: 1) the strength of a country's ties to the West; and 2) the strength of the incumbent regime's autocratic party or state. (Way, 2008, 60)

Thus far, looking at the body of academic literature on colour revolutions in the West, no concrete references to space are evident. Regarding the factors deemed necessary for a colour revolution to occur, we can conclude that there are several and contradicting views on the phenomenon. Three major categories of factors can be identified: 1) micro factors, such as the protesters' motivation and strategic innovation; 2) meso factors, such as the organisational structure of the ruling elite and the opposition; and 3) macro factors, such as the economy and political system.

Additionally, we can add a fourth category, which consists of publications that see colour revolutions as a result of external (i.e. foreign) influences. Beacháin and Polese (2010) have identified two types of this kind of international support: 1) Western, in the form of guidance and training for NGOs and observers; and 2) the mutual "economic, political, military and diplomatic support to besieged autocrats […]" shown by other autocratic leaders in the region. The Kremlin in particular is highlighted as a key supporter of autocratic leaders. Even if external support receives considerable attention in academic literature and in media discourse, the editors go on to underline that domestic factors, such as a well-developed civil society and motivated people, are important factors for colour revolutions to occur (Beacháin and Polese 2010).

Popular Revolutions or (Geo-)Political Technologies? [21]

The leading politicians of Russia and Belarus, Vladimir Putin and Aliaksandr Lukashenka, both perceive colour revolutions as affected by the latter category (external influence). In the aftermath of the Euromaidan revolution in Ukraine (2013-2014), which led to the ousting of Russia-leaning president Viktor Ianukovych, Putin called colour revolutions a form of extremism and "a geopolitical instrument for changing spheres of influence (BBC Russian Service 2014). Lukashenka has also blamed Western powers for attempting to topple the Belarusian state (Nersesov 2017), although in an earlier interview with Russian media outlets in 2016 he did state that, if the standard of living is high in Belarus and Russia, no destructive colour revolutions will occur (Afitsyinyi sait Respubliki Belarus' 2016). Thus, Lukashenka also recognises the third (macro-) category.

Russian academic publications on the subject often voice views similar to those of the political leadership. The Russian political scientist Andrei Manoilo, for instance, sees only external factors. He defines colour revolutions as

> [...] [political] technologies for the implementation of coups d'état and external control of the political situation in a country in conditions of artificially created political instability, during which the pressure on the government is exerted in the form of political intimidation, [by] using a youth protest movement as an instrument of such an intimidation. (Manoilo 2015)

Manoilo (2015) presents colour revolutions as a tool created by Anglo-Saxons in the US (among them Gene Sharp 1973), who have used it as a hybrid weapon in unfriendly countries: in Eastern Europe during the 2000s; in the Middle East from 2011; and in Ukraine in 2014 (the latter is

---

21   The British political scientist Andrew Wilson (2011) provides the following definition of political technology: "[...] a term largely unfamiliar in the West—[it] is the euphemism commonly used in the former Soviet states for what is by now a highly developed industry of political manipulation".

presented as a "dress rehearsal" for destroying Russia with the same 'soft power' weaponry). Manoilo also identifies five distinct phases that colour revolutions go through: 1) A network of organised protest movements in the target country is created; 2) Upon a signal, often after an orchestrated event, the network of people simultaneously goes out on the streets in major cities in the country; 3) Activists in the network of cells turn into catalysts of 'singing protests'[22] in order to engage large sections of the population; 4) The protesters gather in large public spaces in order to create a crowd mentality, through which new values and imperatives are given. Here, the people are reprogrammed, in much of the same way as "Protestant totalitarian sects" brainwash their followers; 5) On behalf of the crowd, ultimatums are sent to those in power under the threat of mass riots and, occasionally, physical extermination. The power holders are either swept away or a rebellion or civil war begins, followed by a military intervention. (Manoilo 2015)

Certainly, some approaches to colour revolutions in Russia are less radical than Manoilo's (see for example Barsamov 2006), and some see geopolitical factors as less important (notably the political scientist Valerii Solovei 2016[23]), yet variations of Manoilo's perspective appear to be numerically the most prominent, and can be found in several publications by other Russian political scientists and sociologists (e.g. Iel'chaninov 2007; Naumov 2016). In Russian media outlets, the understanding of colour revolutions as a geopolitical tool and a threat to the sovereignty of the Russian Federation is often all too obvious (see for example TASS 2019; Krasovskaia 2019; NTV 2019).

---

22   Manoilo is probably referring to the Singing Revolution in the Baltics, particularly in Estonia (1987–1991), against Soviet hegemony; or to the festive qualities of the Orange Revolution and Euromaidan in Ukraine (2004–2005 and 2013–2014); on the latter see Hansen et al. (2019, 33–83).

23   Solovei is one of the most prominent academics in the Russian opposition. Although not explicitly dealing with colour revolutions, in his book *Revolution* (*Революtion*) (2016) he describes seven conditions for a revolution to occur, focusing mainly on micro factors such as the protesters' moral strength, their readiness to face obstacles, and their inner psychology (Solovei 2016, 298–306).

This Cold War frame of mind stems from Russia being perceived (and perceiving itself) as the natural successor to the Soviet Union—the main adversary of the West during the Cold War. The rivalry between these two power blocks was not only fought out in proxy wars; the two also supported protest movements and insurgents in order to damage each other's spheres of influence across the world, and especially in the former European colonies of Asia, South America, and Africa (Kanet 2006, 337; Powelson 2003). The dissent in the Eastern Bloc that eventually led to the collapse of the Soviet Union could be seen as part of this warfare. Hence, given that a new wave of colour revolutions occurred at the same time and place as the EU and NATO were expanding—into areas seen by Russia as *their* sphere of influence—Russia's hostility to mass protests becomes more understandable.

One outcome of the wave of colour revolutions is that autocratic countries have started to perceive nonviolent protest as a serious threat. Since the stakes are so high, the autocrats are readier to suppress political dissent with harassment, increased surveillance, and violence (Beacháin and Polese 2010, 238). Moreover, in Russia and Belarus, pro-governmental youth organisations have formed to counterweight foreign influence on the youth (Matchanka 2014; Hemment 2012; Atwal and Bacon 2012). This effort to combat mass demonstrations has been reinforced since the recent Ukrainian revolution, and colour revolutions are accordingly defined by the military as a threat to national sovereignty, and increasingly defined as 'acts of war'.[24]

The problem with a single focus on foreign influence is that it disregards the other micro-to-macro factors and presumes that external influences alone are enough to create a popular uprising or nonviolent revolution. Ukrainian views on colour revolutions are, perhaps unsurprisingly, often more nuanced than the views held by their Russian counterparts. For example, in the Ukrainian political scientist Oleksandr Romaniuk's (2005) assessment of the phenomenon in Yugoslavia (2000), Georgia (2003),

---

24 See for example the harsh language used by Belarusian and Russian officials during the Third Moscow Conference on International Security in May 2014 (Cordesman 2014; Russian Ministry of Defence 2014).

Ukraine (2004), and Kyrgyzstan (2005), internal factors—such as the decay of the political elite, a worsening of democratic standards, the poor standard of living, and a growing desire for political change among the general population—are seen as the foundation for discontent, which, triggered by election fraud, turned into colour revolutions. Romaniuk adds, however, that all the opposition forces have received moral and sometimes material support from Western democracies (2005, 24).

3.1.4 Non-spatial Factors

At the start of this chapter, two questions were outlined: 1) Which academic literature recognises and/or relates to the links between space and protests? 2) Which approaches and concepts can be integrated into a theoretical model examining the causal relationship between space and protest?

Regarding the former question, there is a tendency in several academic disciplines around protest to overlook spatial factors. For example, in the literature on nonviolent contention, tactical innovation is often emphasised as important; but few if any references are made to the possibilities space provides for such innovation. A spatial perspective is also missing from the literature on colour revolutions, despite the fact that most of these mass actions have utilised a similar form of static spatial occupation.

One exception to this tendency, of course, is Manoilo (2015), who asserts that urban spaces are used to brainwash the people gathered in them. Another (perhaps more realistic) exception is the research on the repertoires of policing, which includes and accounts for space. Even so, compared to the countless examples in history of urban spaces that have played a role in contentious actions, there clearly must be a gap in the literature on protest. In the following section, the search for literature to fill this gap will continue as the focus moves from academic literature on protest to academic literature on space.

Regarding the latter question, several concepts and theories can be integrated into a theoretical model on space and protest. POS theory is particularly relevant, as it emphasises the importance of the political environment, which can be used to account for and examine variables with an effect on protests. However, as noted above, it is difficult to map all factors.

This problem becomes particularly apparent when a comparison is made to the wide range of arguments identified in the literature on colour revolutions.

In order to gain a better understanding of factors that may or may not be of significance in the political environment, these are visualised in the two figures provided below. The first (fig. 7) is a proposed list of micro, meso, and macro factors in the political environment. The second is a diagram in which the three levels are placed next to each other, alongside external influences (such as support for leaders or NGOs) and events (e.g. election fraud), which are added as possible outside effects (fig. 8).

Figure 7: Micro, meso, and macro factors

Micro	**Meso**	**Macro**
Goals	Culture	Political system
Identity, feelings, beliefs, values	Organisations, networks	Economy
Innovation, originality	Communities	Formal organisations
Strategies, tactics, methods	Groups	Etc.
Identity, feelings, beliefs, values	Police structures	
	Political parties	
	Etc.	

Figure 8: The political environment

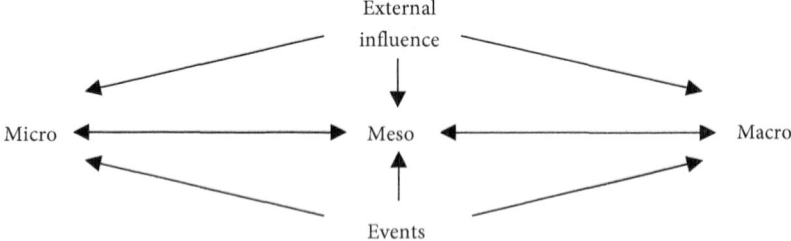

3.2 Space

Having identified some of the main perspectives in the literature on protest, it is necessary to give an overview of the research literature on space and its function in society. This literature, of course, consists of many publications; yet only a small proportion of them is directly related to the two questions stated at the beginning of this chapter. Additionally, I have concentrated on a selection of the literature that can be used to formulate an understanding of what constitutes the nature of space.

This section starts with metaphysical and philosophical space (3.2.1). Here, discussions and understandings of space found in Arendtian and Habermasian texts are defined in reverse chronological order of development (from the least physical [Habermas] to the most physical [Arendt]), followed by various Marxian perspectives, including the terms "public space" and "the right to the city". The next subsection (3.2.2) concerns more physical and concrete approaches found in architecture, urban planning, and human geography. This account is followed by an overview of the prospect-refuge theory, as found in landscape architecture. The final subsection (3.2.3) specifically deals with studies of protest locations. It should be noted that these three categories are neither exhaustive nor mutually exclusive, but serve as guidelines within a larger body of literature.

3.2.1 Public Space

In *The Structural Transformation of the Public Sphere* (1962/1989), the German philosopher Jürgen Habermas introduces the term "public sphere". According to Habermas, a weakening of totalitarian institutions, such as feudalism and the state church, in Western Europe in the eighteenth century enabled more representative forms of government to appear. At this time, a growing middle class had the time and energy to participate in discussions about how the public should be managed, and the public sphere became the transition point between public and private life. Habermas describes the public sphere as an ideal and abstract neutral place for which societies must strive. In this ideal place, people conduct their deliberations, and all opinions are equally valuable; there is also an absence of hierarchy. Habermas refers to coffee houses and salons as early examples of this sphere, and sees mass media as an important tool in the creation of public discourses. The threat, argues Habermas, comes from the powerful organisations that aim to control the discourse which occurs in the public sphere.

The German-American philosopher Hannah Arendt also stresses the importance of the public sphere in democratic societies, but in her works—and especially in *The Human Condition* (1958/1998)—the physicality of such spaces is strongly emphasised. The political scientists Maurizio Passerin d'Entrèves and Ursula Vogel (2005) elaborate on this physicality:

> [One] feature stressed by Arendt has to do with the spatial quality of public life, with the fact that political activities are located in a public space where citizens are able to meet one another, exchange their opinions and debate their differences, and search for some collective solution to their problems. Politics, for Arendt, is a matter of people sharing a common world and a common space of appearance so that public concerns can emerge and be articulated from different perspectives. In her view, it is not enough to have a collection of private individuals voting separately and anonymously according to their private opinions. Rather, these individuals must be able to see and talk to one another in public, so that their differences as well as their commonalities can emerge and become the subject of democratic debate. (d'Entrèves and Vogel 2005, 9)

In other words, opinions are formed, and meaningful exchanges of opinions and debates occur, in physical space; thus, the presence of a location where people can meet, talk, act, and deliberate is vital for the existence and proper functioning of public life and politics. (For more on Arendt's focus on geography, see Howell 1993, 313–316.)

In the book *Democracy and Public Space* (2012), the Dutch political scientist John R. Parkinson takes this argument further. Like Habermas and Arendt, he perceives a well-functioning public space as a premise for working democracy. He identifies four ways in which physical space can be considered public: It 1) "is openly accessible"; and/or 2) "uses common resources"; and/or 3) "has common effects; and/or 4) "is used for the performance of public roles." (2012, 61). Parkinson's definition of public space is thus broad enough to include political institutions, and he argues that the layout and structure of such public spaces affect the ways we interact (Parkinson looks specifically at the layout of parliaments and other political institutions, but also town squares). This type of perspective is concurrent with the prevailing view within the field of political geography (see for example Jones, Jones, and Woods 2004; Van Deusen 2004; and Agnew and Muscarà 2012), but I have found no political geographers who have developed a way to examine the causal relationship between urban space and contentious politics.

"Public Space" and "the Right to the City"
Political philosophy is used to explain not only why space is *necessary* for discussions and debate to occur, but also why urban space is *contested*. Such discussions about the nature of spatial contestation often take a Marxian perspective. In Marxian economic philosophy, social class struggle is sometimes seen spatially, which can generate questions such as "Who owns the city?" and "Who has the right to use it?"

The French philosopher and sociologist Henri Lefebvre raises these questions in two of his influential books on the subject, *Writings on Cities* (Lefebvre 1996) and *The Urban Revolution* (Lefebvre 1970/2003). In the former, Lefebvre discusses the capitalist accumulation of money in urban centres and how this has led to the exclusion of certain groups (ethnic or national minorities, people of certain ages, the disabled, etc.). Lefebvre establishes that all urban inhabitants have the right to use the city they live in and to participate in its creation, and he urges people to reclaim their rights over the city. In the latter book, Lefebvre describes the development and nature of the city, from the Neolithic revolution to his own day. He examines how capitalism has shaped urban space, globally, nationally, and locally. According to Lefebvre, world society is gradually (i.e., at the time of publication in 1970) going through complete urbanisation. By this he means that no part of the world exists in total independence of the urban centres (Lefebvre 1970/2003; see also Lefebvre 1974/1991).

The term "right to the city" has been further developed by at least two other Marxian scholars: the British economic geographer David Harvey and the US geographer Don Mitchell. Harvey explores the relations between capital, politics, and the people (see for example Harvey 1989; 2008; 2012), and develops Lefebvre's arguments about the increasing social and economic injustice in urban centres.

Mitchell also considers inequality in urban space. He is concerned with how contestations occur in space and about space (see for example Mitchell 1998); how wealth is produced and distributed in a city (Staeheli and Mitchell 2008); and the exclusiveness of urban public space, e.g. gated communities and how some groups, particularly the homeless, are left with fewer rights to the public space than others (Mitchell 2011; 2016). Mitchell's recurrent argument is that space is contested by different layers of the population, who constantly negotiate and argue about how it should be used and by whom. This contestation contributes significantly to the Lefebvrian concept of production of space (i.e. how space is given meaning by the acts occurring in it). (See 3.2.3, for more on the production of space).

Public space is thus not only contested in itself, but is a contested term with a wide range of viewpoints and definitions. Interpretations of public space range from the metaphysical to the physical and include informal meeting places, such as cafés and chat rooms, formal institutions, such as parliament buildings, and urban space, such as town squares and parks. In an attempt to create a unified understanding of the concept, the US professor of public administration Charles Goodsell (2003) identifies six defining characteristics of public space, from a variety of academic disciplines:

> [1] Generic definition of public space: A space-time continuum for connected and interactive political discourse. [2] Place-bound public space: The above consisting of face-to-face interaction in a single physical location. [3] Electronic public space: The above achieved at dispersed geographic locations through information technology. [4] Extended public space: The above when broadcast by television, radio, Internet, or other means. [5] Pure definition of democratic public space: The above when open to all, unrestricted as to conduct, and unconditional as to participation. [6] Practical definition of democratic public space: The above when public access is encouraged, the status of state authority is muted, barriers between governors and governed are minimized, staging is arranged by the people as well as officials, and conditions conducive to deliberation are fostered. (Goodsell 2003, 370)

The public space discussed in this book is naturally positioned within Goodsell's second, place-bound definition. The specific definition of public space will be developed in the next chapter (4.2).

3.2.2 Physical Space

Now that we have discerned the importance of public space as the location of discussion and deliberation, as well as the place where contestations occur and meaning is created, it is time to move on to the physical aspects of space. Architecture, urban planning, urbanism, and human geography are four academic disciplines naturally concerned with physical (urban) space, and key studies from each of these can be related to collective action.

Urban Planning, Architecture, and Urban Geography

Goodsell (2003) provides some assessment of the relevant literature in architecture and urban planning. He writes, for instance, that the relationship between political power and people is often expressed in architecture, and "a common theme is how the design and symbols of physical space reinforce political power" (2003, 365). Referring to his own and others' studies of buildings and official institutions, he explains how such places seek to evoke certain feelings, such as that of authority, monumentality, or—in the case of court rooms—legitimacy and equality (2003, 365–366). (For a similar view, see Bismarck 2014.)

In urban planning, public spaces are often seen as places for social interaction and, as in architecture, there is much focus on the perception of space. Additionally, urban planners tend to focus on the utility of spaces, and how the right planning can increase their usage. Some urbanists also frame such usage in a historical context (see US geographer and urbanist Edward Soja 2010).

The US urban theorist Kevin Lynch has influenced writing on urban planning for more than half a century. For his book *The Image of the City* (1960), Lynch conducted interviews with citizens about their daily travels in, and interactions with, public space. He asked the respondents to describe and draw the spaces they went through, what they remember from them, and what feelings they evoked. Lynch used the information he collected to identify five elements of urban space that dominate people's mental perception of it: nodes (places of destination or transition points); paths (the connections to and between nodes, e.g. roads and walkways);

landmarks (reference points, such as monuments and buildings); districts (areas of the city with distinct characteristics); and edges (boundaries and obstacles that hinder movement, e.g. walls and shorelines). (See chapter 6: 6.1.1, 6.1.2, and 6.1.3.)

Groups of scholars, architects, and urban planners are also concerned with identifying what makes spaces inclusive and practical to use. The Feeling of Place project (Nielsen 2017), for example, is an examination of public spaces in Southwark, London, to establish why people respond well to certain places and not to others. The researchers asked respondents in London what they felt about the spaces they were in, using 13 feelings as a framework to evaluate the positive vs. negative value of the spaces.[25] As a result, nine key themes were identified that affect how people relate to space in everyday life: 1) people's awareness of what is in the space; 2) its history and social life; 3) the presence of nature; 4) its level of accessibility for some or for all people; 5) whether or not people are visiting or living in the place; 6) how welcome people feel there; 7) the scale of buildings and activities in the space (as stated by the authors: "Locations with tall towers […] made people feel less happy and were seen as less pleasant than places with lower scale houses. Planting and activities on street level helped people feel that the […] place [was] more pleasant.", 13); 8) complexity and confusion; and 9) changes occurring in the space (Nielsen 2017).

Similarly, the Project for Public Spaces—a cross-disciplinary platform for the promotion of sustainable urban spaces—has identified 10 principles for a successful (i.e. much-used) square: 1) it has a strong image and identity; 2) there are attractions and destinations on or around the square; 3) there is a presence of amenities, such as benches; 4) it has a flexible design, including 5) different designs for different seasons; 6) it is easy

---

25   Happy/unhappy; relaxed/tense; excited/bored; welcome/not welcome; strong/low sense of belonging; familiar/unfamiliar; pleasant/unpleasant; want to approach/avoid; interesting/uninteresting; complex/simple; crowded/empty; understandable/confusing; not stressful/stressful. (Nielsen 2017, 5). However, this method can be criticised for oversimplifying space, as aspects such as 'crowded' have been marked with a positive value, while 'empty' is negative. Arguably, a crowded place might be perceived by some (or in some circumstances) as less positive than an empty space.

to access, preferably on foot; 7) there is a good balance between the outer (i.e. surrounding buildings, roads, amenities) and inner (centre) square; 8) its paths (roads, streets, walkways) reach out "like an octopus"; 9) it is well managed by people who are familiar with the square; and 10) it has diverse sources of funding (Project for Public Spaces 2005.)

The principles identified in the two projects outlined above provide valuable clues as to what variables create pleasant, accessible, and visible space, which are three important aspects of urban protests (see chapter 6). Yet even though the vast majority of architects perceive and utilise the feelings that space and buildings evoke, and urban planners look at the various usages of public space, neither discipline is explicitly concerned with how these qualities affect collective action. A few notable exceptions should be mentioned. One is the US landscape architect Jeffrey Hou, who has edited two books on the subject: *Insurgent Public Space: Guerrilla Urbanism and the Remaking of Contemporary Cities* (Hou 2010) and *City Unsilenced: Urban Resistance and Public Space in the Age of Shrinking Democracy* (Hou and Knierbein 2017).

In the former book, the authors (including anthropologists, geographers, architects, urban planners, and artists) aim to understand the role of public space in the constant changes cities undergo, as well as various attempts to create and control public space: "[P]ublic space has been an important facet of cities and urban culture [...] [Urban spaces] provide opportunities for gathering, socialising, recreation, festivals, as well as protests and demonstrations" (Hou 2010, 2). In the authors' view, the city is constantly changing, both physically and in the ways it is perceived and used: city space can be contested, change meaning, be appropriated, made available or unavailable to some or all groups, new meanings can be attributed to it, and so on.

In the latter book, co-edited with the Austrian landscape architect Sabine Knierbein, the authors put contestations in urban space into the context of neoliberal economic globalisation. As with other scholars, such as Don Mitchell (3.2.1), David Harvey (3.2.1), and the US architect and urbanist Paul Knox (2011), they see urban development as driven by global investors who gentrify urban centres and increase local and global inequalities (Hou and Knierbein 2017, 6). The authors call this tendency "shrinking democracy". This means that, when public space is increasingly controlled by private and commercial actors, its alternative use as an outlet for public discontent against authorities (see chapter 2) is reduced (hence, the utility of space as a safety valve in societies is shrinking).

There is also an emerging interest within human geography and architecture in the physicality, organisation, and structure of protest camps; see for example the British human geographer Adam Ramadan on the occupation of Tahrir Square during the Arab Spring in Egypt. He argues that the protest camp is a public space which functions as a vehicle for political change (Ramadan 2013). Another prominent example is the anthology *Protest Camps in International Context* (Brown, Feigenbaum, Frenzel, and McCurdy 2017), which sees camps as a form of organisation. The authors examine the symbolic value, logistics, and possibilities provided by protest camps across the world, while analysing what the editors call four 'infrastructures': media infrastructures, action infrastructures, organisation infrastructures, and re-creation infrastructures. These studies thus emphasise that static protests are important, and that they are reliant on accessibility and transport networks in order to function properly (see spatial qualities as a variable in chapter 6, 6.2.1).

Prospect-Refuge Theory
Before moving on to studies concerned with particular spaces of protest, one final theoretical approach with a spatial focus should be mentioned: namely, prospect-refuge theory (PRT). PRT was first developed by the British geographer Jay Appleton in *The Experience of Landscape* (1975), in which he explored the aesthetics of open spaces and the forms of landscape people tend to respond well to. According to this theory, which sees human preferences as an evolutionary trait for survival, people feel safe, and thus prefer to stay, in spaces where they can observe the surrounding area and perceive approaching threats or prey (=prospect), but are not themselves easily observed or attacked (=refuge). A high-up position, a narrow space in the shade looking out onto a wider area, or a place by an edge (such as a river, wall or steep mountain) are all preferable to a space

without edges or with few exits (such as a narrow mountain pass), where one can easily be spotted or dangers can converge from several directions.

PRT is also applied to urban environments (see for example Fisher and Nasar 1992; Ramanujam 2007), in which confined and confusing spaces with few exits—such as a narrow and sparsely lit alleyway, or an underground car park—feel uncomfortable while a wide, properly lit street with plenty of exits, or the space in the shade of a grove in a lush park, feel pleasant. The theory has been criticised for not always being applicable to an urban context, where the need for refuge is arguably less psychologically important than in a natural setting (see for example Dosen and Oswald 2016). But this reservation to the theory might not apply in a contentious context, as instincts for personal safety are probably more acute in these situations than in day-to-day life.

3.2.3 Contested Spaces

Having reviewed leading theories of protest in the first section of this chapter; and the various theories about the nature of political and physical urban space in the previous two subsections, I will now turn to case studies of specific spaces, which have been used to explore and illustrate the theories and concepts identified in this chapter (i.e. works specifically concerned with the location of contestation).

The case study literature on contested spaces can be divided into two main groups: 1) publications describing how contentious actions have shaped people's perception of urban space, and 2) publications looking at the effects locations have on contention. As with other categories provided in this chapter, these two groups may not be absolute, and some of the literature discusses both: how contention in urban space shapes people's perception of space, and, at the same time, how space provides people with the conditions of and possibilities for contention. See for example Karl Schlögel's book *Moscow, 1937*, in which Moscow is described both as the setting for the terror and traumas of the Stalin Purges (1936–1938), and as changed by the omnipresence of informants, paranoia, deportations, and executions during that time (Schlögel 2012).

In the first group, urban space is often regarded as a dependent variable. People's perception of space is fluent and constantly changing, affected by the contestations about and within the space.[26] The "production of space" is often a key concept used to understand whole urban areas. See for example: Smith and Mitchell (2018) on how the space in New York City has been produced by the contestations that occurred in the city throughout its history: Yacobi (2004) on the contestations of urban space in 'mixed' Palestinian/Israeli cities; or McCann (1999) on how civic space in Lexington has changed due to spatial (and racial) policies. The "production of space" concept can also be applied to individual spaces, such as a single square or park. See for instance Van Deusen (2002) on the production of Clinton Square, New York.

The scholars in the second group often perceive space more as an independent variable that wholly or partially affects people's possibilities of protest. This includes studies of the symbolic characteristics of urban space, e.g. Örs (2014) on Gezi park and Taksim Square as a public space, and how the attempts by the Turkish authorities to change this symbolic value by redesigning their physical layout triggered the 2014 multifaceted pro-democracy protests in cities across the country. A further example is Gunning and Baron (2014), who not only describe the where, when, who, and whys of the 2011 Egyptian Revolution in Tahrir Square, but also how the square became a shared symbolic focal point for a range of protest movements.

Conversely, several scholars highlight the importance of the physical characteristics of space, such as layout, size, or location. See for example Lee (2009), who argues that Tiananmen Square was chosen by the May Fourth Movement in 1919 because of its physical features and availability, even though it had far less symbolic value than other public spaces. Or Salmenkari 2009, who puts the emphasis on location in her comparison of protest places in Buenos Aires and Seoul, finding that "the majority of

---

26 This being said, other actions—such as public festivals, trade, criminal acts, military parades, and sporting events—might also affect the perception of urban space, as well as who uses the space: e.g. is it public, private, commercial, or official.

protests take place at sites of political authority, places that appeal to the public, places connected with a grievance, and symbolically meaningful places." (2009, 256) She also points out that historical and symbolic sites are often interpreted differently and might not have the same reinforcing nature for all (protest) groups (2009, 257).

Some underscore social features and the traditions around using a space: e.g. Zaazaa (2009) on the cultural, social, and historical significance of Tahrir Square. He argues that, since the central space is in the political centre of Cairo, heavily trafficked and used by thousands of people every day, demonstrations in the square immediately gather local and national attention.

Finally, some see a combination of the three: such as Hatuka and Kallus (2008), who in their study of Rabin Square in Tel Aviv recognise several ways in which the square's social, symbolic, and physical attributes affect protests, albeit with a focus on the physical. All three of these aspects of space (perceived/symbolic, social, and physical) have been introduced as categories in the theoretical model (6.1).

3.3 The Gap

In the previous two sections, I set out to survey research literature which identifies the links between space and protests and how the two relate to each other. However, as the section on protest shows, there is a profound lack of literature making this connection with space, as almost none of the theories examined here have any reference to it; and the few that do (e.g. repertoires of contention) are limited in scope and do not provide a detailed account of the causal relationship between space and protest. Although the connection between the two has been identified in the research literature considered in the second section (on space), and from a variety of viewpoints (such as to the location for discussions, deliberations, and contestations), this literature, too, lacks a generalised approach to assess the use value of space.

This lack of a spatial perspective on political action has been highlighted, among others, by Parkinson (2012, 6–7). Moreover, two chapters in the anthology *The Oxford Handbook of Social Movements* (della Porta and Diani 2015) address this lack within the studies of social movements: chapter 12 (urban dynamics and social movements) and chapter 24 (geography and social movements).

In the former chapter, the authors attempt to define urban movements, the conditions under which they occur, and various forms of urban movements. The authors use POS theory to identify why urban movements appear in some spaces and not in others; and, like David Harvey, Don Mitchell, and other Marxian economists (3.2.1), the scholars focus on economic and political elements in the political environment rather than on pure geography (Andretta, Piazza, and Subirants 2015). In the latter chapter, the British political scientist and geographer Paul Routledge starts by identifying the lack of geography in theories on social movements, and continues by outlining several ways in which urban space is significant. These include: the various associations and feelings people have towards space; the inequalities of society that are reflected in space; how space can provide different POSs for different people in different spaces; the scale of space in which social movements occur; and how these scales might provide "a range of opportunities and constraints" (Routledge 2015, 386). Still, none of these two chapters suggest an approach to analyse the relationship between protesters and the protest space they inhabit.

In his monograph *Space Invaders: Radical Geographies of Protest* (2017), Routledge's focus has moved from social movements to protests, and is thus much closer to the spatial perspective sought in this book. Routledge discusses the acts of planning and realising mass protests from a spatial perspective, and he examines various ways in which people can utilise urban space to their advantage. This includes: 1) identifying and using local spatial qualities in an optimised manner; 2) considering the pros and cons of utilising static and mobile methods of action; 3) using the selected space to create a shared culture with which the protesters can identify; and 4) selecting methods of increasing an action's media exposure, both offline and online. The book is illustrated with examples of spatial strategies from contentious actions across the world, to inspire innovation among prospective protesters.

What the book does not have, however, is a generalised approach to how one can assess the use value, constraints, and limitations that urban spaces provide for mass protest. This shows that there is clearly a lack of generalised spatial perspectives in the literature on protest.

The second aim of this chapter was to find approaches and concepts that can be integrated into a generalised spatial perspective of this type. This question yielded more results, as several of the various findings, approaches, variables, and systems can be identified as valuable for a theoretical model on the causal relationship between space and protest. See for example POS theory and the concept of political environment (3.1), which are integrated into the model in chapter 5 (5.6) and 6 (6.2.2); or see the account of prospect-refuge theory (3.2.2) in chapter 3.

Additionally, in section 3.2, several contradicting understandings of what space is were identified. In the next chapter, I shall present my own definition of space and protest, to a large extent based on the literature presented in this chapter. In the subsequent chapters 5 and 6, I will explain how a spatial perspective on mass protest can be articulated, and how it can contribute to filling the research gap.

4 Definitions and Research Questions

The previous chapter concluded by identifying a gap in the research literature on urban mass protest. Before moving to the development and layout of a theoretical model to fill this gap, the aim of this chapter is to define some key concepts and delimitations. It starts with two sections that provide definitions and delimitations of mass protests (4.1) and urban public space (4.2); followed by a statement of the major research question and a series of secondary research questions (4.3).[27]

4.1 What Is a Mass Protest?

According to Karl-Dieter Opp, a protest might be defined as "[a] joint (i.e. collective) action of individuals aimed at achieving their goal or goals by influencing decisions of a target" (Opp 2009, 38). I have used this definition because it incorporates elements of key sociological perspectives on protest (3.1). The 'target' of the protests might be institutions or people. However, in this book, the main targets of the mass protests are governmental authorities. The 'goal or goals' of the protesters have previously been identified as change of regime, policy, or discourse (I elaborate on the goals of protest in chapter 9, subsection 9.1.3).

Opp's definition is still not specific enough, as it does not include a sense of scale. The word 'mass' has therefore been added to convey that the action is carried out by a large number of people.[28] Even with the inclusion of this additional word, a large number of individuals joined in action in order to achieve a goal can protest in a number of ways that would put

---

[27] Please note that there might be some inconsistencies between the definitions, terms and concepts in these chapters of *Part I* and *Part III* (chapters 1–6 and 10), and in the three accompanying chapters in Part II (chapters 7–9). This is because the spatial perspective has evolved over time, and each of the chapters represents the model at its different stages of development, before these concrete definitions were reached (see chapter 5).

[28] In one of the definitions provided by the Merriam Webster dictionary, 'mass' is described as "a large body of persons in a group" and "the great body of the people as contrasted with the elite—often used in plural". (Mass, n.d.)

them outside the scope of this project (e.g. using petitions, Internet actions, boycotts, graffiti, or civil disobedience). For the purpose of this book, "mass protests" are limited to the physical act of protesting in urban public space. I concentrate on static protests in the form of encampments and spatial occupation, rather than on mobile protests, such as marches.[29] The current study is also limited to protests 'on foot', thus excluding (the usually mobile) protests based on the use of vehicles, such as cars, bicycles, and trucks.[30] The reason for these delimitations is that, in the East Slavic region, static encampments on foot are the most prominent form of mass displays of discontent, and thus the one I had access to.

For the sake of simplicity, I have also tried to avoid the inclusion of violent protests such as riots and revolts, although some of the mass protests described here turned violent (notably Euromaidan). The reason for this exclusion is that, once a mass event turns violent, its nature is radically transformed; and the dynamics between demonstrators, law enforcement agencies, and urban space significantly change.

We thus arrive at the following definition of the mass protests examined in this book:

> Mass collective actions by pedestrians, engaged in static occupation of urban public space and intending to change society by influencing the decisions of a target by nonviolent means.

Mass Protests and Social Movements

Another concept closely related to mass protests is that of social movements, which are often discussed in the same literature as protests. The difference between the two terms is that, while social movements develop over time (and the focus of social movement studies is often on the causes that create the movement, or on its values, identity, and connections), mass protests are independent events or actions that either erupt suddenly

---

29   Since mobile demonstrations often are a tactical part of an encampment protest (e.g. reacting to events by staging demonstrations), the question of how spaces affect demonstrations demands separate attention (see 6.2.1 for mobility as a spatial quality).
30   Such as the truck drivers' strikes in Russia (Obshchaia gazeta 2017), or Automaidan in Ukraine (Kuzik 2014).

or are part of a bigger (social) movement for change. (A more elaborate definition of urban social movements can be found in Andretta, Piazza, and Subirats 2015.)

4.2 What Is Urban Public Space?

In order to succinctly define urban public space, it is first necessary to examine the term word-for-word. Of the three, 'urban' is the easiest part to deal with. According to the dictionary, 'urban' relates to, is characteristic of, or constitutes a city (Urban n.d.). In other words, it describes something in, or of, a city.

However, the next two parts, 'public' and 'space', are more difficult to define, as the two terms cover a broad variety of complex things. The Merriam Webster dictionary, for example, offers 7 and 10 categories of definitions respectively for each of the two categories. Based on these entries, we can deduce that 'public' refers to a collection or representation of the people or citizens of a community or society; or to something happening where it is easily perceived by, or relating to, the population. 'Space' covers an even wider range of phenomena, with distance between points or obstacles as the common denominator. For the purposes of this research project, definitions 2a ("a limited extent in one, two, or three dimensions: [distance, area, volume]") and 2b ("an extent set apart or available") are the closest in nature to the geographical space under examination. (Public n.d.; Space n.d.)

Urban Space and Public Space
When combined with 'urban', 'space' becomes 'an extent set apart in a city environment'; or, in other words, 'outdoor open areas between buildings', such as squares, parks, streets, and walkways.

So what, then, is 'urban public space'? Let us leave 'urban' aside for the moment and take a look at the contested term 'public space' first. Based on the literature on public space (3.2.1) and a discussion I participated in during a lecture by the US geographer Don Mitchell,[31] we can identify six questions that can be asked in order to define whether or not a space is public:

1. Who the space is for: is it for the people or their representatives, or for someone or something else?
2. To whom it is available: do all citizens/inhabitants/individuals/groups have equal access to it, or are they equally represented in it?
3. Who controls it: is it owned by a collective entity, such as a state or a city council?
4. What happens in it: is the space used for communication, interactions and contentious actions, such as protests?
5. How it is perceived: is it perceived as a place for all, representative of all, and/or used by all?
6. What it is used for/what it might become: is it where people's perception of the public is shaped and/or embodied? (Ukrainian national identity has, for instance, to a large extent been shaped by events on Maidan, and most Ukrainians are aware of the potential it has in society.)

Conversely, public space can be defined by what it is not. For instance, public space is not commercial or private space; it is not space reserved for only one or some groups (such as a gated community); it is not dominated by commercial interests or political control (in the form of heavy-handed policing or intrusive surveillance); and it is not perceived as exclusive.

To sum up, public space is a place which, ideally, is equally accessible and open to the whole general population. In order for something to be a truly public space, it must be accessible to everyone, including all individuals, minorities, political and non-political groups, organisations, and so on. This access must also be granted on an equal basis, as outlined by Habermas (3.2.1).

---

31 The lecture was part of the University of Oslo Summer School "Public Space: People, Power, and Political Economy" in 2018.

Urban Public Space

When we add 'urban' to the definition of public space above, we get the following (geographically oriented) definition:

> Urban public space is an outdoor open area between buildings in a city environment, equally accessible and open to everyone in the general population.[32]

Yet since all urban spaces are regulated in some way and, more often than not, are at least partially influenced by commercial, institutional, or political interests, it is possible that no urban public space in this ideal form exists. Even so, the six questions outlined above provide us with a tool for assessing to what degree an urban space is public. Therefore, we might add 'which in its ideal form is' before 'equally accessible and open to everyone in the general population', to underline that this is an idealisation and not necessary a reflection of reality.

In these chapters, the term 'urban public space' (often referred to simply as 'public space') is applied both in a general sense, i.e. to mean all the area between buildings in a city (for instance, the urban public space of Moscow); and a specific sense, for geographically defined areas of the city space (such as Swamp Square).

4.3 Research Questions

Chapter 2 outlined the historical and contemporary context around the act of urban contention. Chapter 3 then related this to the various research publications on the topic, where a gap in the existing research was also defined. Now that the components of the research question have been defined in this chapter, the context is fully developed, and we can return to the research question as stated in the introduction:

---

32 Conversely, Goodsell's *place-bound public space* definition could be used: "In this [...] *space* all persons present are within direct visual and audible range. Their mutual contact is face-to-face, within a reasonable distance. Probably this form of public space is the most efficient in terms of achieving true connection and inter- activity. This is the kind of public space, contemplated by the urban planners for their plazas and the architectural analysts in their ceremonial rooms" (Goodsell 2003, 370).

How are mass protests affected by urban public space?

It can now be expanded by using the definitions developed in this chapter:

> How are mass collective actions by pedestrians, engaged in static occupation of an urban public space and aimed at changing society by influencing the decisions of a target by nonviolent means, affected by this urban public space (i.e. outdoor open areas between buildings in a city environment, which in its ideal form is equally accessible and open to everyone in the general population)?

The question can also be expressed as a causality figure (in which the arrow signifies effect):

Urban public space (independent variable) → Mass protests (dependent variable)

This opens up several secondary questions, which naturally need to be answered, in full or in part, in order to properly answer the main research question:

1. What should a theoretical model exploring the causal connections between urban public space and mass protests look like?
2. What variables does urban public space include?
3. What variables do mass protests include?
4. What other variables can be identified in the causal chain between urban space and mass protests?
5. How can these variables be mapped and measured?

These questions are the subject of the discussion in the next chapters on theory development (chapter 5) and on the variables of the theoretical model and the methods used to find them (chapter 6). The main research question is answered specifically in the three case studies (chapters 7, 8, and 9), and generally in chapter 10.

5 Theorising and Development

This chapter traces the development of the spatial perspective from idea to current model, and provides an overview of the development of the three case studies (see below). It starts by defining some of the processes that brought the model to its current stage of development, including the approaches applied when theorising, and key qualitative methods (5.1). This is followed by a description of two ethical dilemmas and concerns encountered during the planning and execution of this research, as well as their practical solutions (5.2); and a discussion of a major pitfall of geographical determinism that I have aimed to avoid (5.3).

The fourth section (5.4) recounts how the idea for this project was initially conceived and the outline of a relevant research gap was identified, followed by a statement of the initial goals for this study. The theorising process is explicated in the fifth section (5.5), where the background for, and the purpose and development of, the first two case studies are discussed (i.e. the prestudy and the transitional study, in subsections 5.5.1 and 5.5.3, respectively). The sixth section discusses the development of the spatial perspective (5.6), followed by a seventh section (5.7) on the testing of the model in case study 3. The chapter ends with a section on the few minor changes added to the model following the main test study (5.8).

5.1 Approaches to Theorising

In the article "Theorizing in sociology and social science: turning to the context of discovery" the Swedish sociologist Richard Swedberg (2012) discusses the process of developing theories within social sciences. Drawing heavily on the Austrian-British philosopher Karl R. Popper and the German philosopher Hans Reichenbach, Swedberg identifies three elements of theory development: *theorising, theory,* and *testing of the theory*. According to Swedberg, in social sciences—which tend to be overly focused on theory and methodology—there is a lack of emphasis on the first (theorising) element (2012, 4).

Swedberg divides the research process in social sciences into two phases: the prestudy, which includes theorising and an early discovery of a phenomenon; and the main study, including drawing up and executing the research design and writing up the results. The first phase is the subject of Swedberg's article.

Swedberg attempts to lay out some basic rules for the creative act of theorising (see fig. 9). He divides these into two parts: "observation" (part I) and "naming, conceptualisation, using analogies, metaphors, and types, developing a tentative theory, including an explanation" (part II).

Figure 9: Swedberg's basic rules of theorising

Rule # 1 Observe—and Choose Something Interesting
You can only theorize on the basis of observation. Anything that can stimulate to a full view of the phenomenon should be used, from sturdy scientific facts to art in various forms. "*Don't think but look!*" (Wittgenstein)
Rule # 2 Name and Formulate the Central Concept
Give a name to what you observe and try to formulate a central concept based on it. Here as elsewhere abduction (Pierce) is the key.
Rule # 3 Build Out the Theory
Give body to the central concept by outlining the structure, pattern or organization of the phenomenon. Use analogies, metaphors, comparisons—and all in a heuristic way to get a better grip on the phenomenon under study.
Rule # 4 Complete the Tentative Theory, including the Explanation
Formulate or model a full tentative theory of the phenomenon, with special emphasis on the explanation that constitutes the natural end of the theorizing process.

(Swedberg 2012, 17)

In the first part, Swedberg argues, one should not necessarily start theorising in a structured or scientific manner: "[…] one can proceed in whatever way that leads to something interesting—and that means *any way*" (2012, 6). By starting with facts, observing these with the use of heuristic methods, and only then developing a theory to explain the facts, the likelihood of creating original research is, according to the author, much higher. He also recommends avoiding reading too many secondary works early on (2012, 13).

In the second part, Swedberg suggests that the researcher should take the observed facts and give a proper name to the theory; conceptualise; flesh out the theory; give explanations, and so on. The theorising process, he argues, would also benefit from including a prestudy before the main study. (2012, 10)

Applying Swedberg's Theory

My theorising with regard to the spatial perspective has, with few exceptions, followed the approach promoted by Swedberg's (2012) article, which will be used below to illustrate the conceptualisation process.

The first part of the approach—conception of the initial idea and observations—began, as I describe below (5.4), while doing field work in Ukraine for my master's thesis, and the idea that space is important was developed in a case study for the current research project (5.5.1), which became what Swedberg's approach calls "a prestudy". In accordance with Swedberg's approach, my theorising was not limited by an excessive focus on the existing secondary works and theoretical approaches developed by other scholars. My background in area studies gave me the advantage of intimate knowledge of the case studies, while the absence of "theoretical baggage" left me open to theorise freely.

It is my view, however, that any new theory or approach benefits from being scrutinised at all stages of development and from feedback, suggestions, and critique. Receiving this feedback throughout the process was particularly important for the development of this spatial perspective, since I had little previous knowledge in architecture, urbanism, or sociology (subjects that might be perceived as better fits for a project such as this). Moreover, having ongoing feedback helped me to avoid writing about a gap in the literature that does not exist, or omitting important literature from my case studies.

For these reasons, I endeavoured to present my project in as many settings as I could find, to as large and as varied an audience as possible. Over the entire process of the project's development, I gave talks at conferences, seminars, and as guest lectures in Great Britain, Norway, Sweden, Ukraine, and Russia. This produced a great number of critical comments, thoughts, suggestions, and recommendations, some of which were integrated into my theoretical model. Moreover, the doctoral thesis, which this book is based upon, was written as an article-based thesis. The benefit of such a format is that the articles were reviewed by anonymous peers within various research fields (and, as an added bonus, gave me a continuous set of deadlines to meet, which propelled me onwards). Finally, I had the opportunity to present the project to scholars of different disciplines by taking part in a diverse choice of PhD coursework options in Tromsø (UiT) and Oslo (UiO). Particularly valuable in this respect were the two summer school courses at the University of Oslo: "Case Study Research Methods" (2016) by the US political scientist Andrew Bennett, and "Public Space: People, Power, and Political Economy" (2018) by Don Mitchell (mentioned above), which allowed me to present the project to leading scholars from two highly relevant fields.[33]

I used the second part of Swedberg's approach, which includes "naming, conceptualisation, using analogies, metaphors, and types, developing a tentative theory, including an explanation" (2012, 14), when working on the second case study (5.5.3). Arguably, the second case could also be characterised as a prestudy, because it forms part of the theorising process and was written in preparation for a more thorough study of Moscow in case study 3, on which the theory is tested. However, since case study 2 could neither be described as the result of unstructured theorising (i.e. a prestudy) nor as a study with a fully developed theoretical model (i.e. a main study), I chose to call it a transitional study.

The next three subsections describe three main qualitative methods used during the development and execution of this study: field work (5.1.1), the use of respondents (5.1.2), and mapping (5.1.3).

5.1.1 Field Work

Field work for this project was conducted in five cities: Kyiv, Minsk, Chișinău, Moscow, and Paris. The advantage of conducting field work is

---

33 See the section on process tracing (5.6), below, and the section on public space (3.2.1), above.

that the researcher builds an immediate relationship to, and understanding of, the location analysed and events observed: cognitive reference points are created. By being physically present, the researcher might also observe details that are harder to find in maps, conversations, or in academic literature. The main limitations are that field work is time consuming and might not always be practically possible. Moreover, when observing a protest, a researcher cannot be in more than one place at a given time. So, while the information gathered might be detailed, the scope might also be somewhat restricted. The advantages nevertheless greatly outweigh the limitations.

Although much of the data for the first case study was already collected during field work in Kyiv for my M.A. thesis (Hansen 2015), additional field work on Maidan and observations of demonstrations in the city was carried out in late 2015 and early 2016. This field work was done in order to check various aspects of the square and assist the theorising process.

Since I have previously lived in Minsk, I had a good knowledge of the public spaces in the city. Nonetheless, to refresh my memory of the two urban spaces I planned to write about for the second article (October Square and Independence Square), I combined a personal trip to the city in late 2015 with observations of the two squares as well as some of the nearby urban spaces. In order to avoid overstepping any legal boundaries created by holding a tourist visa, I did not observe protests, approach possible respondents, or conduct interviews while in the city. The interviews were conducted at a later point using communication technologies (see 5.1.2).

Figure 10: Great Assembly Square, Chișinău, August 2016

Photo: Arve Hansen

When a series of mass protests erupted in Moldova in 2015–2016, I decided to travel to Chișinău in August 2016 to conduct preliminary field work there. The aim was to check a) whether the city space could become a separate case study for this research project, and b) what could be learned about space and mass protests by observing contention in the city. In Chișinău, as in Kyiv, I already knew which specific urban space should be analysed before I arrived. For reasons I explain below, my field work was concentrated on mapping the Great National Assembly Square (*Piața Marii Adunări Naționale*), although I also observed other urban spaces nearby. I witnessed one small protest against the president at Great National Assembly Square during the Independence Day celebrations on 26 August 2016. I also visited museums in order to better understand the city and the country's history, and conducted interviews. For reasons I also explain below, the city did not become a full case study, but my observations of its urban space, and of contention and policing of protests in the space and city, contributed to the development of the spatial perspective model. (See 5.5.1 for more on Chişinău and its contribution to this development.)

The most structured form of field work was carried out in Moscow in June 2017, as the theoretical model and accompanying methodological approach were almost fully developed at this point. My field work in Moscow had four goals. The first was to get a general feel for the city and what it is like to move around in, and use, its urban public spaces. I did this mainly by walking around the city on foot[34] and using the underground system. The second goal was to collect data from various squares, parks, and other urban public spaces with a tradition of protest or proximity to the country's political institutions. The third and fourth goals were to observe mass protests in the city and how the authorities prepared for and reacted to them. I had several opportunities to do both.[35] I did not, however, have the opportunity to observe any protests or policing strategies on Swamp Square, the urban space ultimately chosen for case study 3. My data

---

34   I walked around Boulevard Ring and most main streets within it, notably Tverskaia Street. I also spent a great deal of time in the area around the Kremlin (Borovitskaia Square, Aleksandrovskii Garden, Manège Square, Red Square, Theater Square/Revolution Square, Chinatown). I walked around most of the western parts of Swamp Island (west of Greater River Mouth Bridge), and the four main streets between Rampart Street and Swamp Island (Greater Iakimanka Street, Greater Glade Street, Greater Ordynka Street, Piatnitskaia Street). Additionally, I walked to other places of interest, such as Academician Sakharov Avenue, the area around the Russian White House (government building), and the Arbat district.

35   At the time, a mass rally against President Putin was planned for Russia Day, June 12, 2017, which was sanctioned to be held at Sakharov Avenue. The night before the action, I observed the massive preparations beforehand, including the construction of physical obstacles in a large perimeter around the Avenue and the setting up of block posts with metal detectors and police command posts. Immediately before the action, the opposition leaders announced that the protest would be held at unsanctioned Pushkin Square instead, and that they would march on Tverskaia Street. This led me to observe how quickly the police efficiently blocked off the whole area around Tverskaia, dividing its southern parts from Pushkin Square. During the action, the police successfully diverted the protesters (and their energy) away from the announced place of action by enforcing one-way movement in a large number of streets. Being on the southern part of the police blockades, I spent more than an hour trying to get around to the other side, ultimately without success. The next day I observed a small protest against police brutality outside the State Duma (Federal Assembly, lower house).

collection included photographing, drawing, and keeping a journal where I recorded data about spatial elements (explained in subsection 6.1).

In Paris field work was conducted on 5 and 6 January 2019, during two of the demonstrations by the Yellow Vests social movement. The aim of this field work was threefold: 1) since Paris has a long and well-known history of urban contention, I wanted to see how various repertoires of contention and policing involved the city; 2) I also wanted to test whether the spatial perspective model could be applied to protests I knew little about, in a city I had never been to before; and 3) I wanted to test whether a Western protest could provide any new insights that could be added to the spatial perspective. I observed the Yellow Vests on 5 January outside Musée d'Orsay, where they were stopped by a wall of riot police on their way to the National Assembly, and the clashes that ensued. The next day, I observed a smaller and more peaceful demonstration on Republic Square (*Place de la République*), where the Yellow Vests' first women's march congregated before they gradually marched towards Champs-Élysées (more on this in chapter 10).

5.1.2 Respondents

A significant part of the qualitative data set used for this book comes from 30 interviews conducted with protest participants, politicians and protest organisers, observers, and experts. (See References.)

This subsection includes 1) a discussion of the benefits and limitations of using interviews; 2) an account of the use of respondents for each of the case studies; and 3) an outline of the main interview structure.

The interviews generated invaluable data for understanding not only specific protest events and how specific urban public spaces are shaped, perceived, and used, but also how protesters and organisers relate to space when planning and carrying out collective actions. In addition, observers and political scientists have contributed with accounts of events from the sidelines. From these interviews and conversations, I have identified several variables of space and protest, as well as the goals of protesters. I achieved a nuanced understanding of the mindset of protesters and protest organisers, and tested some of my hypotheses on them. Hence, my theorising has benefitted a great deal from interviews and conversations. The limitations of qualitative interviewing are mainly related to the time and effort it takes to prepare, conduct, and process them. Interviews, especially in semi- to fully authoritarian states, also require some significant ethical decisions (5.2).

The interviews used in the prestudy on Maidan were conducted for my M.A. thesis in 2014. The interviews did not have a unified layout, covered a variety of topics, and consisted, with few exceptions, of open-ended questions. The in-depth interviews were with four participants in Euromaidan (three Ukrainian and one Belarusian), and two observers of the revolution (one Ukrainian and one Norwegian). I also had a large number of conversations in and around the protest camp at Maidan in the course of events, with both protesters and observers, and a number of pilot interviews and unstructured conversations (some of which are included under References). Since most of the interviews included questions about the respondent's subjective understanding of Maidan and about the square's function in Ukrainian society, they gave me enough material to act as a basis for the arguments presented in the prestudy about the function and symbolic value of the square.

For the research on Great National Assembly Square, I carried out six interviews with three political scientists (one Moldovan, one East European, and one Scandinavian), one observer (from Scandinavia), and two interviews with one protest organiser/activist. The interviews were semi-structured around a number of open-ended questions, adapted to each individual interviewee, about the situation in the country, the various political actions that had already occurred, and the Great National Assembly Square. Some questions were based on Lynch's (1960) methodology for mapping people's perception of urban space (see the outline of the interview structure, as stated below; and 3.2.2 on Lynch). I also had a number of informal and unstructured conversations with protesters and other people I met while in the city.

For the transitional study on October Square and Independence Square in Minsk, I interviewed five respondents who had participated in protests, three politicians/protest organisers, and one observer. All were Belarusians. These interviews were semi-structured with open-ended questions about the political situation in the country, their activism or actions they have witnessed, and about the city and the two specific urban spaces. At the end of the interviews I would often include my own thoughts and hypotheses about the role of space in general and about the effect of the two squares on the 2006 and 2010 protests in particular. This frequently generated new discussions, as the interviewees were often sceptical of my hypotheses. But, as they had "warmed up" with their own accounts of past events and entered a spatial mindset by describing the two squares to me, several new aspects of space and the effects of space on protests were identified in discussion.

One significant variable in the interview process was the location in which the interviews were conducted. Whilst most of the interviews for Maidan and Great National Assembly Square were conducted face-to-face (in parks and cafes), all the interviews about the squares in Minsk were dependent on communication technology (video calls, telephone, and e-mail) (see section 8.1).

For the main study on Swamp Square in Moscow, I decided not to interview respondents for two main reasons. One was ethical, relating to the safety of my respondents (5.2); another practical, relating to the planned layout of the third case study (5.7). Before I decided not to carry out interviews, I conducted one pilot interview, but the data generated from this was not used in the article. Not including interviews had several consequences, most importantly a smaller qualitative data set. I would also potentially miss important information about events and aspects of Swamp Square, and would not be able to fully map the perceived (i.e. subjective, see 6.1.1) elements of the urban space or to test all of my hypotheses about Swamp Square. To add to the data set, I sent out a Google Forms questionnaire on a social media platform I use on and off.[36] The survey

---

[36] YouTube (Hansen n.d.). At the time of writing, the channel has 30,000 subscribers (mostly Russophone and Ukrainophone). YouTube does not provide information about the number of Muscovite subscribers, but 50 % of the channel's views are from Russia.

mainly consisted of questions about how citizens of Moscow and other people with knowledge of Moscow perceived the city, and one open question about the effect Moscow has on public actions, such as demonstrations and parades. The object of the survey was to map the perceived and social elements of the city (6.1.1 and 6.1.3), and see what ideas people had about spatial effects. Although the questionnaire generated 154 responses of varying quality and length, and the answers presented a number of viewpoints about the effects of space (ranging from "I have never thought about that" or "we have no space to demonstrate in" to "[Moscow affects protests] as a bucket of water on quarks"), these were not included in the case study, as the scientific value of the survey was questionable. Instead, my research (based on field work, mapping, and academic literature) was complemented with informal conversations about my hypotheses with colleagues and acquaintances with a knowledge of the city.

I decided not to carry out any conversations or qualitative interviews with respondents on Republic Square in Paris, as I have little command of French. Besides, my time in the city was greatly limited.

The Main Interview Structure

All interviews started with my telling the respondent about the project, what it was for, and their rights as a respondent. Most importantly, I asked the respondents whether they consented to my use of the information they provided (this point is further elaborated in subsection 5.2.1). The respondents were then asked to share with me their

1. description of the political situation in the country today;
2. account of actions they had attended or observed.

Once they had spoken about these actions in their own words, I would ask about goals, important events, and impact, in order to obtain

3. a description of the physical space where the action occurred;
4. a description of the social space (i.e. who uses the space, at what time and for which purposes);

5. a description of the perceived space (i.e. the respondents' subjective opinion about the space).

If any elements (physical, social, or perceived) were left out, I would sometimes prompt the respondents with questions like "What exits were available to you during the protest?".

6. Often, I would present some of my findings to the respondents and ask them to comment on them. These questions often stimulated a whole new discussion about the importance of space, the impact of which the respondents initially downplayed almost without exception, yet which often produced new insights.[37]

The semi-structuring of the interviews was due to my not knowing exactly what I was looking for at first; most of the variables were not yet identified at this stage, and the independent variables had not yet been thoroughly defined. My aim was to get the respondents themselves to tell me about the protest in the space and to identify the variables they found important, before looking into the specific spatial elements and qualities.

5.1.3 Mapping

The maps used for this project were created using the vector programming tools Affinity Designer and Adobe Illustrator CS6 and based on a wide range of sources, including: online mapping services, such as OpenStreetMap, Google Maps, and Yandex Maps; field notes and drawings; research literature; news articles; Wikipedia; and protest sites, groups, and channels on social media platforms (mainly Facebook and YouTube). All the case studies have benefitted from the use of mapping as a tool at four stages of development:

As preparation for field work. Mapping was of great assistance to me while creating a list of points of interest and routes to walk while in the city (although, once on site, I often deviated from these lists and routes for

---

37 See for example this excerpt from the conversation with a respondent by the name of Pauliuk: "Come to think about it, [we associate the square…] with the authorities, with failed desires, dreams, […] yes, and with disappointment."

various reasons). In Minsk and Chișinău I knew exactly which spaces to analyse, and in Paris I had a general idea (Republic Square, Champs-Élysées, and Bastille Square), but mapping these spaces identified districts, spots, and objects I marked as interesting. Mapping was especially important for the study of Moscow, as I had only a few initial ideas about which public spaces to include in the main study.

During field work. Digital or hand-drawn maps were used on location in all the spaces analysed as part of the field diary. In the diary, notes about elements and other aspects of urban spaces were continually added for later reference.

During analysis. The mapping of cities and urban spaces facilitated the process of examining sites, as maps can function both as visual guides to places and events and as reference points while writing the analysis.

Presenting the results. The developed maps also functioned as illustrations for paper presentations and in the articles. The unnecessary parts of the maps were removed in order to leave only the relevant points; the reader should, if I have done my job properly, be presented with a simplified illustration of the points I make about the space under consideration.

5.2 Ethical Considerations

Researching mass protests in authoritarian countries is no easy matter and requires a number of practical and ethical decisions. This study is no exception, and two key dilemmas had to be resolved. The first concern is how to handle respondents with proper care, respecting their rights and protecting them from potential repercussions. The second is related to the possible misuse of my research.

The decisions I have made are based on The National (Norwegian) Committee for Research Ethics in the Social Sciences and the Humanities' "Guidelines for Research Ethics in the Social Sciences, Humanities, Law and Theology" (NESH 2016). Although all the committee's guidelines have been read through and form the ethical foundation for this study, chapters B "Respect for individuals" and C "Respect for groups and institutions" are of particular importance.

5.2.1 Interview Ethics

While preparing for and carrying out the interviews, as well as processing them, the rights and safety of the respondents were always my highest priority. An account of how the interviews were conducted in this regard is provided below. This is followed by a discussion about gaining access to Russia and one practical implication of being open about my work.

Pre-interview

Before the interviews, I did my best to inform the respondents about my project, where I worked, how the respondents' information would be handled and where it would be published. They were also informed that, up until the moment of publication, they had the right to review their answers or withdraw them altogether, and that I would not question their decision to do so.

I informed the interviewees in advance that they would be given pseudonyms. Exceptions were made for some of the elite interviewees (politicians, observers, and experts), who participated as public figures; they were explicitly informed that I would attach their names to their answers. None of the respondents thus informed had any objections to being referred to by name, and no one withdrew their participation. This is probably because elites—and particularly high-profile politicians—already have a visible and well-known political standpoint. Leaders of the opposition talk to foreign media and researchers on a regular basis, and this project would not worsen their situation in any notable way. Moreover, the extra publicity such a study might produce can be beneficial for a politician or opposition leader.

It must be noted, however, that even though some public figures were identified, I have omitted any irrelevant or personally sensitive information I may have acquired during these interviews.

If, for some reason, I was unable to inform the respondents of some or all of these aspects in advance of the interview, these were explained at the start of the interview itself and the respondents were given the opportunity to take some time to think this over and, if they wished, to discontinue the interview.

Interview

At the start of each interview, I once again informed each respondent about the project and their rights as a respondent, and asked them if they consented to participate. I told them how the interviews would be conducted and about their rights to withdraw from participation at any moment without needing to provide a reason for doing so. I also informed them how their personal and sensitive information would be handled afterwards.

Post-interview

The interviews were processed by myself alone, and personally sensitive information that could be used to identify the respondents was stored on a password-protected external hard drive accessible only by me. The information was not stored for any longer than strictly necessary. At the time of writing, all personal and potentially sensitive information has been permanently deleted.

Russia

Gaining access to the countries in which I intended to conduct field work usually did not pose any practical problems. Both Ukraine and Moldova have a visa-free regime for citizens of EEA countries; the visit to Minsk, a city I know very well, was (as stated above, 5.1.1) limited to observations; and France is located in the EU. By contrast, I did not have the same access to Russia, as travel to the country requires a visa. Nor did I have the same previous knowledge of Moscow as of Minsk and Kyiv, since I had only visited the city for shorter periods.

I wanted to be open about my work in Russia, especially as I was co-organising a seminar at the Norwegian University Centre in St. Petersburg on the centenary of the October Revolution, where I wanted to talk about my project. The decision had some practical implications, however, and I was determined to act with extra caution in case the Russian authorities took an interest in my work. I could no longer be absolutely sure that conversations and interviews with respondents would not come to the attention of the authorities and so put respondents in a difficult situation. For this reason, as well as the practical reasons explained in section 5.7, I concentrated on the development of the theoretical aspects of the spatial perspective, which by that time had become more important than the qualitative interviews.

5.2.2 Practical Utility

When presenting this project, I have often been confronted with the potential consequences and misuses of my results. One critical argument has been that my study could be used by authoritarian leaders to design public spaces in such a way as to ease the suppression of mass protests. Another has been that my research could be used by radical groupings and violent mobs in order to overthrow peaceful governments and stable democracies.

I believe such criticism to be naïve.

The short answer to the first argument is that my research probably does not provide authorities or police strategists with any new knowledge of importance. In all three case studies, I have shown examples of authorities using space in order to limit public protests (7.2.1; 8.5.1; 8.5.2; 9.2.5). It is only natural that law enforcement agents sit down before a planned march or protest to discuss the possibilities and limitations that various spaces provide and how to avoid damages, minimise injuries, etc. What I might have done, however, is provide them with updated language to discuss such space more efficiently. Moreover, taking the long view, rebuilding a city so as to avoid protest would require great time and effort. It is, of course, a possibility which cannot be excluded; but I highly doubt that any future dictator would look at my book and design a city full of Swamp and October squares.

My response to the second argument is similar. Although protesters may not think about spatial features in the same way as the police do, my research shows that protesters are aware of their surroundings and instinctively know which possibilities and/or obstacles they might encounter. My contribution is making these observations available for academic study.

5.3 Geographical Determinism

Before I proceed to delineate the process of conceptualising and theorising the spatial perspective model, I must mention my main reservation. Often, when examining the causal effects of geography, it is easy to become caught up in the geographical context, finding cause only in geography and disregarding other factors. Few if any illustrate this problem of deterministic argumentation better than the British journalist Tim Marshall who, in his book *Prisoners of Geography* (2015), demonstrates how the researcher can be trapped by the geographical argument.

In the book, the world is presented as a geopolitical battleground, a zero-sum game for resources and strategic positions between superpowers. Yet, even though most of Marshall's ten geopolitical case studies arguably *are* affected by geography, it is by far not the only factor in international relations, and Marshall often exaggerates its importance. An example of this is his case study of Russia. In his assessment of the country's geography, Marshall states that Russia's foreign policy has, historically and presently, been determined by the country's lack of warm-water ports as well as the lack of a prominent mountain range between Russia and the rest of Europe. Viewed in isolation, these statements probably hold true; but the argumentation disregards a number of other factors, such as the effectiveness of rulers, religion, random events, etc.

Marshall proceeds to explain the Russo-Ukrainian conflict on the basis of this same geographical argument. He presents the conflict largely as a result of, firstly, Crimea and the Black Sea Fleet's strategic importance for Russia; and, secondly, NATO and EU meddling in Russia's sphere of influence. Therefore, Russia's invasion of Ukraine was allegedly the only viable option open to Putin, and the crisis was near-inevitable. Moreover, Marshall's argument is supported by oft-repeated simplifications of two complex and multifaceted countries. Ukraine, for instance, is presented as a country with two clearly definable regions (shaped, of course, by geography), a pro-European West and a pro-Russian East, even though this is far from the case;[38] the whole formal political opposition to Yanukovych is called "anti-Russian", although the majority of it (represented by the UDAR and Fatherland political parties) was decidedly not so; and Ukrainians are depicted as pawns in a geopolitical chess game, without a will of their own.

The upshot of this argumentation is that geography and geopolitical interests are indeed to blame for the Ukrainian crisis. But such a one-dimensional macro perspective cannot possibly explain by itself Russia's interventions in Ukraine. At the least, the claim should not be made without first examining alternative/complementary explanations of the conflict.

Having read Marshall's book,[39] I became very aware of the dangers of such a deterministic argumentation; and I decided early in the theorising process not to become yet another prisoner of geography. This is one of the reasons why the importance of the political environment is emphasised in this study (5.6).

5.4 Conception

In the introduction to this book, I described one of the many moments during Euromaidan when I experienced first-hand the value of using Maidan for protests. During the events in Kyiv, I observed that the square was not only an ideological platform, as the place where Ukrainians demand more democracy and civil rights. The architecture, history, and geography of the square also reinforced the protesters, both practically and symbolically. This realisation made me want to investigate this phenomenon closer, to pinpoint the characteristics that made Maidan so special.

---

38 See for instance Barrington and Herron (2004) and Onuch and Hale (2018).
39 I feel obliged to add that I thoroughly enjoyed the book. Despite its oversimplifications, it was easy to read, informative and witty.

5.4.1 M.A. Thesis

Although I have presented this as an eureka moment, more development was needed before I could start theorising. I had travelled to Kyiv in June 2013 because I wanted to write my Master's thesis about some of the contention in the region, which had fascinated me ever since I first moved to Belarus in 2006. Mass protests were frequent when I lived in Belarus, Ukraine, and Russia, but their means, methods, and results were often different.

By chance, I arrived in Kyiv five months before Euromaidan began, and I was able to witness the 2013–2014 revolution from its early beginning through to its political aftermath. Fascinated by the events that were unfolding in the Ukrainian capital, I decided in December 2013 to change the topic of my M.A. thesis to an examination of the driving forces of Euromaidan.

In the introductory chapter to that thesis, I wanted to address the space where the revolution occurred and explain some of its historic and socio-political significance. The reason for this was threefold. 1) The protesters made many references to Maidan. The protest was called *Euromaidan* (Ukr. *ievromaidan: ievro* [Europe] + *maidan*), and the protesters were *maidanovtsy* (*maidan* + *ovtsy* [people of]). A group of mobile protesters in cars contributed to the protests, and this was called *Avtomaidan* (*avto* [automobile] + *maidan*). And the pro-governmental countermovement was called *Antimaidan*, and often used derogatory terms for the *maidanovtsy*, such as *maidaunovtsy* (*maidan* + *daun*, for the medical condition Down's syndrome). 2) The protesters talked about the square with reverence, as if it were a physical manifestation of an ideal democratic institution. Several of my respondents perceived Maidan as a modern form of medieval public assemblies, such as the Old Slavic *Viche* or the Old Norse *Thing*. 3) Some of the physical characteristics of the square indicated that it was suitable, not only as a symbol, but also as a strategic location for protests.

In order to better understand the importance of Maidan, I turned my attention to concepts in political philosophy, such as Habermas's *public sphere* and Arendt's *public space*, and to architecture and urban planning (Kevin Lynch 1960); but I did not find a satisfactory explanation for the success of Maidan Square as a protest space. At the same time, while working on the other (main) parts of the master's thesis, I realised that the chapter on Maidan was growing and threatening to become the main subject of the thesis. For this reason, I narrowed down the chapter and put some of my findings aside for a future project.

5.4.2 PhD Proposal

From the first project draft, one of my main aims has been to examine the power of space, while at the same time researching the opposition in a region I know well and am very much intrigued by. The three countries (Ukraine, Belarus, and Russia) have—despite a similar historic and political background—very different forms of opposition, and the three capital cities are quite different from each other. Starting from this proposition, the original research questions were stated in the research proposal as follows:

> Are there urban spaces [similar to Maidan Square] in Russia and Belarus, in which the population can express their discontent? If so, where are these spaces located, what characterises them, how do they function [as public spaces] or why do they not function?[40]

These initial questions are not far removed from the current research question:

> How are mass protests affected by urban public space?

The difference is that the current question is more generalised, while the original questions were embedded within each of the case studies, expressed (with some variations) in the following, condensed manner:

---

40 From the research proposal (in Norwegian): "Finnes det tilsvarende rom i Russland og Hviterussland hvor befolkningen kan uttrykke sin misnøye? Hvor er i så fall disse, hva kjennetegner dem, hvordan fungerer de eller hvorfor fungerer de ikke? Dette ph.d-prosjektet tar sikte på å kartlegge, analysere og sammenligne offentlige byrom som brukes, eller inviterer til å brukes, til protester i Moskva, Minsk og Kyiv."

How is the opposition in Ukraine/Belarus/Russia affected by the urban public space in Kyiv/Minsk/Moscow?

The initial hypothesis, formulated in the research proposal was that…

> […] not only reprehensible social, political, and economic conditions need to be present for larger demonstrations to occur, gain momentum/popular support, and persevere for a long time. The access to a symbolic gathering place that possesses a variety of practical and physical properties is probably a necessary condition, too.

Based on the methods, ethical considerations, and reservation described above, the next four sections describe how the initial hypothesis developed into a full-fledged theoretical model, from the various stages of theorising (5.5), through a development of a causality model (5.6), to the main study of Moscow (5.7), ending with the adjustments made to the theory after the main study (5.8).

5.5 Theorising

Starting from the initial hypothesis stated above, I had to conduct some initial examinations of the effects of urban public space on oppositional activity in order to identify the phenomenon's variables. The best option, by my estimation, was to perform a prestudy of Maidan (Independence Square), which I knew very well as a place with positive spatial characteristics.

5.5.1 Prestudy

Without much previous theoretical knowledge from urbanism, architecture, or sociology, I set out to describe Maidan's effect on mass protests. Interestingly, even though spaces of contention had been discussed in a variety of cases (3.2), I could not find a theory that addressed why some locations were more suitable for protest than others. For this reason, I used Kevin Lynch's (1960) theories of urban planning (3.2.2) as a loose frame of reference to identify some key physical and social features of the square. This framework formed the basis for discussing the value of these features.

The lack of a strict theoretical framework allowed me to cast my net wide and identify as many explanations as possible as to why Maidan had become Ukraine's preferred urban public space for mass protest.

The field work and interviews conducted in Kyiv during and after Euromaidan contributed considerably to my theorising and to my assessment of how the square was perceived in Ukraine. I also looked into academic literature on the square's history, daily uses, layout, and position, as well as its local and regional significance, and found that there were several reasons for the special significance and symbolic value of the square: Maidan's history, architecture, symbolic monuments, landmarks, and location all signify that it is a central part of Ukrainian history and represents a majority of the population. Its current and previous names[41] imply a revolutionary quality that can be perceived as a protest against Russian hegemony. Its visibility in the centre of the city, in a location of local, regional, and geopolitical significance (political, religious, and cultural), attracts national and international attention to protests, including media coverage. Additionally, it is easily defendable, hard to supress with normal policing strategies, and easy to get to and get away from. In Ukraine, Maidan is perceived as a safety valve in a corrupt and dysfunctional political system: the only place where the actions of the people are viewed as having a real impact on politics.

The first case study thus served to open up the field and identify some key categories in the relationship between space and protest. It confirmed that, in the Ukrainian context, my initial hypothesis was—at the very least—not wrong. Urban public space had a positive impact on contentious actions in the city, and my findings indicated that the spatial qualities of the square contributed to the success of Euromaidan. Moreover, since there seemed to be few theoretical approaches to the analysis of protest spaces, it led to the realisation that a new theoretical model was required if I was to take the analysis of urban space to the level I wanted.

---

41   October Revolution Square, 1977–1991; Maidan Nezalezhnosti, since 1991.

5.5.2 Formulating a Theory

The knowledge I gained from the prestudy led me to what Swedberg's terminology (2012) identifies as the second part of theorising: "naming, conceptualisation, using analogies, metaphors, and types, developing a tentative theory, including an explanation" (2012, 14). Swedberg argues that naming, if possible, should be descriptive but simple, and he urges caution in inventing new words and expressions (2012, 19–20). I chose to name my model "a spatial perspective on mass protests" because this describes the essence of what I am trying to do—looking at mass protests from the viewpoint of space—and also employs accessible, clear, and consistent language.

Swedberg proposes a wide range of heuristic methods to conceptualise and "flesh out" the theory, to help the researcher understand the phenomenon he or she is studying. (Swedberg 2012, 23–24) I used analogies, such as comparing public space to democratic and/or representative institutions, or, in the case of an occupation protest, as a separate society. Another of Swedberg's suggested methods is testing explanations using counterfactual arguments. To take one example: a square with many entrances (such as Maidan) is arguably hard to control by the authorities. The counterfactual argument would be that a square with *few* entrances would by default be *easy* to control by the authorities.

Categorisation and typologies also emerged as efficient tools of theorising. Based on data from field work and interviews, 18 new elements with particular relevance to mass protests were added to Lynch's (1960) original five, and these were divided into three categories: perceived, social, and physical elements (see fig. 11). By naming the different parts of urban space and dividing them into categories, it became easier to discuss space based on its variations, but also to identify how different spaces contain many of the same or similar elements (floor, exits, entrances etc.). Categorisation was especially fruitful when combined with the counterfactual tool of "ideal types" (Swedberg 2012, 25). What might be considered a perfect space for protests? What might be considered a functional space for displaying the might of the authorities, while also discouraging protests? This method highlights the use value of the different elements and categories of public spaces. Observing protests in Kyiv and Chișinău also led to the discovery that non-physical elements—such as the history of a space, people's relation to the space, its traditions and day-to-day usage, and so on—can affect protests, and should therefore also form part of the theory.

Figure 11:   Elements of the city, first version

Perceived elements	Social elements	Physical elements
History	Paths	Location
Ideological symbols	Nodes	Size
Buildings	Buildings	Shape
Landmarks	Landmarks	Entrances
Monuments	Districts	Exits
History of protests	Traditions	Walls
	Official use	Floor
		Objects
		Obstacles
		Edges
		Public works
		Focal points

Following this unstructured conceptualising, the updated theoretical model consisted of mapping the spatial elements which, if properly identified and examined, would be a good foundation for discussing the space's value as a protest location. Once this was combined with field work, interviews, and academic literature on history and past collective actions, I would be able to create a fuller picture of the possibilities and limitations that a given space provides.

5.5.3 Transitional Study

In order to test my post-Kyivan spatial perspective, I needed a second case study. I had already planned a study of public space in Minsk, but it so happened that in 2016, while I was conceptualising and developing my model, mass protests flared up in the Moldovan capital Chișinău.[42] Still living in Kyiv, I decided to travel to Chișinău in August 2016 to establish whether the urban public space of Chișinău would make a suitable second case study.

Chișinău

There seemed to be many similarities between the Ukrainian and Moldovan cases. The international media had dubbed the social movement in the city "the Moldovan Maidan" (Călugăreanu 2015; International Business Times 2015), partly because of the similarities with the initial Euromaidan protests in Kyiv in 2013 and partly because in Chișinău, too, the protesters occupied a central square. In 2015, they had established an encampment on Great National Assembly Square (*Piața Marii Adunări Naționale*), and parts of the opposition were working on organising a similar event in 2016. Both Moldova and Ukraine are post-Soviet countries with a history of widespread corruption. Both had experienced a colour revolution in the 2000s (Ukraine in 2004, Moldova in 2009), the aftermath of which still affected both countries. Both had a square in their capital cities where there was a tradition of mass protest. And Russian is spoken by a large minority in both countries, too.

However, when I arrived in Chișinău in August 2016, it immediately became clear to me that this would be a more difficult case study than Kyiv. First of all, even though many Moldovans speak English, Russian, or Ukrainian to a sufficient level, I encountered several Moldovans (especially young ones) who did not know or did not want to speak the two latter languages, while speaking very basic English. As I do not speak Romanian, I would not have access to a significant part of the population. Secondly, while Chișinău is a small city of approximately 686,000 inhabitants (Biroul național de statistică n.d.), Kyiv is a metropolis with 2.9 million registered citizens (Holovne upravlinnia statystyky 2019). (The actual number of

---

42 These were part of a continuing protest movement against corruption in one of Europe's poorest countries. The protests of 2015–2016 were triggered by the disappearance of 1 billion USD from Moldovan banks, and were largely directed against the oligarch Vladimir Plahotniuc (see Calus 2016).

inhabitants is probably a great deal higher [100 realty 2019].) Additionally, although the centres of both cities were badly damaged during the Second World War and rebuilt as examples of Stalinist Soviet classist architecture, the architecture of the remaining parts of Chișinău differed a great deal from the architecture of Kyiv (topography, size of buildings, width of streets, layout, etc.). Thirdly, in Moldova, the culture (both traditional and popular) also came in no small degree from neighbouring Romania, which differs from Slavic, and especially Russian, culture. Fourthly, while Moldova is no more ethnically diverse than Ukraine, the tensions between Moldovans, Romanians, Russians, Ukrainians, and Gagauzians have been a bigger part of the political picture than ethnic tensions in Ukraine (at least up until 2014). Moldova has an unresolved conflict (from 1992) between Russia-supported separatists in the Transnistria Region in the East and an autonomous Gagauzian territory in the South, which in 2014 held a non-binding referendum in favour of declaring independence if Moldova joins the EU. Last but not least, there is a large social movement among Moldovans identifying themselves as ethnically Romanian, which calls for Moldova to unite with neighbouring Romania.

Although the goal of my second article was to create an approach that, in theory, would be applicable to all cities, it would complicate the theorising process and make comparison more difficult and speculative if I did not have a thorough knowledge and full command of my research material. I therefore decided to leave Great National Assembly Square and Chișinău as a possible case study for a later point. Nonetheless, I used the time allotted in Moldova to practice mapping the central square; learning about Moldova's political, cultural, and architectural history; conducting interviews; and talking to people I met about the situation in the country and their views about life, which, as stated repeatedly in this chapter, assisted me in theorising about space and protests in general.

Minsk

Leaving Chișinău aside, I turned my attention to Minsk, where I already had a network of friends and contacts. As I explored in chapter two, Minsk and Kyiv have many similarities (2.2), which make the differences stand out even more. While Ukraine's two revolutions of 2004–2005 and 2013–2014 were successful, the two attempted Belarusian colour revolutions of 2006 and 2010 were violently suppressed, and virtually no mass protest in Minsk has achieved any political impact during Aliaksandr Lukashenka's 25-year reign. Moreover, the Belarusian opposition did not have a single preferred protest space. This could be attributed to the fact that Minsk was built post-Second World War as a model Soviet city, with wide avenues, massive buildings and open spaces—a style that Belarus' only president so far, Lukashenka, has continued to endorse.

Based on the methods described above (5.1.1–5.1.3), I analysed two urban public spaces, October Square and Independence Square, which were used during Minsk's two failed Belarusian colour revolutions. This case study showed that the three categories (6.1) had (almost universally) a negative impact on mass protests in the city, and that there is little room for protests in Lukashenka's meticulously controlled and highly Sovietised space. Finally, the case study demonstrated that there was room and possible utility for my approach, even in places less suitable for protest, and that a spatial perspective could provide new insights into the difficulties facing the Belarusian opposition today.

5.6 Causal Chains

At this point, the spatial perspective had developed from the observation of an idea into a hypothesis about the importance of urban public space, which had then been tested on a prestudy, developed into a tentative theory, and applied to a second case study.

Importantly, the transitional study identified some structural weaknesses in the model. It is one thing to provide a detailed description of a city and its spaces and then, in relation to previous actions, to discuss how protesters and protest organisers perceive the said space. An approach like this might give a good indication of the practical (dis-)advantages of a square. To prove a causality relation or effect is another matter. The model required a theory that linked the independent variable (urban public space) to the dependent variable (mass protests).

I therefore turned to process tracing (PT). Inspired by the methods used in criminology, PT was developed by the US political scientists Andrew Bennett and Jeffrey Checkel to study causality in political sciences and international relations. PT systematically traces causal mechanisms by finding and examining evidence for every observable point within causal chains between independent and dependent variables. Key pieces of evidence are described and analysed in order to prove (or falsify) a correlation between the variables of case studies. Additionally, PT recommends that all parts of a causality relationship are tested thoroughly and suggests using a mix of different methods, depending on the case study at hand. (Bennett and Checkel 2015)

In *Process-Tracing Methods: Foundations and Guidelines*, Beach and Pedersen (2013) criticise the lack of a unified way to implement the PT approach, and provide a set of guidelines to overcome this limitation. They identify three main uses of process tracing, of which theory-testing PT and theory-building PT are of particular relevance to this research project. On one hand, theory-testing PT starts with a phenomenon and the mechanisms which propose to explain it, and examines case studies in order to find evidence supporting or undermining the hypotheses in the theory (2013, 14–16). Theory building PT, on the other hand, starts from the other side, with the case studies, and uses evidence to generate hypotheses for the mechanisms that create a phenomenon. In turn, these hypotheses are used to create a theory (2013, 16–18). Both approaches are adopted in my spatial perspective model.

From this point onwards, I expanded and regrouped the independent variables (i.e. the spatial elements).[43] I also found that the spatial elements could be assessed on the basis of the spatial qualities they formed. By analysing past events in Ukraine, Belarus, and Moldova, I identified

---

43   Three elements (emotions, feelings, associations) were added to the perceived elements and put in a separate subcategory, based on methodology (6.1.1); one element was removed (obstacles); one was added (open/empty space), and one element changed name (from traditions to traditional use). These changes were made in order to clarify the independent variables.

seven such spatial qualities: accessibility, mobility, defensibility/policeability, sense of safety, visibility, symbolic value, and motivation.

The dependent variables could in turn be subdivided into more practical units. I found that all mass protests have a preparation phase, an execution phase, and some level of impact. This could be used as a tool for assessing three areas potentially affected by urban public space: the emergence, realisation, and impact of mass protests.

Another key element of process tracing is that one should be equally thorough with all theories applied to a target phenomenon. Proving or falsifying one's own hypotheses is not considered more important than proving or disproving other people's hypotheses. These hypotheses are, essentially, other factors that may or may not affect the dependent variable. To identify such factors and other explanations of why protests sometimes occur and have great impact, I looked for explanations in academic literature on specific case studies, as well as the general conditions that could be found in the relevant literature on sociology and on colour revolutions (3.1).

For the model to work, it had to examine not only how spatial qualities affect the emergence, realisation, and impact of mass protests, but also the impact of space on other factors. For example, in the case of Belarus, research literature often finds that the sense of national identity within the country is prevalently weak (e.g. Törnquist-Plewa 2001, 81; Rudling 2008). Rather than dismissing this as a rival hypothesis to explain the low impact of previous mass protests, the Belarusian identity—which to a large extent is based on Belarus's Soviet past and Lukashenkian present—could be examined with a view to how it is reinforced by the city's perceived elements (6.1.1). The Soviet monumentality of the city creates an urban space that confirms the grandeur and immortality of the stable status quo, and might lessen people's motivation to go out and join a protest.

Because such spatial and non-spatial factors might have a correlative effect on mass protests, the factors have been grouped together as the collective term "political environment"; a term originating in POS theory. See subsection 3.1.4 for an overview of the political environment.

The model is illustrated with two figures. Figure 12 (below) is a (theoretical) diagram of the causality, while figure 13 (next chapter) explains how the causality (methodologically) can be found. The figures demonstrate that the combined effect of spatial qualities (shaped by the spatial elements) and other factors in the political environment can significantly affect urban mass protests.

Figure 12: Causality diagram, second version

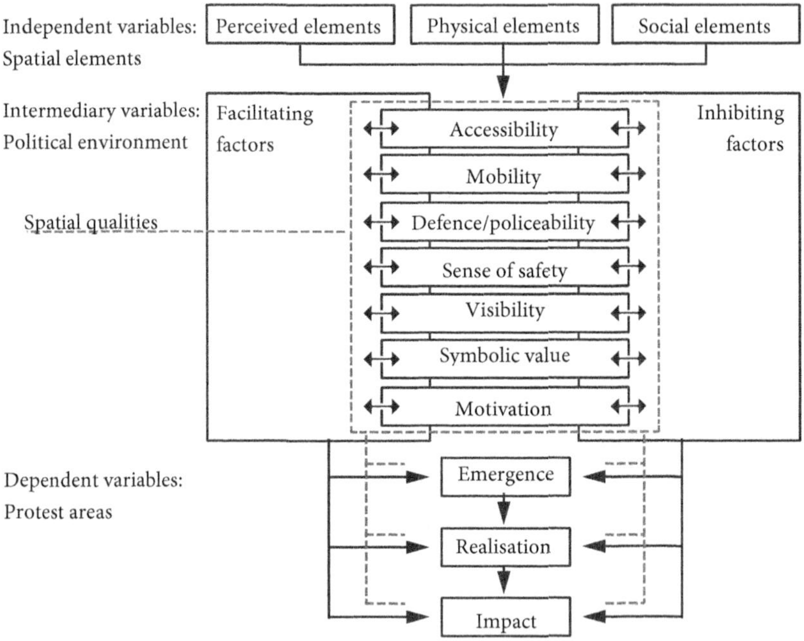

Independent variables: Spatial elements	Perceived elements	Physical elements	Social elements

Intermediary variables: Political environment	Facilitating factors	Accessibility / Mobility / Defence/policeability / Sense of safety / Visibility / Symbolic value / Motivation	Inhibiting factors

Spatial qualities

Dependent variables: Protest areas → Emergence → Realisation → Impact

Arrows (→) signify effect

5.7 Main Study

The third step of theory building consists of testing the model to see how it works when applied to a case study. In addition to the similarities and differences between Moscow, Kyiv and Minsk (see 2.2), the Russian capital was chosen because it is a metropolis consisting of a wide range of different spaces. Moreover, while Maidan is a space almost universally suited for protest, and October and Independence squares in Minsk almost universally unsuited, there are multiple urban public spaces in Moscow that have a history of protest, with varied outcomes.

The third case study of Moscow became more theoretical than the previous two case studies, as the object was not only to see how space in the city creates opportunities and obstacles for the Russian opposition (which had been done in the transitional study), but primarily to test the more complex theoretical model and argue that the spatial perspective is useful as a methodological tool. An argumentation of this type needs plenty of room. It was therefore necessary either to apply the model to only one urban space, or to discard most descriptions from the within-case studies conducted. The former option seemed the most logical, as the argumentation needed examples in order to be effective, and so the main study was divided in two parts: one theoretical, which describes the model; and another practical, in which the model is applied.

Swamp Square was chosen from five possible within-case studies (Manège Square, Triumph Square, Pushkin Square, Sakharov Avenue, and Swamp Square), all urban spaces in proximity to the political centre, or—as is the case with the latter two—spaces which were previously sanctioned by the authorities for mass demonstrations. Because of its location, Swamp Square was chosen for the March of Millions collective action during the *For Fair Elections* protest wave in Russia in 2011–2012, which would have negative consequences for the Russian opposition for years to come. My major reservation about choosing this within-case study was that, like the two squares in Minsk, it provided almost universally negative spatial qualities. Yet, compared to the two squares in Minsk, it was negative for a different set of reasons[44] and, since my goal was to study an urban space that had been significant for the outcome of previous protests, Swamp Square emerged as an obvious choice. Additionally, both to make space for the theory and for practical/ethical reasons (5.2.1), I decided not to use respondents for the third case study.

44　A major difference is that while October Square and Independence Square in Minsk are wide-open spaces, with little room for the protesters to move or hide, Swamp Square is claustrophobic since it is closed on all sides and offers only limited visibility.

The case study of Swamp Square demonstrates that the square's physical, perceived, and social spatial elements form qualities that might discourage people from starting or joining an action in said square. Swamp Square has a negative symbolic value, is not particularly visible in spite of its central location, and its layout greatly affects the protesters' room to manoeuvre (amongst other things). The spatial qualities of Swamp Square create obstacles to the realisation of protest, and the space does little to increase the impact of the protest on national politics or society.

On a more general level, the case study shows that the spatial perspective could be used as a tool for assessing the use value of urban public space for mass protest, and that it can provide new insights into the understanding of the political and spatial contention in the city. It can also provide a practical "wrapping" for descriptions of how political control is asserted.

5.8 Post-test Theorising

Some minor tweaks to the theoretical model were added following the main study of Moscow (chapter 9), and these require comment.

Firstly, the causal connections in the model are more fully explained in section 5.6 and in chapter 6 than in the chapter itself. Secondly, the spatial qualities have been expanded with a proposed list of elements and other qualities thought to have a hypothetical impact, as well as some key questions that can be asked in order to assess various spatial qualities (6.2.1). Thirdly, the methodological structure of figure 13 has been added to clarify the process of identifying points in the causality chain. Fourthly, a list of micro, meso, and macro factors which may or may not influence protests, and an overview of the political environment (fig. 7 and 8, respectively), have been added to systematise the non-spatial factors in the political environment. And fifthly, the causal mechanisms described in figure 12 have been updated with a separate line between the spatial qualities and the protest areas. This is to emphasise that these qualities may have a direct impact on protests regardless of the other factors in the political environment (e.g. the size of an urban space).

6 Variables and Methodology

The previous chapter provided a description of the theorising process, including an overview of the three case studies and an explication of the spatial perspective. This chapter proceeds to a detailed elaboration of the variables in the model. The independent variables are described in section 6.1, the intermediary variables in section 6.2, and the dependent variables in section 6.3, in addition to the specific methods used to gather information about the variables.

Figure 13 outlines the methodology used to trace the causal relationship between urban public space and mass protests.

Figure 13: Methodology

A		Urban public space can be observed, and a variety of qualitative methods can produce empirical data for describing single elements and categories of elements.
B		When spatial elements are seen in combination, certain spatial qualities can be induced on the basis of logical reasoning.
C		Based on the spatial qualities, three main types of hypotheses can be made:
	1	Hypotheses about the effect of spatial qualities on three protest areas (emergence, realisation, impact).
	2	Hypotheses about the correlation between spatial qualities and non-spatial intermediary variables in the political environment—i.e., how they affect each other.
	3	Hypotheses about the cumulative effect (of spatial qualities and non-spatial intermediary variables in the political environment) on three protest areas.
D		The hypotheses may be confirmed or disproved by:
	1	Observation
	2	Interviews
	3	Research literature
E		Finally, all other non-spatial factors should be examined with a view to their effect (independent of space) on the three protest areas.

6.1 Independent Variables

The independent variables need to be reintroduced in their current form, since their categorisations have changed several times during their development. Notably, figure 24, which is used in the chapter on Minsk (chapter 8) differs from figure 14, below (from chapter 9) (5.6fn. for an accurate description of the changes made).

Figure 14: Elements of the city, second version

Perceived (subjective) elements		Physical elements	Social elements
Measurable:	Abstract:	Measurable:	Measurable:
History	Emotions	Location	Traditional use
Ideological symbols	Feelings	Size	Official use
Buildings	Associations	Shape	Districts
Monuments		Entrances	Paths
History of protests		Exits	Nodes
Landmarks		Walls	
		Floor	
		Objects	
		Edges	
		Public works	
		Focal points	
		Open/empty space	

To facilitate the gathering of data and the analysis itself, the elements have been divided into three categories which are described in the following three subsections, together with the main methods used to gather information about them. It should be noted that the definitions of these elements may occasionally be fleeting and overlapping. This is especially true for the perceived elements, which are mostly cognitive in nature. However, the purpose of identifying and describing the elements is not to create a definite categorisation of separate elements, but to provide a detailed enough data set for a systematised induction of spatial qualities.

6.1.1 Perceived Elements

The first category of elements contains the non-physical objects of urban public space that are experienced subjectively. Some of the perceived elements come in physical forms, such as monuments and buildings. When the physicality of such perceived elements is discussed, they are categorised as physical elements, such as objects and walls (see corresponding elements below, 6.1.2).

The perceived elements have been divided into two subcategories based on the methods that can best be utilised to map them. While the first category contains measurable elements that can be found by reading research literature and by analysing their meaning and possible impact, the second subcategory involves personal emotions, feelings, and associations (i.e. mental connections)—elements that can only be found qualitatively in conversations and interviews with protesters and organisers, or in research literature and museum exhibitions based on such qualitative sources.

Perceived elements should also be examined with a view to who perceives them. Two groups might, for example, relate to a symbol in widely different ways (see for example Thornton 1996, on the perception of the Confederate flag in the Southern US). The researcher's own subjective perception (through field work) of a space might be added as a complementary source. Although data of this type might not provide an accurate representation of how the space is perceived by the general population, it can form the basis of discussion with respondents.

History includes the circumstances in which an urban public space first came to be; who created it and for what purpose; who has used it and for what purposes since; previous names of the space; what destructions or reconstructions have occurred in it and in its proximity.

Ideological symbols might appear in the form of monuments or buildings with special significance, but could also include abstractions about the status of a place or an object: for example, the Bastille in July 1789, or the abstract notion of Maidan as a popular assembly.

The **buildings** in a space can, as explained in subsection 3.2.2, express power. Who owns the buildings in and around the space, what they signify and what feelings the architecture invokes might all be meaningful in order to understand how they are perceived by the various actors in society.

The potential power of **monuments** lies in their ability to evoke feelings and emotions, in much the same way as architecture. But monuments are also references to points in history or historical persons, and they often have a pragmatic (i.e. unifying) purpose. This might, however, not always be the only effect. See, for example, how the Independence Monument in Kyiv is referred to by nicknames such as "the pole" (7.3).

The **history of protests** is closely related to the history element. It is singled out as a separate element because it contains important information about the history and repertoires of contention (or lack thereof) in a given space. Which protests have occurred in the space and in the city? What was the result of previous protests? What are the traditional repertoires of contention and repertoires of policing here (3.1.1), and what changes have they undergone?

Kevin Lynch defines **landmarks** as points of reference that people do not enter. "Some landmarks are typically seen from many angles and distances, over the tops of smaller elements, and used as radial references. [...] Other landmarks are primarily local, being visible only in restricted localities and from certain approaches." Thus, Lynch differentiates between major landmarks, such as towers and tall monuments, and smaller landmarks, such as "signs, store fronts, trees [...]". (Lynch 1960, 48)

Emotions and **feelings** represent two complex and interconnected elements that may be generated by space. While there is no clearly defined difference between the two, the former is usually seen as instinctive and the latter as a combination of emotions and thoughts (i.e. processed emotions). Both can trigger physical and psychological reactions and influence people's behaviour.

Finally, space often comes with a single **association** or sets thereof. These associations might be connected with past events, monuments, architecture, social and physical elements (see next subsections), etc.

6.1.2 Physical Elements

In contrast to the first, the second category of elements is tangible and fully measurable. The most important method for gathering data about physical elements is mapping (5.1.3), from which a great deal can be learned about an urban space. Field work should also be part of the examination, in order to fully describe the physical elements involved; and interviews could be added to gain information not easily mapped or found during field work. A respondent can, for example, inform the researcher of alternative entrances that are not visible, or easily located by the uninitiated.

The **location** of an urban space is to a large degree defined by its distance from practical or symbolic points of interest, including proximity to political institutions (see for example Lee 2009 on the location of Tiananmen Square), to physical manifestations of whom or what the protests are directed against (e.g. Wall Street during OWS), and to nodes (6.1.3).

The **size** and **shape** of urban space are important for a number of practical reasons, including walking distances, the number of people that can fit into the space simultaneously, their overview of the space, and how visible they are within it.

Entrances and **exits** are often the same thing, but are kept as separate categories because they might facilitate one-way movement only (e.g. a police blockade which only allows for movement in one direction).

Walls are a form of tall edges that potentially limit movement. The shape and layout of the walls can affect a number of qualities, including visibility, sense of safety, policing, etc.

The urban **floor** might consist of various materials (cobblestone, asphalt, grass), colours, obstacles (fences, signs, kiosks), heights, etc. The floor affects the overall feel of a place, might hinder or enhance movement, produce noise (e.g. traffic on cobblestones), or become improvised weaponry (cobblestones again).

Virtually all **objects** in an urban space may have an effect on crowds, and should therefore be examined. For instance, kiosks, benches, signs, and fountains, which might appear as obstacles, platforms for addressing a crowd, etc. The element is included in this list because it is important to map, or at least consider, everything.

According to Lynch, **edges** are "linear elements not used or considered as paths [...]." They include, but are not limited to, "railroad cuts, edges of development, walls", water fronts, rivers, and façades. They "may be barriers, more or less penetrable […], or they may be seams, lines along which two regions are related and joined together." (1960, 47).

Public works are infrastructure, resources, public buildings, services, and utilities, "constructed for public use or enjoyment especially when financed and owned by the government" (Public works n.d.). Electricity, sewage, schools, tram rails etc. are included in this category. This element may be of importance for the maintenance of a protest that continues for weeks or months.

Focal points can be defined as "a center of activity, attraction, or attention" (Focus n.d.): in other words, the most prominent elements (e.g. landmarks, monuments, and buildings) that attract a viewer's attention. Examples include the Independence Monument in Kyiv (7.3) or the Palace of the Republic in Minsk (8.3.1)

Finally, **open/empty spaces** might be important, too, as they can be used both for movement and to contain people or vehicles. Therefore, they should also be mapped with regard to size, shape, etc.

6.1.3 Social Elements

The third category consists of various uses of space, and the social elements are based on the architectural and urbanistic literature reviewed in subsection 3.2.2. The collection of data on social elements is mainly based on field work and mapping, but the data can be checked and improved by presenting and discussing findings with respondents.

Traditional use describes the traditions connected with the usage of a space by the public (i.e. the citizens). This includes daily and cultural uses and interactions (e.g. shopping, dates, tourism, rites and rituals, etc.), whether recurrent (such as ice skating, yoga or parkour) or sporadic (e.g. unofficial fairs and flash mobs). The difference between traditional use and history (perceived element) is that, while history represents the past, traditional use is in the present. This element also includes who uses particular bits of space and when.

Official use is similar to traditional use, since it also describes the daily, recurrent or sporadic uses of the space. The difference is that the latter is arranged by local, regional, or national authorities. Examples are festivals, religious celebrations, parades, etc. The data can be complemented by official sources (e.g. government websites).

Districts are described by Lynch as "medium-to-large sections of the city, conceived of as having two-dimensional extent, which [one] mentally enters 'inside of,' and which are recognizable as having some common, identifying character" (Lynch 1960, 47). Different districts are used by different people at different times, and the perception of an urban public space in a district might be affected by the general feel of said district and vice versa.

Paths are "the channels along which [one] customarily, occasionally, or potentially moves. These may be streets, walkways, transit lines, […]" (Lynch 1960, 47). This element shows how people move in relation to the space.

Nodes are "points, the strategic spots in a city into which an observer can enter, and which are the intensive foci to and from which he is traveling" (Lynch 1960, 47). Nodes therefore include transportation hubs; meeting places; places were paths start, stop, or cross; places of interest, and so on.

The three latter elements (districts, paths, nodes) all have a great potential effect on protests, particularly on their visibility. In a contentious setting, the users of the district within which the space is located will have a greater chance of noticing a mass action; the same applies to the people who use paths on or along the protesters' space. The visibility is even greater when a number of paths end or intersect on the space, and thus constitute nodes. Compare, for instance, the visibility of Manège Square and Swamp Square in Moscow. The former is located in a district frequented by large amounts of people, in proximity to a number of paths, several of which intersect and end (as nodes) on Manège Square itself. Conversely, the latter is in a sparsely used district with few paths nearby and with virtually no nodes of importance (9.2.3).

6.2 Intermediary Variables

The second level of causality consists of the intermediary variables, which include both spatial qualities and non-spatial factors in the political environment.

6.2.1 Spatial Qualities

The spatial qualities can be found by means of inductive reasoning. Some of the qualities are testable (e.g. accessibility and visibility), while others are less concrete (e.g. symbolic value and motivation). Here, the object of reasoning is to create a sense of the facilitating and/or inhibiting factors collectively provided by spatial elements.

The following list is retrieved from chapter 9 (9.1.1), and has been expanded with a proposed list of elements and other qualities of hypothetical impact, as well as some key questions that can be asked in order to assess various spatial qualities.

"**Accessibility** affects several aspects of a protest, such as getting to a location, furnishing protesters with necessary supplies, and the opportunity for people to join the protest spontaneously."

- Accessibility may be affected by physical elements (location, entrances, walls, objects, edges, public works) and social elements (paths, nodes).
- Questions to pose: How easy is it to get to the space? How is it controlled and by whom? Is it public (i.e. open to all)?

"**Mobility** is closely related to accessibility, but includes the protesters' ability to move and be flexible once in situ. Some tactics, such as demonstrations starting out from a space occupied by protesters, are harder to organise if the public space has few exits, many obstacles, or can be easily surrounded by police forces."

- Mobility may be affected by physical elements (location, shape, entrances, exits, walls, objects, edges, public works), social elements (paths, nodes), and accessibility.

- Questions to pose: How easy is it to move from the space to other places? Are there many possibilities for movement? What means of transportation are available?

"The level of difficulty in **defending** and/or **policing** a space is important for the realisation of protests in societies where protest is either unsanctioned or has a high probability of being met with hostility, provocations, violence, and/or arrests."

- Defensibility/policeability may be affected by physical elements (size, shape, entrances, exits, walls, floor, objects, edges, open/empty space), and spatial qualities (accessibility, mobility, motivation).
- Questions to pose: How vulnerable is the space to police tactics? Is the space easy to surround and 'kettle'? How easy or difficult is it to block movement to the space (i.e. are there many roads that need to be blocked)? Are there any physical obstacles that would stop police vehicles or inhibit police movement? How are coercive, persuasive, and informative policing strategies (3.1.1) affected by the space?

"The **sense of safety** is shaped by the physical layout of a space (see for example Dosen and Oswald 2013, on prospect refuge theory), as well as the protesters' actual ability to defend themselves (for example against heavy-handed policing)."

- Sense of safety may be affected by perceived elements (history of protests, emotions, feelings, associations), physical elements (location, size, shape, entrances, exits, walls, objects, edges, open/empty space) and spatial qualities (defensibility/policeability, mobility, visibility (internal).
- Questions to pose: Does the space induce feelings of protection and/or refuge (3.2.2)? Does the space provide protesters with opportunities to get away if they are met with provocation or violence?

Figure 15: Maidan, Kyiv, January 2014

Photo: Arve Hansen

"One aspect of **visibility** is the protesters' ability to be seen externally by the public, the authorities, and national and international observers and audiences (including media outlets). Visibility may therefore affect the number of people who notice the action. The other aspect of visibility is internal: the protesters' ability to see what is going on around them. This aspect affects their coordination and communication within the protest camp."

- Visibility may be affected by perceived elements (monuments, landmarks), physical elements (all), social elements (all), and spatial qualities (accessibility, mobility).
- Questions to pose: How noticeable are protests in the space, by whom are they noticeable, and in which parts of the city? How much can protesters see within the space? How much can they perceive of what is going on outside the space?

"Several elements influence the **symbolic value** of a space, ranging from the physical (e.g. its proximity to the institutions targeted) and the social (whether the protesters are occupying a space commonly used by others) to the perceived (such as the history of the space and the outcome of previous collective actions held there)."

- Symbolic value may be affected by perceived elements (all), and a physical element (location).
- Questions to pose: What does the space mean, and for which sections of the public? How important is the space?

"Finally, **motivation** is perhaps the most important of the spatial qualities, since it has a direct impact on the number of participants in a collective action and their belief in the likelihood of achieving their goals" (I will elaborate on the goals of protests in chapter 9, 9.1.3). "This quality is shaped both by physical and perceived elements, as well as other spatial qualities (e.g. sense of safety—if it feels safe, the chances of going out to protest might be higher)."

- Motivation may be affected by perceived elements (all), social elements (all), and spatial qualities (defensibility/policeability, sense of safety, visibility, symbolic value).
- Questions to pose: Are people more or less willing to join in when the protest is taking place in this particular space?

6.2.2 The Political Environment

The political environment is understood as "a generic term used variously in the literature of political science to refer to, among other things, aspects of formal political structure, the climate of governmental responsiveness, social structure, and social stability" (Eisinger 1973, 11). In other words, it is the context of and location in which contention (might) occur, and it comprises a wide range of factors and conditions. The methods for identifying such factors may differ from study to study. However, for research on a post-Soviet region such as this, McFaul's (2005) seven conditions (or a similar type of checklist) is a good starting point (see 3.1.3 and 3.1.4). It should nevertheless be complemented by case-specific research literature.

Having identified the presence or absence of factors in the political environment, two questions can be asked about their correlative effect: 1) How do these factors affect the spatial qualities? and 2) How do the spatial qualities affect the factors?

This correlative effect can be illustrated by an example from chapter 8: McFaul states that a necessary condition for a colour revolution to occur is that there must be a modicum of independent media. In Minsk, where virtually all media outlets are controlled by the government, this condition is not present (8.6); which, according to McFaul, diminishes the chances of a colour revolution occurring. Additionally, the visibility of Minsk's two main protest squares is limited, which enhances the effect of McFaul's condition, since protests in areas with little visibility are more dependent on mass media to get their message out.

6.3 Dependent Variables

The third level of analysis brings in the systematic creation of hypotheses about the political environment's effect on three areas of mass protests, as well as the testing of these hypotheses. The testing includes observation and/or interviews with protesters, protest organisers, and observers.

6.3.1 Emergence

"Emergence" means the protesters and protest organisers' ability to "organise and implement an action" (9.1.3). This includes planning, informing, and mobilising people to protest. This crucial part of protest is probably more affected by non-spatial factors in the political environment (such as intolerable living standards or the presence of widespread election fraud) than by spatial qualities, and should therefore be identified by other means (e.g. sociological: POS, CAT, RMP, etc.). Space should nonetheless be considered as a contributing factor. As demonstrated in all three case studies, spatial qualities such as *motivation* and *sense of safety* may encourage (7.1) or discourage people from protesting (8.1, 8.3.2, 9.2.5).

The optimal way of testing whether the spatial qualities affect the emergence of protest would be to conduct qualitative interviews with a large number of protesters, during or right after a protest. However, this may not always be practically possible.

6.3.2 Realisation

"Realisation" is understood here as "the protesters' ability to execute their planned action (their level of communication, coordination, and organisation, how they are resisting aggressive policing, and so on)" (9.1.3). This area of protest is affected by all the spatial qualities and may greatly facilitate and/or inhibit protest. Nevertheless, non-spatial independent variables may also have an effect here, and these should be analysed as well.

Hypotheses formed about the spatial qualities are best confirmed by direct observation of protests in the space, but research literature, video footage, and/or interviews with participants or observers of an action might also provide data to corroborate or contradict these hypotheses.

6.3.3 Impact

"Impact" means the protesters' "ability to be seen and to use this visibility effectively in order to change public discourse, policy, or leadership." These three points flow directly from the protesters' goals, which I identified through my qualitative interviews with members of the opposition in Ukraine, Moldova, Belarus, and Russia. Based on these conversations, the goals of virtually all mass protests relate to change: change of public discourse, change of policy, or change of regime. These goals are interrelated and overlapping, and one goal often evolves into another (9.1.3).

Three spatial qualities have a direct influence on a protest's impact: namely visibility, defensibility/policeability, and symbolic value. External visibility naturally affects the number of people who notice the protest; as does defensibility, especially in authoritarian regimes where the length of time people stand and protest (and thus get noticed) is greatly affected by their ability to withstand coercive policing strategies. Finally, the symbolic value of the space may influence impact, which is why most protest organisers prefer to protest outside political institutions (e.g. Manège Square in Moscow) or in urban spaces with a history of successful protest (Triumph Square), rather than a secluded space with an unimpressive name (Swamp Square).

As with emergence and realisation, impact too may be influenced by other, non-spatial factors in the political environment, such as popular support of the regime, levels of control over the media, etc. These factors may be identified with the help of sociological methods (e.g. POS theory), and possibly also discourse analysis.

* * *

In the next part of this book, I shall provide a practical demonstration of how the spatial perspective has been applied to three case studies at different stages in the perspective's development. The first is a prestudy of Maidan (Independence Square) in Kyiv, the second a transitional study of October and Independence squares in Minsk, the third a main study of Swamp Square in Moscow.

Part II

Figure 16: Tverskaia Street, Moscow, June 2017

Photo: Arve Hansen

7 Prestudy

Maidan, Kyiv

This prestudy is based on a modified translation from Norwegian into English of the article "Majdan Nezalezjnosti: symbolikk og funksjon" (Eng.: Maidan Nezalezhnosti: Symbolic Value and Function, Hansen 2016).

Abstract
Much has been said and written about the Ukrainian revolution of 2013–2014, yet research on Maidan Nezalezhnosti, the protests' most iconic location, has so far been rather limited. This case study analyses the history, attributes and symbolism of this particular city space. What function does Maidan have in Ukrainian society? In the course of my fieldwork on the recent revolution, which I conducted in Kyiv between 2013 and 2015, I found that Maidan has many features that make it a particularly suitable site for protest. In this chapter, I argue that several factors related to the square's physical space—from its location between the religious, historical and political centres of Ukraine to its proximity to important landmarks, as well as its infrastructure, shape, architecture, and size—make Maidan both a symbolic and a practical choice of space for people demanding change. Since the collapse of the Soviet Union, Maidan has acquired a special significance for Ukrainians. The name of the square itself could be interpreted as a protest against Russia, and the many protests and three revolutions that have taken place on Maidan have given it a particular revolutionary significance. I argue that Maidan functions as a socio-political safety valve—a place people turn to, and turn up at, to demand change when formal political institutions fail to deliver.

In the centre of the Ukrainian capital, Kyiv, lies Maidan Nezalezhnosti (Independence Square), one of Kyiv's larger open urban spaces. In the winter of 2013–2014, Maidan attracted much attention during the Euromaidan protests, which, over three dramatic months, saw at least 82 demonstrators killed (Ukrainian Ministry of Health 2014) and a political power shift on a national level. The protests also became a prelude to Russia's annexation of the Crimean Peninsula and the war in Donbas. Thus far, the war has claimed more than 9100 human lives (UN News Centre 2015), 1.38 million people have been internally displaced (UNHCR 2015a), and 1.1 million have fled the country (UNHCR 2015b, 2).

In the course of my fieldwork in Kyiv from November 2013 to May 2015, which examined the driving forces behind the protests, I noted several aspects indicating Independence Square's important symbolic meaning for Ukrainians. The most prominent example is that the protests themselves were given the name *Euromaidan*—a combination of the words *Europe* and *Maidan*. Yet it is perhaps even more telling that the first attack by riot police on the demonstrations in Kyiv was referred to in Ukraine as the "Attack on Maidan" (Ukr.: *Rozhin Maidanu*).[45] The attack took place during the night of 30 November 2013 and led to a surge of popular support for the protests amongst Ukrainians (Hansen 2015, 44–45). It was also interesting to see that "Maidan", as a concept, was not limited to the physical space of Independence Square alone, but also became a generic term for the areas occupied by the protesters as so-called *maidan-y* began to appear in other Ukrainian cities. A respondent, the local historian *Serhii*, describes Maidan as something mobile: "After the attack on Maidan […] a funny expression [emerged]: 'Maidan has moved to Mykhailivs'ka Square' […] that is, 'Maidan' is not attached to the space—it already means an act of protest. It doesn't matter where it is." [46]

While international attention has subsequently moved to a significant extent from Kyiv to Donbas, Maidan is still a subject of discussion in Ukraine. In connection with the presidential and parliamentary elections in 2014, and before the local elections in October 2015, oppositional parties and other groupings threatened to "go to Maidan" if the Poroshenko administration did not end the war and speed up the reform process. The authorities have, in turn, attempted to show that the symbolic value of Maidan is important to them. During the summer of 2015, a large-scale architectural competition to reconstruct the city space was launched, with

---

45 *Rozhin* could be translated as scattering, driving away, dispersal, storming, or attacking. But since the context is a square, neither scattering nor driving away fit here; the "dispersal of Maidan" does not capture the serious nature of the event; and the "storming of Maidan" has already been used for the police action of 18 and 19 February 2014. I have chosen to define the incident as an attack.

46 "Posle razgona Maidana […] byla takaia fraza smeshnaia: 'Maidan peremestilsia na Mikhailovs'kuiu ploshchad' […] poluchaetsia, chto Maidan ne priviazan k ploshchadi – eto uzhe protestnaia aktsiia. Nevazhno, gde on."

extensive funds made available—the faltering economy notwithstanding (Terra Dignitas 2015). Among other things, authorities and activists discussed what the memorial to Euromaidan and the fallen demonstrators should look like.

In order to understand the turmoil that occurred in Kyiv in February 2014, and thus the background of the events unfolding in the country at present, it is necessary to look more closely at what Maidan means for Ukrainians. Why do protests appear on Independence Square? What does Maidan symbolise? Which functions does the square have in Ukrainian society?

Figure 17: Maidan, Kyiv, August 2016

Photo: Arve Hansen

Due to space constraints, the scope of this chapter is limited to protests in Kyiv, and the relation between them and the city space in which they were most frequently organised. My analysis does not include other urban spaces, nor do I examine the structures and/or organisation of individual protest actions.

This chapter is divided into three sections. The first (7.1) looks at the physical layout, position, local history, and daily use of Independence Square. The second (7.2) discusses the symbolic meanings associated with Maidan. Finally, I discuss the functions of Maidan in Ukrainian society today (7.3).

I will argue that Independence Square has become a natural place of protest and that, despite a couple of disadvantages, it is well suited for larger crowds. In addition, Maidan has a special symbolic significance as *the people's square*—a location associated with several revolutions, and the only place where people feel they have a direct influence on the country's politics. My findings support the idea that Maidan today functions as a socio-political safety valve in a dysfunctional and corrupt political system.

Methods and Theory

This analysis of the physical layout of Maidan is based on my own observations in Kyiv between November 2013 and July 2015.[47] The theoretical framework for the analysis is derived from Lynch's (1960) theories about the functionality and significance of cities.[48] During the revolution, I made 23 field trips to Maidan and established contact with numerous people. From these contacts I chose six respondents for seven semi-structured in-depth interviews. Excerpts from these interviews are used in this chapter.[49] Since I have had two longer periods of residence in Kyiv (from January to June 2011, and from July 2013 to December 2015), and travelled regularly to the city (from May 2007 onwards), I have also had many experiences of my own in the city. I refer to these here as "personal experiences".

---

47 I have used much of the same qualitative source material as in my master's thesis on Euromaidan (Hansen 2015).
48 Lynch emphasises, among other things, people's regular and possible patterns of movement (*paths*); landmarks and points people go to or through, and/or to which they relate (*landmarks* and *nodes*); things that hinder movement (*edges*); and areas in the city with distinct characteristics (*districts*). These terms are not employed directly in this text, but they still form the basis of my analysis.
49 For the safety of my respondents, their names have been pseudonymised and are listed in the text in italics. However, this does not apply to Ukrainian photojournalist Oleksandr Klymenko, who wanted to appear under his full name.

The existing literature includes in-depth analyses of the relationship between democracy, protests, and individual urban spaces (see Parkinson 2012). More specifically, the Occupy movement's relations to occupied space in cities in the West have been analysed (Hammond 2013); the space occupied by the Gezi Park protests in Istanbul in 2013 has been thoroughly discussed (Göle 2013a, 2013b; Inceoglu 2014, 2015; Örs 2014); and the same applies to several protests in urban space during the Arab Spring from 2011 to 2012 (see, for example, Lopes de Souza and Lipietz 2011), the protests on Tiananmen Square in 1989 (Hershkovitz 1993; Lee 2009) and so on. However, few analyses of urban space have been undertaken in connection with the protests in Kyiv. Whilst analyses have been made of the layout and history of Independence Square—such as the discussion of the square's post-Soviet transformations (Hryshchenko 2013) and publications on the history of the city and the Euromaidan protests in a historical perspective (Cybriwsky 2014a and Cybriwsky 2014b, respectively)—there has been, so far as I am aware, no in-depth discussion of the relationship between the layout, symbolic value, and function of Maidan.

7.1 Physical Space

The capital of Ukraine is centrally located in the country, between Poland in the west (440 km from Kyiv) and Russia in the east (300 km). Kyiv is more central than any other city in Ukraine, even though it is closer to Belarus (95 km), for example, than to regions such as Donbas and Crimea (600 km and 550 km respectively). Its centrality is due to its connectivity with the country's infrastructure, such as roads, railways, and the river Dnipro.

According to legend, Kyiv was founded in 482, and is considered the historical basis for the three modern nations of Ukraine, Belarus, and Russia. It was in Kyiv that Grand Prince Volodymyr converted Kievan Rus' to Christianity in 988, and the city therefore remains important for a number of Orthodox denominations.[50] Some of the holiest buildings of Orthodox

---

50 The city is particularly important for: the Russian Orthodox Church; the Ukrainian Orthodox Church, whose leadership is located in Kyiv even though it is a subject of the

Christianity, including Saint Sophia's Cathedral and the cave monastery Kyievo-Pechers'ka lavra, are located in the city. In addition to being an important historic and religious centre, Kyiv also houses several of Ukraine's most important political institutions, as well as some of the country's oldest and most prestigious universities.

Independence Square is located in the middle of Kyiv, between three hills, high up on the western (right) bank of the Dnipro. Six small streets (Borys Hrinchenka Street, Taras Shevchenko Alley, Sofiivs'ka Street, Mala Zhytomyrs'ka Street, Mykhailivs'ka Street, and Kost'ol'na Street) fan outwards from the north-western part of the square (henceforth, the NW part) towards the city's historical and religious centre on Starokyivs'ka and Zamkova hills. From the south-eastern part of the square (henceforth, the SE part) two streets (Instytuts'ka Street and Architect Horodets'kyi Street) point to the political centre on Pechers'ka Hill, where the Presidential Administration, Verkhovna Rada (the Parliament), the House of Government, the Central Bank, and several party headquarters are located. The 1.3 km main street, Khreshchatyk Avenue, crosses Independence Square on its way between European Square in the north-east and Bessarabs'ka Square in the south. Independence Square is large, about 370 metres long and between 110 and 200 metres wide (depending on how and where it is measured). Khreshchatyk Avenue, with its eight lanes and 60-metre width, pavements included, is also an intrinsic part of the urban space. Overall, square and avenue provide plenty of room for hundreds of thousands of people. In the area around Independence Square there are a number of meeting places, including parks, large squares, and educational institutions.

7.1.1 Spatial and Urban History

One way to trace Kyiv's development through the ages is through the many names of its central square. The area where Independence Square is

---

Moscow Patriarchate; the Ukrainian Orthodox Church with its own patriarchate in Kyiv; the Ukrainian Greek Orthodox Catholic Church (this is officially Catholic, but follows the same Byzantine Rite as Orthodox believers do); and the Ukrainian Autocephalous Orthodox Church.

presently located was not developed until the mid-eighteenth century; although *Liads'ki Gate*—one of the city's three entrances in the medieval period—was also situated there. The Mongols allegedly invaded Kyiv through this gate in 1240, marking the end of Kievan Rus'. From the middle of the nineteenth century, the city grew rapidly. The small square was initially named *Khreshchatyk Square* in 1869 after the densely built commercial street. When the city Duma was built in 1876, the name of the square changed to *Duma Square*.

After the Bolsheviks came to power in 1919, the square changed names several times. First, it became *Soviet Union Square* and then, from 1935, *Kalinin Square* after the Soviet politician Mikhail Kalinin. Between 1941 and 1943 the square was renamed *Nineteenth September Square*, after the date when Nazi Germany first occupied the city. And when the city was reclaimed by the Red Army, it became *Kalinin Square* once more.

136   Arve Hansen

Figure 18:   Maidan and the surrounding area (map)

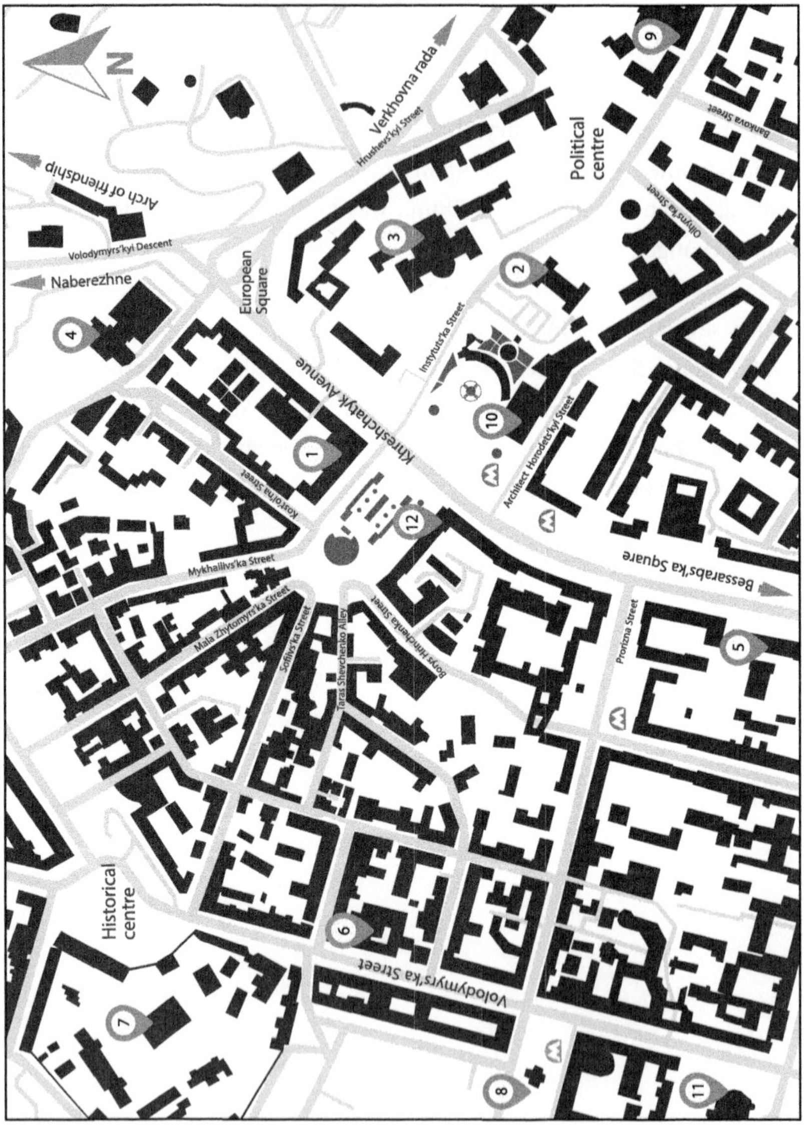

1: Trade Unions Building. 2: Hotel Ukraine. 3: October Palace. 4: Ukrainian House. 5: City Administration. 6: Security Service of Ukraine (SBU). 7: Saint Sophia's Cathedral. 8: Golden Gate. 9: Central Bank. 10: Conservatoire. 11: Opera House. Illustration: Arve Hansen

Before the 60th anniversary of the October Revolution in 1977, the urban space was renovated and given the name *October Revolution Square*. The NW part, which until then had been heavily trafficked and had many physical obstacles, was converted into an open, green area with park-like qualities, with less traffic and plenty of opportunities for large crowds to gather. At the end of the SE part, a large monument was erected in memory of Lenin and the October Revolution (Hryshchenko 2013, 86). After the fall of the Soviet Union in 1991, the square changed its name to *Independence Square*, the name it still has today.

The façades of the urban space also show some of the transitions the city has undergone. Only the October Palace (now a performing arts centre), which stands at the top of a large grass hill at the eastern end of the square, and the Conservatoire are left from before the Second World War. The lack of pre-war buildings bears witness to the destruction the city and people suffered during the war years. After the war, Stalin redeveloped the city in Soviet classicist style using the forced slave labour of prisoners of war: Khreshchatyk became a wide Soviet avenue, and Kalinin Square became the city's central square. The Duma had burned to the ground during the war and was not re-erected. The buildings along Khreshchatyk Avenue and in the NW part of Kalinin Square were all built using a type of yellow natural rock in the same vein of majestic design (sarcastically called *Stalin Cream Cake* [-style] by the city's inhabitants).[51]

The death of Stalin in 1953, however, brought an abrupt end to this architectural neoclassicism. Khrushchev rejected the grandiose plans and completed the reconstruction in a much simplified form. *Hotel Moskva* (from 2001, *Hotel Ukraina* [Hotel Ukraine]), illustrates this simplification well. The hotel, which stands on top of the hill in the end of the square's SE part, was meant to be built as one of the Stalin *vysotki* (skyscrapers), but was finished quickly, standing lower than planned and without the classicist decor. The two largest buildings on the square, the Central Post Office and the Trade Unions Building, are in stylistic contrast with one another. The Central Post Office is built in a traditional Soviet classicist style, while

---

51   From an excursion with the firm Interesnyi Kiev, 27 July 2013.

the Trade Unions Building is a postmodern structure topped by a 24-metre-high digital clock tower.

Figure 19: The Independence Monument, Kyiv, May 2019

The monument is 62 metres tall and portrays Berehynia: the protector, a female spirit from Slavic mythology. Photo: David-Emil Wickström

After the fall of the Soviet Union, Kyiv went through a rapid transition to capitalism. Today, there are large illuminated advertising billboards on top of all the buildings on the NW part of Independence Square. Before the Trade Unions Building was completely destroyed during Euromaidan, its façade was covered by enormous advertising posters. On the ground level, banks, fast food restaurants, and kiosks now dominate the cityscape.

During the winter of 2000–2001, a redevelopment of urban public space began on a grand scale. As part of this redevelopment, a shopping mall was built on Independence Square. The shopping mall is two floors deep and extends underneath the whole NW part of the square. A six-metre-tall glass dome at the end of the square sheds light downwards into the mall. At the other, south-eastern end of the square is an enormous mirror glass façade, which is three floors high. This is the second part of the shopping mall, located in front of Hotel Ukraine. The shopping mall was strongly criticised for damaging the appearance of Maidan, and even the developer, Hari Korohodskyi, stated in 2007 that he agreed with the criticism (*Fokus* 2007). In parallel to the construction of the shopping mall, numerous new monuments were erected portraying Ukrainian historical and mythical figures. This was part of a nationalization project by Leonid Kuchma, intended to unify the country around a shared historical memory.

Hryshchenko has written about the reconstruction of the urban space and recounts how the square went from being a green gathering space to a grey and inaccessible area that has lost much of its charm. The fact that the Independence Monument—the city's most famous landmark—is often referred to by nicknames, such as "the pole," "the lady with the twig," or "Batman" is indicative of the general unpopularity of Kuchma's nationalisation project among the wider population (Hryshchenko 2013, 86–87).

Figure 20: Kyiv within the Ring Road (map)

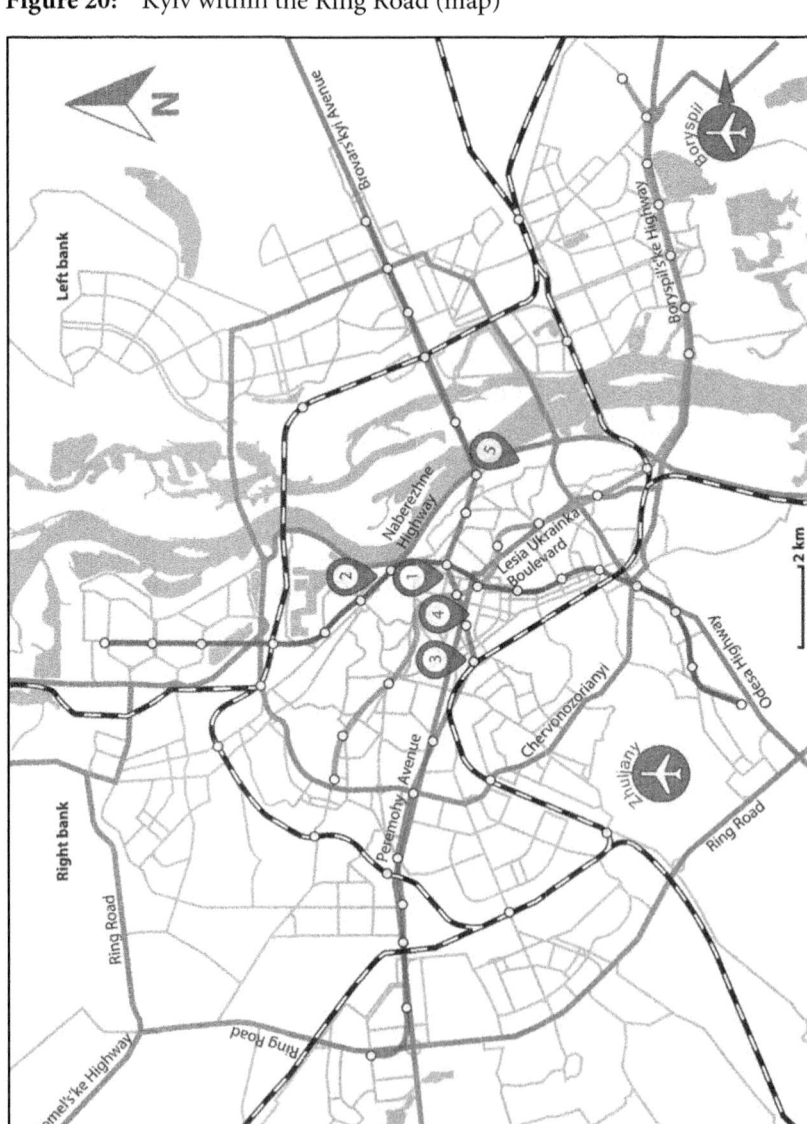

1: Maidan. 2: Kontraktova Square. 3: Main railway station. 4: Taras Shevchenko National University of Kyiv. 5: Cave Monastery Kyievo-Pechers'ka lavra. Illustration: Arve Hansen

7.1.2 Daily Use

Despite a somewhat messy layout, the urban space of Maidan is used by a vast number of people every day. Khreshchatyk functions as the natural thoroughfare between several important roads: Naberezhne Highway—which runs along the Dnipro on its right bank; Taras Shevchenko Boulevard—a prolongation of Peremohy Avenue, which is an important traffic artery from the western parts of Kyiv to the city centre; and Baseina Street, a continuation of Lesia Ukrainka Boulevard, which runs from the south east to the centre of the city. All of these are wide, heavily trafficked roads. Instytuts'ka Street, which crosses Khreshchatyk Avenue and leads on to Mykhailivs'ka Street, is also well trafficked, and is an important path from the political centre out into the city.

Kyiv has three rapid transit circuits: red, blue and green. The interchange between Independence Square Station (on the red circuit) and Khreshchatyk Station (on the blue circuit) is located beneath Independence Square. There is also a short walking distance to Golden Gate Station (*Zoloti vorota*, on the green circuit). There are bus, minibus and trolleybus routes crossing Independence Square, and the main railway station is approximately 3.5 kilometres away.

Many pedestrians also use this urban space. The Independence Monument has become a natural meeting place for people in the area, whether they want to stroll in one of the parks in the city centre or go shopping in one of Kyiv's increasing number of shopping malls. There is also a multitude of cafes, restaurants and nightclubs in the area, which attract crowds during the day and evening. At weekends, Khreshchatyk is closed for traffic and becomes a pedestrian zone as far as Bohdan Khmel'nyts'kyi Street (not shown on map), with ice cream parlours, street musicians, entertainers and much else. Independence Square is also one of Kyiv's most frequented places for tourists, not only because of its history, location, and social and cultural events, but also because several of the city's hotels are located on and around the square.

Since the urban space is large and centrally located, it is also used for festivals, concerts, and on commemorative holidays. Rallies and military parades are arranged on Labour Day (1 May), Victory Day (9 May), and Independence Day (24 August). On 1 December every year, a large New Year tree is erected on the square.

7.1.3 Protest Space

There are many practical advantages of using Independence Square for protests and demonstrations. The large number of parks, expansive urban spaces, and educational institutions within a short walking distance of the square make it possible to arrange simultaneous rallies in several places in the city and, later, to lead them down to Maidan when they are large enough to fill the square. The park in front of Shevchenko University, Kontraktova Square, and Mykhailivs'ka Square have often been used in this way, e.g. during the "Revolution on the Granite" in 1990 (see below), the Orange Revolution in 2004–2005, and Euromaidan in 2013–2014.

Independence Square has become a natural meeting place for different groupings and organisations because it has enough room for a large number of people, and because it is a short distance from the political centre. A protest encampment based at Maidan can react quickly to the actions of politicians. During Euromaidan, for example, the demonstrators responded to new laws and the imprisonment of activists by arranging demonstrations in front of Verkhovna Rada and the city courthouse, among other locations.

Since Independence Square is used by a large number of people, any protest located there soon draws notice and can potentially grow fast. Due to Kyiv's political, religious, and symbolic importance—within Ukraine as well as among its neighbours—protest actions in the city often attract both national and international attention. Additionally, the many plateaus over the SE part give the media, and anyone else who might wish to take photos of the protests, a good overview of what is going on at Maidan.

Nonetheless, the square presents protesters with some disadvantages. The ten entrances to the square and its large size make it easy for demonstrators to access the square, but also make the area vulnerable to attacks from police and other law enforcement agencies. This is mainly true for smaller demonstrations. Conversely, large crowds of people have shown themselves particularly difficult to remove. Even when military vehicles and firearms were deployed in February 2014, the government did not manage to clear more than a fraction of the Euromaidan protestors.

However, it is all the physical obstacles that appeared on the square after the reconstruction of 2000 that constitute a real challenge for large protests. The many fences, fountains, and benches in the NW part prevent movement across the square and reduce both outward visibility and room to move. The SE part is more open and higher up than the NW part, making it a natural focal point for people on the square. This part would therefore be the obvious place to put a stage from which protest leaders can address the crowds. But space in the SE part is constrained due to the position of the Independence Monument and other objects. For this reason, the protesters often set up their stage close to Khreshchatyk Avenue, facing the SE part and the press vantage points, with its back to the NW part.

Even so, the disadvantages of organising a protest at Independence Square are outweighed by the advantages. It is very likely that the square's physical suitability has been an important factor in the successful outcome of large protests there (including, among others, the Orange Revolution in 2004–2005 and Euromaidan in 2013–2014). The physical qualities by themselves do not, however, explain why Maidan has become such a powerful symbol in Ukraine. Nor do they explain what functions Maidan has in Ukrainian society.

Figure 21: Maidan, Kyiv, November 2013

Photo: Arve Hansen

7.2 Symbolic Value

Maidan Nezalezhnosti consists of two words: *maidan* and *independence*. The word "maidan" became part of the Ukrainian language during the Mongol period, and it derives from the Middle-Persian and Arabic word ميدان (meydân [Persian], midān [Arabic]). Maidan means space or arena in Middle Persian and volume, sphere, or a place for games in Arabic (maidan, 1989). In Ukrainian there are two words for square/open urban space: *maidan* and *ploshcha*. A maidan is, unlike a *ploshcha*, a larger arena with many entrances (Vasianovych 2011).

The word "maidan" does not exist in Russian, which has only one word, *ploshchad'*. After the collapse of the Soviet Union in 1991 and Ukraine's declaration of independence, October Revolution *Square* (ploshcha) changed name to Independence *Maidan*. The new name thus not only symbolises Ukraine's independence but also emphasises that the country is not Russian.

In addition to the name of the square, there are several other aspects that reinforce the sense of Maidan belonging to the people: 1) In the apparent mess one finds at Independence Square—monuments, buildings in a variety of architectural styles, enormous advertising boards and plenty else—are symbolic markers of the city's and the country's history. 2) The Trade Unions Building—the large cornerstone structure in the NW part of the square—serves as a symbol of the fight for labour rights. 3) The cultural life of Ukraine is represented through the Art Centre and the Conservatoire. 4) It is Maidan that is regarded as the centre of the capital, not Pechers'ka Hill (the political centre) or Zamkova Hill (the religious centre).

7.2.1 25 Years of Protest

The first mass protest in this specific urban space (then known as October Revolution Square) took place in October 1990. Ukraine was, like many other Soviet republics, ravaged by a faltering economy, corruption, and widespread lack of goods, in addition to the consequences of the Chernobyl Catastrophe in 1986. Gorbachev's perestroika and glasnost' reform projects now made demonstrations possible and, accordingly, two student organisations from Kyiv and Lviv staged a hunger strike in front of the Lenin Monument on the granite-paved square. This was called the Revolution on the Granite. The students demanded, among other things, Ukraine's exit from the Soviet Union, a parliamentary re-election, and that conscripts should not be required to serve in hot spots such as Afghanistan and Nagorno-Karabakh. The protests, which begun with a few hundred students, soon grew large; and when miners from the Donbas region joined them, the authorities began to react. The biggest achievement of the Revolution on the Granite, after 16 days of hunger strike, was that the leader of the Kyivan student organisation, Oleksandr Donii, was granted speaking time in the Verkhovna Rada. During the live broadcast, he repeated the protesters' demands. Conscripts were also promised that they would serve within Ukraine (Divaki production 2011).

One year after the Revolution on the Granite, the Soviet Union ceased to exist, but this newly won independence did not mean that everything suddenly improved. A rapid transition to a capitalist system, uncontrolled privatisation, and some hasty economic decisions led to inflation and shortages of goods (Morrison 1993, 686). In the wake of the economic crisis, corruption and crime rose. Three rival oligarch clans (the Kyiv clan, the Dnipropetrovsk clan, and the Donetsk clan) were established during the 1990s, and these remained in economic—but, quite often, also violent—conflict (Matuszak 2012, 13–15).

The second president of Ukraine, Leonid Kuchma, was able to stop the economic chaos that had ravaged the country during President Leonid Kravchuk's term. In the course of his first presidential term (1994–1999), Kuchma stabilised the economy, introduced the country's first constitution, and oversaw a large growth of the middle class. In Kuchma's second period (1999–2005), however, the positive developments ended and the oligarchs increased their power. Corruption boomed, and the president tightened censorship of the mass media (Dyczok 2006; Hansen 2015, 15–16).

In 2000, Kuchma was at the centre of a huge scandal. Three weeks after Heorhii Gongadze, a journalist critical of the regime, was found tortured and beheaded in a forest outside Kyiv, sound recordings from the president's telephone were leaked by the president's former bodyguard Mykola Mel'nychenko. The recordings allegedly confirmed that the president, among other things, ordered the killing of Gongadze, and that he was behind election fraud, corruption and numerous other criminal acts (Kuzio 2007, 42). The so-called *Cassette Scandal* triggered the *Ukraine Without Kuchma* protests in the winter of 2000–2001, during which thousands of demonstrators demanded the president's resignation. The protesters initially settled at Maidan, but the above-mentioned substantial redevelopment of the square became a pretext for the authorities to relocate the protest camp. The demonstrators had to move to the park in front of Shevchenko University, where they stayed for almost three months until the encampment of tents was brutally demolished by riot police in March 2001. Cybriwsky (2014a, 167) asserts that the authorities used the work on

Maidan that winter in order both to remove the protests and to reconstruct the square to make it less suitable for protest.

Despite these new obstacles, Independence Square was the setting of the Orange Revolution in 2004–2005. After a dramatic election campaign between Kuchma's preferred candidate, former prime minister Viktor Ianukovych, and Governor of the Central Bank Viktor Iushchenko, Ianukovych was declared the winner. Iushchenko had been poisoned during the election campaign but survived, and there were many reports of election fraud (Wilson 2005, 70–121). The biggest protest in Ukraine up until that point was led by Iushchenko and Iuliia Tymoshenko. After two months at Maidan, which at times was populated by hundreds of thousands of demonstrators, the authorities agreed to change the constitution and to hold new elections. The new elections were won by Iushchenko.

During his campaign, Iushchenko had pledged to reform the country, eliminate corruption, and improve the economy, but both he and the new economic elite turned out to be a big disappointment. The president struggled to implement the reforms and could not cooperate either with the parliament or with Tymoshenko. The latter criticised Iushchenko increasingly vocally, and the two soon became political adversaries. In 2010, five years after Iushchenko was elected president, he had achieved little. Corruption had soared, the value of the Ukrainian Hryvnia fell by 38% in relation to the dollar (*BBC* 2009), the murder of Gongadze remained unsolved, and the oligarchs had at least as much power as before. In the presidential elections of 2010, Ianukovych returned as a candidate and won against Tymoshenko with 48.95% against 45.47% of the votes. Iushchenko lost the race in the first round with a mere 5.5 % support (Kireev 2007)

Ianukovych soon attracted criticism from many sides. He was accused of promoting the renewed Russification of Ukraine (Kuzio 2012; *Zik* 2010) and exacerbating the obstacles facing small businesses (Hansen 2015, 19), and held responsible for the increased levels of corruption and crime and for weakening the position of human rights in society: redacting the judicial system, obstructing the work of NGOs and committing human rights offences, among other things (Zakharov 2014, 13–28, 161–173). Several protests against the authorities were held on Maidan. Some of the biggest were the Tax Maidan in 2010, against an increase in the government's control over small- and medium-sized businesses; the Freedom for Iuliia demonstrations (*Iuli voliu*) in 2011, against the criminal prosecution directed at Tymoshenko (Ianukovych's rival); and the Vradiivka protests, directed against legal officials accused by the demonstrators of protecting one of the police officers suspected of involvement in the abduction and brutal gang rape of a woman in a little town called Vradiivka (Hansen 2015, 19–20).

Euromaidan was, therefore, only the last of several protests against Ianukovych, and one of a large number of protests to take place at Maidan since Ukraine achieved independence. The protests described above include only some of the most widely known protest actions, and a tradition of going to Maidan to protest against the authorities has been firmly established.[52] Because Maidan can simultaneously be associated with four revolutions, the space also has a revolutionary symbolic value. The Revolution on the Granite, the Orange Revolution, and Euromaidan all took place at Maidan, while the October Revolution was the square's namesake until 1991. The photojournalist Oleksandr Klymenko believes that the name of October Revolution Square was one reason why students chose it as their location for the Revolution on the Granite in 1990. This revolutionary symbolic value was only strengthened after a large number of demonstrators died in the clashes in February 2014. The demonstrators killed are now represented as heroes in Ukraine, collectively known as the Heavenly Hundred (*Nebesnia sotnia*)—a symbol of the willingness of Ukrainians to die for the sake of effecting change in their country.

Of course, Maidan is not the only urban space in central Kyiv that can be used for protest. The urban spaces of Sophia Square and Mykhailivs'ka Square can, taken together, accommodate a large number of people, and their close proximity to one another makes this possible. Shevchenko Park, in front of the university of the same name, has great symbolic value because the poet Taras Shevchenko (1814–1861) is considered one of the

---

52   During my two periods of residency in Kyiv as well as my frequent trips to the city, there were apparently "always" ongoing or planned protests on Independence Square.

most important figures for the opposition. Parliament Square, in front of Verkhovna Rada, is centrally located in proximity to various political institutions. All these urban spaces can and have been used for demonstrations; but, as I mention above, they are used to a lesser extent, and often as auxiliary spaces for bigger demonstrations at Maidan. Their layout and locations are probably important reasons why they have not been used as often as Maidan (Hansen, 2015, 37–38), although the heavy symbolic value of Maidan probably is an even more important reason.

Figure 22: Maidan, Kyiv, March 2014

Flowers in memory of the Heavenly Hundred. Photo: Arve Hansen

7.3 Function

What functions, then, does Independence Square have in Ukrainian society? Many of my respondents state that they perceive the square as a vital part of the political system. *Hanna*, an Internet activist, believes that Maidan first occurred as a reaction to the corruption in the political system, and has now turned into a movement to get rid of it:

> Our politics is corrupt on such a level [...] that Maidan has become a necessity for us. [...] Maidan is a spontaneous reaction, a protest, a reflex [...]. But subsequently, a shared goal emerged: to completely change the corrupt system. You could say that this is a social movement against corruption, or against the ghost of the Soviet Union.[53]

When I asked my respondents what function they believe Maidan has, several of them compared Maidan to various political institutions. Both the photojournalist Oleksandr Klymenko and the local historian *Serhii* (who have seen a number of protests on the square over time), as well as *Stanislaw* (a Belarusian activist who came to support Euromaidan), call the space a form of people's parliament, where one goes to resolve problems. *Serhii* compares Maidan with two forms of popular assemblies:

> [...] the word "Maidan" has simply begun to mean some kind of mass action. Like a type of the Old Russian phenomenon *viche*. Or like the Norwegian word *thing*. In other words, this is a popular assembly that takes some kind of important decision [italics mine].[54]

The American history professor Timothy Snyder draws a similar parallel to the Greek Agora:

> [...] a maidan now means in Ukrainian what the Greek word agora means in English: not just a marketplace where people happen to meet, but a place where they deliberately meet, precisely in order to deliberate, to speak, and to create a political society (Snyder 2014).

Several others, including the Ukrainian journalist and blogger Volodymyr Zolotoriov, also emphasise Maidan's role as a place for discussion: "Maidan is social training for collective action and joint

---

[53] "Nasha polityka nastilky korumpovana, [...] shcho nam prosto neobkhidnyi Maidan. [...] Maidan – tse spontanna aktsia, protest, refleks [...]. Ale zhodom ziavylas' spil'na meta – povnistiu zminyty korumpovanu systemu. Mozhna skazaty, shcho tse sotialnyi rukh proty koruptsii abo pryzraku Radianskoho Soiuzu."

[54] "[...] slovo Maidan prosto stalo oznachat' imenno kakuiu-to mnogoliudnuiu aktsiiu. Kak tipa drevnerusskoe iavlenie veche. Ili podobnoe k norvezhskomu slovu ting. To est' eto narodnoe sobranie, kotoroe prinimaet kakoe-to reshenie vazhnoe."

communication. Ukrainians are learning to become a society, act collectively and communicate together." [55]

It is, of course, possible to questions claims about Maidan being a *thing* or an *agora*. During Euromaidan, of course, the various protest groupings discussed questions about the political situation and what was to be done, but there was little during my field work to indicate that Maidan was primarily a place for discussion. The government and those who supported the authorities were not given access to the debates at Maidan, and the attendees were usually in broad agreement about what and whom they were against, even if they occasionally disagreed about the methods. Therefore, Maidan was more a space for action than a democratic institution.

It might, however, be less relevant to ask whether or not Maidan functions as a people's assembly, and more important to ask which functions Maidan does have in Ukraine. Since this is a location where people often go to take action against the authorities, it performs an important role: protests appear at Maidan when there is great discontent with a given issue and Ukrainians are not satisfied with how the authorities are dealing with that issue. We can therefore see Maidan's primary function as a form of safety valve for Ukrainian society—a place where Ukrainians can feel that they have a real possibility of affecting the political process directly once discontent reaches a critical level.

Anyone can occupy Maidan, and different groups and segments of the population have started protests on the square. During the Revolution on the Granite in 1990 and Euromaidan in 2013–2014, it was students who started the protest. However, protests have also been started by politicians, for example, such as the Free Iuliia Tymoshenko movement in 2011; by businessmen, such as the Tax Maidan in 2010; and by people from minor towns, such as the Vradiivka protests in 2013. The broad appeal (or otherwise) of a given issue is what decides whether other social groups also join

---

[55] "Maidan – eto sotsialnaia praktika vzaimo-deistviia, so-obshcheniia. Ukraintsy uchatsia byt' obshchestvom, vzaimo-deistvovat' i so-obshchat'sia [sic]."

in and, as they say in Ukraine, "a new Maidan begins" (*novyi Maidan pochynaetsia*).

7.4 Conclusions

At the start of this chapter, I asked what makes Independence Square the primary protest space in Ukraine, what symbolic value it holds, and what functions it performs in Ukrainian society.

Protests have been part of the political landscape in Ukraine for a long time. During 25 years or so of social discontent and 30 years of economic hardship, trust in the country's political institutions has worn thin. Corruption and crime within the country's small elite have led many Ukrainians to see politicians as representing only their own personal interests, not those of the people. The disappointment that followed the Orange Revolution contributed to the perception that all politicians are like this, even the opposition. When people start to feel that politicians are doing a poor job of protecting their interests, they go out to Independence Square. Despite attempts at the start of this century to make the urban space less suitable for large crowds, it remains the place where people gather to protest.

Independence Square is physically well suited as a protest space. It is strategically located between several key meeting places in the city, which facilitates the possibility of organising demonstrations at several places in the city simultaneously and leading them down to Maidan, and it is only a short distance from the political centre on Pechers'ka Hill. The collective urban space of Maidan and Khreshchatyk Avenue is also a large one, allowing huge crowds to demonstrate at the same time. The many main roads and entrances to the square make it easy to get to Maidan, and the authorities have a hard time controlling actions on the square. The square's layout makes it very difficult to clear people off it once they have been able to set up camp there.

Independence Square is also well suited for protests from a symbolic and cultural viewpoint. The square's name symbolises a distance from Russia, as both the words *maidan* and *independence* are interlinked with the independence of 1991. The square is located downhill from Kyiv's central political, religious and historical landmarks, yet still in the centre of the city. This gives it a peculiar symbolic value as a people's space. This symbolic value is enhanced by the Trade Unions Building, the cultural institutions, and all the local history in the shape of buildings and monuments. Maidan is simultaneously associated with four successful revolutions, three of which are directly connected with the square; reminding both city and country dwellers of the possibilities the square affords them.

It is to Maidan that Ukrainians go to be heard when their political institutions fail, and Maidan can be seen as a kind of safety valve—a place where people congregate to reject their rulers when those deviate too far from the people's will. The sheer number of protests at Maidan bears witness to the importance of this safety valve, and the difficulty of reforming Ukrainian society. The goal of most of these protests has been to remove corrupt leadership, but it is not a given that a new leadership will bring in a new and reformed society.

The current political leadership of Ukraine knows the significance of Maidan. These politicians acquired their positions after the presidential and parliamentary elections in 2014 were expedited owing to the revolution. Therefore, when the Poroshenko administration is threatened with a new Maidan, it knows the implications of this very well. In a climate ravaged by war and instability, but also unsettled by a number of reforms, it will be interesting to see how Maidan will be used in the times ahead.

Figure 23: Maidan, Kyiv, February 2014b

An old man in front of the monument to the founders of Kyiv, in the aftermath of the final clashes during Euromaidan. Photo: Arve Hansen

8 Transitional Study

October Square & Independence Square, Minsk

This transitional study is based on the article "Public space in the Soviet city: A spatial perspective on mass protests in Minsk" (Hansen 2017).

Abstract

In many capitals, the central public square is the place where people go *en masse* when they wish to voice their discontent. The squares used for such collective actions are diverse. Each square has its own unique combination of symbols and history; they are each used in different ways by the public; and they often have distinct physical characteristics. However, in the social sciences, space is often overlooked when determining what makes collective actions successful.

In this case study, I present an approach for analysing public space in relation to mass protests. I then apply this approach to the Belarusian capital Minsk, where virtually no protests have been successful during the post-Soviet period. In what ways are mass protests in Minsk affected by the perceived (symbolic), social and physical elements of the city's public spaces? I examine the centre of Minsk in general, and analyse two central squares in particular. My study is based mainly on qualitative, semi-structured interviews with protesters, observers and opposition leaders; on research literature; and on my own fieldwork and experiences from living in Minsk.

I conclude that space contributes to the difficulties facing the Belarusian opposition in several ways: 1) The perceived elements of Minsk and the two main squares present a symbolic value that favours the regime. 2) The social elements of the city show that the political centre is generally avoided by the public, thus making protests less visible. 3) This latter point is important, given that the physical elements of the squares make policing a demonstration particularly quick and easy. These physical elements also limit the protesters' communication, movement and flexibility. I argue that a spatial perspective should be included in research on collective actions.

In the concept of democracy, the *square* has a central position. Historically, when people started to live in urban societies, the town square often became the natural meeting place—a space in which people would deliberate, make policies and decide on a course of action. Examples of this are the ancient Greek *agora*, the medieval Scandinavian *thing*, and the Slavic *vecha* [Bel.: *веча*].

In our day and age, most decision-making has moved from the town square into political institutions, and the squares have been assigned other uses, such as recreation and celebration. But every so often, people return to the square's original function. To mention just a few recent examples, we have seen people gather on and occupy several squares in modern history, from Tiananmen in 1989 to the squares of many post-Soviet cities during the wave of 'colour revolutions' in the 2000s. We saw massive uprisings start on squares throughout the Arab world from 2010; and, from 2011, there were Occupy protests in many large cities in the West. In Kyiv, protests in the winter of 2013–2014 led to regime change in Ukraine for the second time in less than a decade.

Belarusians, too, have taken to the central squares of Minsk to protest against Aliaksandr Ryhoravich Lukashenka, the country's only president since 1994. Most notably, thousands of Belarusians went to October Square in 2006, and to October and Independence squares in 2010. However, these and many other similar actions were rapidly supressed by the authorities.

The Success and Failure of Mass Protests

In the social sciences, a number of theories have been advanced to explain what makes collective action successful or otherwise. The sociologist Susan Olzak (1989) sets out the factors used to analyse events such as a mass protest or revolution: the duration of the event, the number of participants, and the presence or lack of violence. The importance of such factors has been the subject of much discussion in the relevant research literature.[56]

During the wave of colour revolutions in the early 2000s, new research was done on the conditions in which some of these protests had led to regime change. Political scientist Michael McFaul (2005) lists seven external conditions necessary for a colour revolution to occur.[57] Others

---

56 See for example Chenoweth and Stephan (2011) on nonviolent resistance.
57 1) The regime has to be semi-autocratic, rather than fully autocratic; 2) there has to be an unpopular incumbent; 3) the opposition needs to be united and organised; 4) there must be independent electoral-monitoring capabilities available; 5) there must be a modicum of independent media; 6) the opposition must have the capacity to mobilize

analyse the internal conditions; such as the political scientist Joshua Tucker (2007), who focuses on motivation, arguing that electoral fraud was a primary trigger for all the colour revolutions.

But one aspect of mass protests has not been thoroughly analysed: namely, public space. In what ways does public space affect collective actions?

8.1 A Spatial Perspective

Public space is diverse. From one city to another, the characteristics of urban public space differ greatly. Firstly, every square has its own unique history, traditions and ideological symbols; secondly, spaces are used differently depending on their connection and proximity to infrastructure, buildings, landmarks, and so on; thirdly, there are physical differences such as shape and size, elevations, monuments, layout, entrances, and much more.

In the research relating urban public space with mass protests, authors are mostly concerned either with urban spaces of protest in general or with the uniqueness of some urban space in particular. The former usually leads to a discussion of modern political philosophy, referring to Habermas's *public sphere*—the space in which people meet to talk and deliberate; to Arendt's more physically oriented *public space*; or to Lefebvre's *right to the city*.[58] Discussions also tend to centre on aspects such as the privatisation of space and/or exclusion from it of certain segments of the public (i.e. homeless people, youth, drug users).[59] The latter category analyses the uniqueness of specific public spaces, such as Taksim Square or Tiananmen Square.[60]

---

significant numbers of protesters; 7) and there must be a split among the "guys with guns." In other words, the opposition must have some support in the state apparatus.

58 See Goodsell (2003); Frenzel, Feigenbaum and McCurdy (2013); Göle (2013); Harvey (2012). Also relevant are Howell (1993) on historical geography; and Parkinson (2012) on public space, political institutions and democracy.

59 See Kohn (2013); Mitchell (1995); Mitchell (2017); Köksal (2012).

60 See for instance Örs (2013) on the history and symbolic importance of the Taksim Square in Istanbul; Gillham et al. (2013) on the policing of Occupy protests; Ramadan

What I believe to be missing in the literature, however, is a general approach to the question of *how* to analyse public spaces and evaluate how they enable (or fail to enable) public protest. Since the goal of this book is to establish and develop such an approach, the aim of this chapter is to demonstrate that space is, potentially, an important condition for collective action. This is the context for the following analysis of the public space of Minsk, which asks in what ways the central squares of the Belarusian capital affect the course and nature of mass protests, and how Minsk's central squares facilitate and/or inhibit protest.

Research Question, Approach, Methodology

In the previous chapter, I applied the architectural theory of Lynch (1960) to describe how people in Kyiv relate to Independence Square. This approach identifies and describes the different 'elements of the city' (paths, nodes, landmarks, edges and districts), using interviews to establish how these elements affect day-to-day life in the city: how people use landmarks for navigation, which paths they take, and so on. In this chapter, I expand on Lynch's theory in order to better suit a perspective on mass protests. I add several new elements and divide these into three categories: perceived elements, social elements and physical elements.[61] How do these perceived, social, and physical elements affect stationary mass protests in Minsk?

Between October 2015 and March 2017, I had many conversations and discussions with Belarusians from my extended circle of contacts (I elaborate on this below). From these, I chose nine observers, organisers and protesters to conduct eleven qualitative interviews.[62] The interviews

---

(2013) on the importance of Tahrir Square in Egypt; Lee (2009) on the making of Tiananmen Square a political space.

61 These elements were identified in the course of preparing my previous publications (Hansen 2015; 2016) and during my work on this chapter. Although I have tried to make this list as complete as possible, it can never be exhaustive. I discovered new elements during my work on Kyiv and Minsk, and I expect more will emerge in subsequent case studies.

62 I interviewed one Belarusian journalist (Vital'); five Belarusians who participated in protest actions (Dzmitry, Katsiaryna [twice], Piatro, Yaraslaw [twice], Pawliuk [who is also a member of the LGBT movement]); and three politicians (Stanislaw Shushkevich, Belarus' first head of state and presidential candidate in 1994; Aliaksandr Milinkevich,

were conducted in Russian and Belarusian via Skype, telephone, and email.[63] All the interviews, except for the email correspondence with Milinkevich, took the form of semi-structured conversations with open-ended questions. I asked the respondents to tell me about the general situation in Belarus; about Minsk and its spaces of protest; and about particular protests (mainly the mass actions of 2006 and 2010). I paid particular attention to instances when the elements of the city were mentioned, then prompted the respondents with questions such as *"How accessible was October Square for you in 2006?"*

Figure 24:   Elements of the city, first version

Perceived elements	Social elements	Physical elements
History	Paths	Location
Ideological symbols	Nodes	Size
Buildings	Buildings	Shape
Landmarks	Landmarks	Entrances
Monuments	Districts	Exits
History of protests	Traditions	Walls
	Official use	Floor
		Objects
		Obstacles
		Edges
		Public works
		Focal points

In addition to the interviews, the current chapter is based on a recent period of fieldwork in Minsk;[64] research literature on the politics of

---

the joint opposition's presidential candidate in 2006; and Mikola Statkevich, a presidential candidate in 2010). The names of all respondents, except those of the politicians, have been altered. The interviews are referred to by the respondent's surname or pseudonym either in-text or in brackets. The number of respondents is limited because this chapter is part of a bigger project including several cities. Nevertheless, I believe that my selection of an observer, politicians and protesters is sufficient to map how space is perceived in Minsk.

63   The interviews were conducted online or by phone, to minimize the risk of our contact being noticed by the government, potentially leading to repressions. The interviews were recorded in audio only after obtaining prior permission from the respondents.

64   The fieldwork was conducted in October and November 2015.

Belarus, the history and architecture of the city; cinema and television documentaries;[65] my own experience of living in Minsk;[66] and from work-related contact with the Belarusian opposition in Kyiv and Vilnius.[67]

I use these data to describe the city and the elements of its main squares, and I identify instances where the elements of the squares have affected the opposition's conduct. I argue that Minsk is a particularly difficult place for protest because: 1) the city is shaped by Lukashenka and embodies both his success and the mainstream and official view of history—while, at the same time, alienating the pro-European opposition; 2) the two main squares (October and Independence) are places most people tend to avoid, making protests there scarcely visible to the population at large; 3) the squares give little shelter or safety to protesters and impede their communication, and are also easily controlled from the outside.

8.2 Belarusian Protests from Glasnost' to Lukashenka

The first major protests in Belarus in the 1980s were enabled by Gorbachev's reform policies. The main concerns for protesters at the time were the effects of the Chernobyl disaster (1986); increasing economic difficulties; and the question of independence—fuelled by the discovery of one of Stalin's killing fields in the Kurapaty Forest on the outskirts of Minsk (Marples, 1994). Protests continued during the post-Soviet 1990s. More often than not, these were concerned with economic problems and food shortages.

The current regime in Belarus is by and large personified by Aliaksandr Lukashenka—commonly referred to in the West as 'the last

---

65   Obyknovennyi prezident (Khashchavatski 1996); Lekcja Białoruskiego (Dembiński 2006); Ploshcha (Khashchavatski 2007); Belarusskaia mechta (Kibal'chich 2011); Banda (Mikhailowskaia 2015).
66   As a language student in Belarus in 2006–10.
67   During my internship at the Norwegian embassy in Ukraine (2011), I worked with many young people from the Belarusian opposition in Ukraine and Lithuania. They had been expelled from Belarusian universities for participating in the protests of 2006, and given funding by the Nordic Council of Ministers to continue their education in Ukraine and Lithuania.

dictator in Europe', a phrase coined by Condoleezza Rice in 2005 (Nielsen 2012). Lukashenka won the first Belarusian presidential elections in 1994 with over 80 percent of the votes (Vardomatskii 1995, 49). Initially he was regarded as an alternative to five other candidates who, in the eyes of the Belarusian electorate, represented either inexperience or corruption or both.[68] Soon, however, new reasons for protest emerged. During Lukashenka's first term in office (1994–2001), one of these was the reintroduction of Soviet symbols, as well as the president's increasing authoritarianism and suppression of the political opposition.

It took Lukashenka ten years to consolidate his presidency: he increased presidential powers and weakened the parliament through two referendums in 1995 and 1996 respectively (Wilson 2011, 168–86). Meanwhile certain of his political and ideological opponents disappeared or died in unclear circumstances (Bennett 2011, 70; Mikhailowskaia 2015). Protests against Lukashenka increased as colour revolutions against authoritarian leaders spread through a number of post-Soviet countries. Large-scale protests were staged against a proposed union with Russia, which was never realised (Statkevich); and, in 2004, people protested against a referendum that removed the two-term limit on the presidential rule. Significantly, large numbers of people went out to protest against the alleged fraud in the presidential elections of March 2006 and December 2010, attempting to achieve a Belarusian colour revolution. Both attempts were brutally suppressed by the authorities.

David Marples (2006) points out that Belarus in 2006 lacked every single one of McFaul's (2005) conditions (see above), arguing that the president had a firm grip on the official ideology and had been able to maintain his popularity with large segments of the population through his control over the media, his repressions of political opponents, and by

---

68 Of his main opponents campaigning for the presidency, three are worth mentioning: 1) The prime minister, Viacheslaw Kebich, who represented the status quo. 2) Zianon Pazniak, who represented the nationalist new political force, while promising a radical Belarusification of society and government. 3) The former head of state, Stanislaw Shushkevich, who represented the more conservative new political force. Initially very popular, he lost because of the accusations of corruption directed at him (Shushkevich).

maintaining close relations with Russia (Marples 2006). To this, Barbara Törnquist-Plewa (2001) adds the (highly) successful Russification under the Russian Empire and then the Soviet Union, and a weak Belarusian identity. By playing on the post-Soviet nostalgia of Belarusian citizens, Lukashenka has built an official national myth on the Soviet past of his country, which emphasises the special position of Belarusians in the narratives of the Soviet Union and the Second World War (known in the former Soviet Union as the Great Patriotic War). Lukashenka's Soviet-oriented and pro-Russian worldview has pushed the majority of the opposition into the pro-European camp. However, in spite of its common contempt for Lukashenka and its shared pro-European values, the opposition shows little unity, conforming to its description by Törnquist-Plewa as "weak and fragmented" (2001, 81). My own experience of working with members of the Belarusian opposition confirms this view.[69]

Since the spring of 2011, Belarus has faced mounting economic problems. The combination of a nationalised and planned economy, poor decision-making on the part of the government (Romanchuk, 2011) and a weakened Russian rouble (from 2014) has led to several devaluations of the Belarusian rouble and to shortages of goods. In early 2017, protests erupted in many Belarusian cities against the economic hardship and the introduction of a new law 'on social parasites', which taxes the unemployed. However, since March 25—when a large demonstration in Minsk was suppressed by riot police and opposition leaders arrested—protests have, for now, ceased. (Bylina 2017)

My respondents repeat many of the observations presented in the research literature regarding the situation in Belarus, such as authority-controlled media and a Belarusian mentality similar to that of a Soviet

---

69   In spring 2011, after the violent crackdown on protests in December 2010, I arranged a meeting at the European Humanitarian University in Vilnius. The meeting was attended by staff members of the Norwegian embassy in Ukraine and the Nordic Council of Ministers, as well as Belarusian students studying in Kyiv and Vilnius. The different opposition groupings, as represented by the students, appeared to be aggressively opposing each other and showed few signs of unity.

citizen who values short-term stability over freedom. Statkevich agrees with Tucker (2007) that only presidential elections have the potential to unite the opposition and motivate large numbers of people to take to the streets: "A small chance appears on the night of the presidential elections [...]. Belarusians are a rational people, very rational. If there's no chance, why take the risk?"[70] To this, my respondents are prone to add that Lukashenka has built a police state that cannot be overthrown by a popular protest or revolution. "Here, the KGB secret service, a large police apparatus and the possibility of using internal troops work well to suppress any public actions."[71] (Pawliuk). Several of my respondents also emphasise differences in national character between Belarusians and Ukrainians: "We don't have the same mentality as Ukrainians. They are good at it." (Yaraslaw). "Maidan is the national character of Ukrainians, not Belarusians." (Piatro). "Our national identity is the same as that of people in Eastern Ukraine [...]".[72]

Thus, there are many arguments which, taken together, might offer plausible explanations of why the Belarusian opposition has failed to achieve success. Nevertheless, I wish to add space as another relevant factor in this picture. In the following section, I will turn to the first group of elements in the city and examine how these also affect the opposition's possibilities.

---

70 "Malen'kii shans pridvigaet noch' prezidentskikh vyborov [...]. Belorusy – ratsional'nyi naro, ochen' ratsional'nyi. Esli netu shansa, zachem riskovat'?"
71 "Zdes' khorosho rabotaet spetssluzhby KGB, bol'shoi apparat militsii i vozmozhnost' ispol'zovat' vnutrennie voiska dlia podavleniia liubykh publichnykh aktsii"
72 "U nas net takogo mentaliteta, kak u ukraintsev. U nikh eto khorosho poluchaetsia." (Yaraslaŭ). "Maidan iavliaetsia natsional'nym kharakterom ukraintsev, ne belorusov." (Piatro). "U nas natsyianal'naia identychnast', iak u liudzei va wskhodnikh ablastsiakh Ukrainy [...]" (Dzmitry).

Figure 25: The Belarusian Great Patriotic War Museum

Photo: Julian Nyča / Wikimedia Commons. Licensed under CC-BY-SA 4.0 (https://creativecommons.org/licenses/by-sa/4.0/deed.en)

8.3 Perceived elements

Minsk is well known for looking 'Soviet', and a first-time visitor is struck by just how much of the Soviet architecture has been preserved. The city is characterised by wide avenues, a Stalinist architectural style, prominent red stars and Soviet slogans, huge squares and monuments to the 1945 victory.

There are several reasons why Minsk is infused with such a strongly Soviet identity, but perhaps the most significant relates to the Great Patriotic War, which reduced the city to rubble. This enabled Soviet architects to rebuild Minsk as an example of what the socialist experiment could achieve (Bohn 2013, 6). With the building boom of the 1940s and 1950s, the infrastructure was developed further, with industry, educational institutions and more. Only a small proportion of the city's original inhabitants returned to Minsk after the war, while Russians and rural Belarusians moved in to take their place. This contributed to a Russification of the city.

In addition to the monumental celebration of Communist heroes, such as Lenin, Dzerzhinsky and Kalinin, the war became an important theme of the public spaces of Minsk—not least after it was granted the status of 'hero city' in 1974 (Bohn 2013, 30). Analysing the memory of the war, Per Anders Rudling states that "in no other country does the war occupy such a central place in the national historiography as it does in Lukashenka's Belarus." (2008, 57). 10 per cent of the toponymy of major streets, parks and squares in the city centre relate to the War, in addition to 60 per cent relating to other Soviet events and persons (Titarenko 2008, 38). These names often replaced the ethnic ones (i.e. from the significant pre-war population of Jews and Tatars).

The city's historic markers went through a similar 'cleansing'. In an article on the phenomenon of Minsk, Larissa Titarenko and Anna Shirokanova describe how the majority of symbolic markers were either destroyed during the fighting or removed by Soviet architects. Prominent examples of this are the levelling of Castle Hill (*Zamchyshcha*), where a wooden castle long stood as a distinctive landmark, and the river Niamiha, now channelled through underground pipes. (Titarenko and Shirokanova 2011, 31) The latter is especially noteworthy since Minsk's first appearance in a historical text is in the Primary Chronicle for the year 1067, which reports a battle near Minsk on the river Niamiha (Cross and Sherbowitz-Wetzor 1953, 145–46). The river Svislach has since taken the Niamiha's place as the main waterway of Minsk.

Most of the capital city's official institutions are placed along the 15-km-long, eight-lane-wide Independence Avenue (*Praspekt Nezalezhnastsi*). The avenue runs from Independence Square in the western part of the city centre to the city's border in the northeast, crossing four further squares after Independence Square. The first of these is October Square; then the avenue bridges the river Svislach, becomes a roundabout where it crosses Victory Square, passes the third, Iakub Kolas, and cuts through Kalinin Square (see fig. 26).

Since Lukashenka came to power, a number of new monumental building projects have been launched. At October Square, the unfinished Palace of the Republic had stood untouched since 1984, when economic problems brought a halt to the project. In 2001, after 17 years as a construction site, the building was completed and the square reopened. Even more grandiose projects include the National Library (2006), the Stalitsa Shopping Centre on Independence Square (2006), and the new museum to the Great Patriotic War (2014), to mention but a few. These building projects are similar to the Soviet brutalist monumental style. It could be said that Lukashenkian architecture carries on the Soviet tradition of aiming to represent the success and prosperity of the country's leadership.

Figure 26: Minsk City Centre (map)

1: Independence Square. 2: KDB (KGB). 3: GUM Shopping centre. 4: October Square. 5: Victory Square. 6: Niamiha. 7: Zybitskaia. 8: Ianka Kupala Park. 9: Gorkyi Park. 10: Main Train Station. 11: Presidential Administration. 12: Iakub Kolas Square. 13: Kalinin Square. Illustration: Arve Hansen

Capitalism has also made its mark with the introduction of advertising and brand names. However, compared to neighbouring capitals such as Kyiv, Riga, and Vilnius, Minsk has escaped the extremes of post-Soviet marketing. Sarna (2008) describes the current authorities' attempt to make Minsk a 'glamourous heaven' by removing everything unsanctioned and disorderly, such as intrusive advertising boards, litter … and even political dissent. In other post-Soviet countries, Minsk enjoys a reputation as a clean and orderly city.

Still, protests do occasionally occur in the city, and two central squares in particular have been used by the opposition for mass protests: October and Independence squares (see below for my explanation). In the following two subsections, I will look more closely at the perceived elements of these two squares.

8.3.1 October Square

October Square is named after the Bolshevik Revolution of 1917. It is the most geographically central square in Minsk; between 1949 and 1984, it was named Central square (*Tsentral'naia*) and was intended as the heart of the city (Bohn 2013, 49). The global positioning of Minsk and of October Square is marked on the square's only monument, a tiny pyramid called the 0-km Sign, which displays the distances from Minsk to other major cities of the world.

The centrepiece of the square is the Palace of the Republic, where officially sanctioned concerts and receptions of foreign delegations are held. This is also where Lukashenka has been inaugurated four times since 2001 (the 1994 inauguration took place in the House of Government) (Naviny 2015). The palace is perceived as a monument to the success and economic stability achieved during Lukashenka's first term in office, and Milinkevich calls it "almost a sacred place for the authorities".[73] The city's inhabitants like to call it *the giant sarcophagus*, because of its brutal but simplistic design reminiscent of a vast coffin. Piatro confirms that the uneasiness of the metaphor is appropriate: "The Palace of the Republic evokes

---

73 "amal' sakral'nae mestsa dlia wlady"

a feeling of horror. It's a sarcophagus that blocks the view to [Verkhni horad District]". [74]

Figure 27: The Palace of the Republic, Minsk

Photo: Grisha / Colourbox

After the presidential elections in March 2006, in response to an appeal by Aliaksandr Milinkevich, people went to October Square in large numbers with the slogan "Freedom, Truth, Justice"[75] (Milinkevich) to protest against alleged election fraud. In the West, the protests are known as the Denim Revolution.[76] In Minsk, however, the protesters tried to change October Square's association from Lukashenka and the October Revolution to something more ideologically appealing. They started to call it Kalinowskyi Square (*Ploshcha Kalinowskaha*), after Kastus' Kalinowskyi—a key person in the 1863 January Uprising against the Russian Empire.

---

74 "Dvorets Respubliki vyzyvaet chuvstbo uzhasa. Eto Sarkofag, kotoryi zakryvaet vid na [Verkhnii gorod]"
75 "Svaboda, Prawda, Spraviadlivasts'"
76 Wilson explains that the Belarusian 'colour revolution' was given the symbol of denim, because "it would be difficult for the repressive local police to victimise people for wearing it." Wilson then criticises the symbol for being too common (2011, 211). Judging by my respondents, the name "Denim Revolution" is rarely used.

Usually, though, the square is simply called 'Ploshcha' (Bel.: *плошча*), which is Belarusian for 'square'. By choosing a Belarusian word, the protesters distance themselves from the largely Russophone leadership. At present, when members of the opposition say "We'll start the Ploshcha," or "go out to the Ploshcha", they mean starting a large protest at October Square. The way in which the opposition uses the word is similar to how Ukrainians use the word 'maidan' (from Ukrainian, meaning 'square') (7.2.1).

> 'Ploshcha', that's because of Maidan. In the beginning we called it Maidan, but the Belarusian media has successfully used Maidan to scare everyone. Both in 2004 and later in 2013 [...]. For many people it has a negative association, therefore we didn't call it Maidan. But at the same time we wanted to come up with something of our own. [...] The simplest solution was 'Ploshcha'. [77] (Piatro)

Despite these attempts to appropriate the space and change the association from the Bolshevik October Revolution to a people's revolt against Russia, the Ploshcha of 2006 did not turn out like the Ukrainian Maidan of 2004, and the protests ended with massive arrests. According to Milinkevich, following the protests, 1500 people lost their jobs, 1200 were sent to jail and 500 students were expelled from their higher education institutions. Today, none of my respondents seem to associate the square with revolution. When I asked about their feelings around October Square, several spoke of disappointment and failure. "[October Square] is associated with the authorities, with failed desires, dreams, [...] yes, and with disappointment." [78] (Pawliuk)

8.3.2 Independence Square

The next mass protests in Minsk took place on 19 December 2010, after yet another re-election of Lukashenka. Triggered by claims of election

---

[77] "'Ploshcha' – eto potomu chto Maidan. V nachale nazyvali Maidan, no Maidanom uspeshno v belorusskoi media vsekh zapugali. I togda v 2004 i potom v 2013 [...]. Dlia mnogikh eto imelo negativnuiu assotsiatsiiu, poetomu Maidanom ne nazyvali. No pri etom khoteli chto-to svoe pridumat'. [...] Samoe prostoe eto bylo 'Ploshcha'."

[78] "[Oktiabr'skaia] assotsiiruetsia s vlast'iu, s neudavshimisia zhelaniiami, mechtami, [...] da, i s rozacharovaniem."

fraud, the opposition announced a new "Ploshcha" and marched to October Square, where tens of thousands of people gathered. After remaining at October Square for a couple of hours, the protesters then decided to move the protest down to Independence Square to protest outside the House of Government.[79] On the way to Independence Square, the crowd grew, and several of my respondents claim that the whole kilometre of Independence Avenue linking the two squares was filled with people.

Figure 28: Independence Square, Minsk

Photo: Zedlik / Wikimedia Commons. Licensed under CC-BY-SA 3.0 (https://creativecommons.org/licenses/by-sa/3.0/deed.en)

One attraction for the opposition is the square's symbolic name—Independence Square, which could be interpreted as independence from Russia and from Lukashenka. The Catholic *Church of Saints Simon and*

---

79   None of my respondents could give a concrete answer why. Several of them talked about going to protest outside the Central Electoral Commission in the House of Government, next to Independence Square (Piatro, Yaraslaw, Katsiaryna), "where evil is being done" ("tam dze robitstsa zlo") (Katsiaryna). Statkevich suggested that marches are more effective than stationary protests. Dzmitry and Milinkevich talked about the possibility that the KGB planted the idea among the protesters, so that they could carry out the well-planned police operation at Independence Square and remove the political opposition once and for all (see below).

Helena, commonly known as *The Red Church*, could also be considered an ideological symbol, especially for the Polish and Catholic minorities in Belarus.

Yet the perceived elements of Independence Square remain problematic. Despite its 1991 renaming from Lenin Square to Independence Square, Lenin is still present as a seven-metre-tall statue looming in front of the House of Government. A bust of the Bolshevik leader also decorates one of the entrances to the metro station, which is still called Lenin Square Station (*Stantsyia Ploshcha Lenina*). My respondent Pawliuk perceives the square as a constant struggle for independence from Lenin, more than anything else. Even as a place for political protest, the square has lost much of its value since Lukashenka stripped the national assembly of political power. "The parliament [in the House of Government] is considered to be in the pocket [of Lukashenka]. They just wait for the president's orders."[80] (Piatro). In addition to this, the Ploshcha of 2010 was even more brutally supressed than the Ploshcha of 2006, adding failed protests to the associations inhabitants of Minsk have with the square.

---

80 "[…] Parlament [v Dome pravitel'stva] schitaetsia karmannym. Prosto zhdut ukazov prezidenta."

Figure 29: The Red Church, Minsk

Photo: Arve Hansen

Minsk's two main protest squares, October and Independence, are associated by the city's inhabitants with the success of Lukashenka and with the failure of the opposition protests. The attempt by the opposition to reappropriate October Square by changing its name has not been successful: Independence Square still represent Lenin and Belarus's Communist past, while the House of Government is not seen as the place where real power is located.

In sum, the perceived elements of Minsk are intended to reinforce the authorities' official version of history and Belarusian identity. The vast majority of the city's main features represent Lukashenka and the Soviet past; be it the architecture, the reputation as a clean city, or the many monuments to ideologically 'correct' people and events. As such, the city is not a particularly inviting place for the pro-European opposition, whose meetings can easily appear alien and misplaced amidst the glamour of the socialist city, surrounded by the evidence of Lukashenka's apparent success.

8.4 Social Elements

Although Minsk—as the perceived elements above demonstrate—might offer an uninviting environment for the opposition, its people have turned to protest on several occasions. I will now look at the social elements of the city and its protest spaces in order to assess their visibility. My respondents all agree that, once you're out to protest, your main objective is to be seen and heard. "We're going to the square to show that we exist. […] That we are many, that we do not agree with what is happening in the country." [81] (Dzmitry). This statement is typical for the respondents but, in a country where the media are controlled by the government, it is difficult to be seen; by authorities, by the media and by fellow citizens. The visibility of a given location therefore emerges as decisive.

8.4.1 The Political Centre

The importance of being seen by the political authorities dictates which areas are suitable for political mass protest. To be in, or in proximity to, the political centre is regarded as a necessity. There is also symbolic value to be gained from occupying a space close to the place where political decisions are being made. This helps demonstrators express that the space belongs to them, too; that they represent the people; and that the political institutions are not doing their job.

On this basis, it is not surprising that the largest political protests have centred in the vicinity of Independence Avenue, on October and Independence squares. The House of Government is situated on Independence Square, and October Square is close to the presidential administration. When asked why protests have been held at these particular squares, my respondents unanimously agree: "[October Square] is simply a central square where the administration of Lukashenka is located." [82] (Dzmitry)

---

81 "My zbiraemsia na ploshchy, kab pakazats', shto my iosts'. […] Shto nas shmat, shto my ne zhodnyia z tym, shto adbyvaetstsa w kraine."
82 "[Kastrychnitskaia –] heta prosta tsentral'naia ploshcha, na iakoi razmeshchana administratsyia Lukashenka."

The closest alternative to October Square and Independence Square is Freedom Square (*Ploshcha Svabody*), about 200 metres to the northeast of October Square. Freedom Square has been used several times by opposition leaders for protests, despite obvious shortcomings:

> Freedom square is an uneven space [...] It is inaptly named, not square at all, with very little open space for mass gathering, and no focal point. People tend to collect on the pavements, steps and pathways and continually threaten to spill onto the roads [...]. (Bennett 2011, 233)

However, according to Milinkevich and Statkevich, two elements of the square still make it a suitable space for protest: "Protests occur on this Square when their organisers do not expect that there will be a large number of participants. In addition, it has a very attractive name." [83] (Milinkevich). "Firstly, it has its symbolic value. Secondly, it is smaller than October Square. Because we don't [always] see that there's a chance that tens of thousands of people will come." [84] (Statkevich). Freedom Square is, therefore, mainly suited for smaller protests.

Still, one can imagine other alternatives to October and Independence squares. There are several large squares located along Independence Avenue: Victory Square, Iakub Kolas Square and Kalinin Square. Some of these have a certain history of protest, but only Victory Square is close to the political centre. However, Victory Square is archetypically Soviet, and can easily be blocked off from the political centre by closing the bridge over the Svislach river. Pryvakzal'naia Square, in front of the main railway station, has also been mentioned as an alternative, but my respondents tend to speak of it as a place to gather before marching to the city centre. A lush verdant city with several large parks, Minsk could potentially offer its green lungs as meeting places for large crowds. What makes parks less suitable for protest are trees and other objects, which limit visibility and

---

[83] "Na hetai Ploshchy adbyvaiutstsa pratesty kali ikh arhanizatary ne spadziaiutstsa, shto budze vialikaia kol'kasts' udzel'nikaw. Akramia taho, iana mae vel'mi prybavnuiu nazvu."

[84] "Vo-pervykh, est' svoia simvolika. A vo-vtorykh, ona men'she, chem Oktiabr'skaia. Potomu chto my ne [vsegda] vidim, chto est' vozmozhnost', chto pridut desiatki tysiach chelovek."

mobility. This leaves only a few public spaces that are useful for mass protest. As my respondent Piatro states, "There are not many open public spaces. There are not many options for gatherings: Independence Square [...], Freedom Square [...], yet October Square is considered the main square of Minsk." [85]

8.4.2 The People's Centre

As we have seen, there are good reasons why political mass protests tend to be held at October or Independence Square, in plain view of the ruling powers. To what extent, then, are actions at these two squares visible to ordinary people? When out walking, citizens tend to use the city's green areas, or stroll along the banks of the Svislach rather than along the avenues or across the large, empty squares of the city centre. The popular café district is also concentrated in a secluded area on Zybitskaia Street, down by the Svislach, and in the Verkhni horad district—a reconstructed part of the old town between Internationalists Street and the Niamiha region. Only commercial businesses have some proximity to the squares (Stalitsa shopping centre is under Independence Square, the GUM warehouse two blocks from October Square). But shopping is not limited to these areas.

Whether intentional or not, the political centre—especially the area around October Square—has become a district through which people pass only occasionally. Yaraslaw sees the city centre as "[...] a place you won't go without an especially good reason. It's a nonspace." [86] Everything interesting, Katsiaryna confirms, is going on a safe distance from the political centre:

> On central squares in Vilnius and in Kyiv there are some festivals, some fairs, people gather there. [...] They have stuff happening, but we've only had something similar for a couple of years. That is on Karl Marx Street, and it's so small, mobility is tight

---

85 "Ne tak mnogo mest otkrytogo publichnogo prostranstva. Sobrat'sia variantov nemnogo: Nezavisimosti [...], Svobody [...], no Oktiabr'skaia schitaetsia glavnoi ploshchad'iu Minska."

86 "[...] mesto, kuda bez osoboi prichiny ne idut. Eto nicheinoe prostranstvo."

[…]. It's far to get to Kupalawskaia (metro), to October Square. And there is nothing going on there. [87] (Katsiaryna)

My respondents state that their aim is to be seen, by the people and by the authorities. However, in a society with a very few, struggling free media outlets and a political centre that most people tend to avoid, the visibility of political protest is limited. Still, the largest protests in post-Soviet Minsk have been held in the political centre, at October and Independence squares. I will now take a closer look at the social elements of these two squares. How have they been used for protests? How are they used in the everyday?

8.4.3 Independence Square

Belarus' first head of state, Stanislaw Shushkevich, explains that until the end of the 1990s, protests usually occurred outside the House of Government. On the other hand, Mikola Statkevich, one of the opposition leaders, claims that they organised protests all over Minsk during the 1990s and not only on Independence Square; but he agrees that many of the largest protests were on that particular square.

Some of Independence Square's social elements might be perceived as increasing visibility. Several paths cross Independence Square or are in close proximity to it. Public transport (trolleybus, bus, and metro) is located both on and under it (the Lenin Square Metro Station), and the main railway station is only 550 metres away; and several avenues and streets from the eastern and southern parts of the city meet next to where Independence Avenue begins. Students also travel daily to the Belarusian State Pedagogical University and to six of the Belarusian State University's faculties located on and around Independence Square. Hotel Minsk, and important landmarks such as the House of Government, the Lenin statue and

---

[87] "У Vil'niuse i w Kieve na tsentral'nykh ploshchakh prakhodziats' neikiia festyvali, neikiia kirmashy, tam liudzi zbiraiutstsa. […] U ikh pravodziatstsia neikiia shtuki, a w nas tol'ki paru hadow pravodzitstsa neshta padobnae. Heta na vulitsy Karla Marksa i iana takaia malen'kaia, rukh malen'ki […]. Dabratstsa da Kupalawskai, da Kastrychnitskai ploshchy tam dalioka. I tam nichoha ne pravodzitstsa."

the *Church of Saints Simon and Helena*, are popular places to visit for tourists. All this makes the square more visible than October Square.

However, although Independence Square is a travel node, this is only the case for some people, such as students and tourists; less so for the ordinary inhabitants of Minsk. There are large flowerbeds, benches and fountains on the square itself, but people don't tend to gather there spontaneously. Some reasons for this may be the large walking distances involved and the fact that the square offers little recreational infrastructure and no protection from the elements (sun, rain, snow etc.). Between 2002 and 2006, Independence Square was closed to the public, while Stalitsa—a huge 75 000 m², three-storey shopping centre—was constructed beneath the square. Although Stalitsa now attracts some shoppers, it has not quite become the popular attraction its size suggests it was meant to be.

Independence Square might therefore be characterised as a place where several paths meet, but as a node only for some. This means that it offers less visibility than the opposition would ideally want.

8.4.4 October Square

In 2006, by the time the reconstruction of Independence Square was completed, the preferred space for protests had moved one kilometre up Independence Avenue to October Square. This was made possible by the reopening of October Square in 2001, but the main reason was probably Lukashenka's moving into the former Communist party headquarters on Karl Marx Street shortly after becoming president, arguably because it was the tallest and most central point in the capital.

The square functions as a node for travel. Cars drive past it on the highly trafficked Independence avenue, and Minsk's two metro lines have their transit point under October Square. However, people rarely stop at the square, merely pass underneath any event that may be happening on the surface above.

The buildings on October Square include the Palace of the Republic; the Palace of Culture; a construction site where the museum to the Great

Patriotic War stood until 2014;[88] and a business centre. Across Independence Avenue, between October Square and the presidential administration, lies Aliaksandrawski Garden Square: one of Minsk's oldest parks, dating from the nineteenth century. In the area, there are several institutions of high culture: the Ianka Kupala National Theatre, the Music Academy, the Palace of Culture and the House of Officers—now mainly used as a concert house. Some concerts are also held in the Palace of the Republic. The common denominator for virtually all the buildings on and around the square is that they are government-controlled.

Even though October Square is large, central, and surrounded by several buildings housing cultural institutions, it is not widely used by people in general. It is a place where—except for the 'giant sarcophagus' itself—there is nothing to look at, virtually nothing going on, and nowhere to sit.[89] There are some cafés and a Belarusian language club in the Palace; but, as mentioned above, people prefer the cafes on Zybitskaia Street.

On this basis, October Square could be considered not so much a node as a place where a small number of paths happen to intersect. Despite its central location, it is underused. Respondents describe it as empty, Soviet and cold, and less visible than Independence Square.

In summary, people tend to avoid the central parts of Minsk, along Independence avenue, where most of the political institutions are situated; and even though both protest squares, October and Independence, are located along the paths some people tend to follow, they are rarely used as nodes: few people will travel to get there specifically. On this basis, we can conclude that the social elements of Minsk are not particularly helpful in directing public attention towards protests and making them visible.

---

88   It has now moved to Victors' Avenue (Praspekt Peramozhtsaw), and it is unclear what will take its place. One proposed project is an administrative office centre in a traditional imperial style, similar to the style of the Palace of Culture (Onliner 2016).

89   A few times, while living in Minsk, I agreed to meet people by the 0-km sign. I vividly recall how boring the square seemed as a meeting place, especially if my friends were late.

8.5 Physical Elements

In this final section I will look at the physical elements of the two squares, October and Independence. I argue that the physical attributes of these squares contributed to the failure of the mass protests in 2006 and 2010.

8.5.1 October Square and Ploshcha 2006

As shown above, October Square is a large urban space totalling approximately 27400 m². The vast majority of this space (approximately 22000 m²) is a large, open, rectangular area in front of the Palace of the Republic. The northernmost side of the square has two narrow openings to Internationalists Street on either side of the palace. The left side is bordered by Engels Street; the right by two buildings and a construction site; and the remaining side by Independence Avenue. The spaces on the left and right sides of the palace are narrow, partly because of a parking lot on the left and a pool of fountains on the right. The virtually impenetrable façades on the left and right sides limit movement on the square to and from Internationalists Street and Independence Avenue.[90]

Milinkevich lists three reasons why the protesters chose October Square for their Ploshcha in 2006: "It is central, the authorities hold most of their celebrations on it [...] and in addition, it could fit up to 50 thousand citizens."[91]

---

90 It is unclear whether there are entrances to October Square on the right. None of my respondents could tell me whether there are ways to enter the square from this side. Yaraslaw recollects a tall fence between the buildings.
91 "[Iana] tsentral,naia, na ioi adbyvaetstsa bol'shasts' sviatochnykh uladnykh merapryemstvaw [...] i da taho zh tam mahlo zmiastsitstsa da 50 tysiach hramadzian."

Figure 30: October Square, Minsk (map)

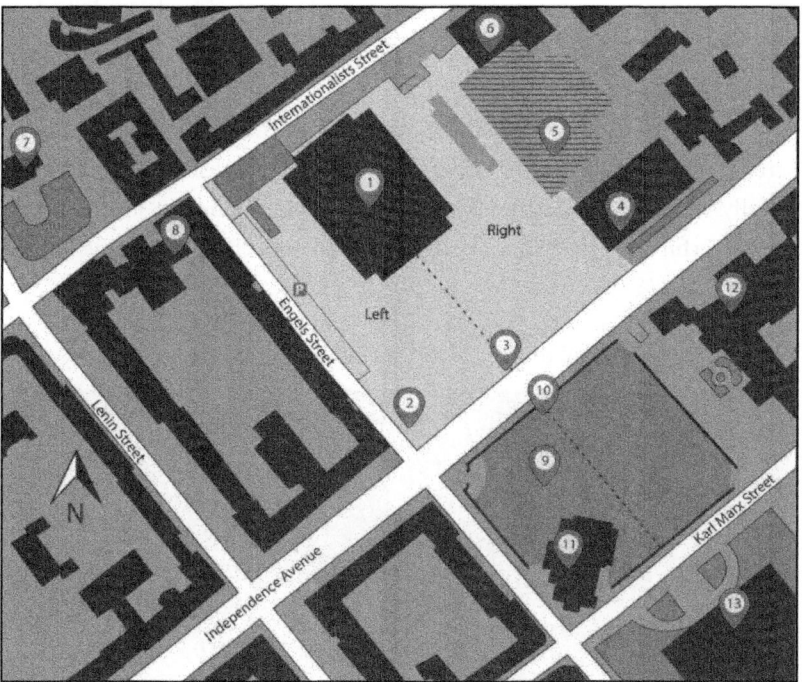

1: Palace of the Republic. 2: Screen. 3: 0-km Sign. 5: Construction site. 6: Business centre. 7: Freedom Square. 8: Music academy. 9: Aliaksandrawski Garden Square. 10: Tribune. 11: Ianki Kupaly National Theatre. 12: House of Officers. 13: Presidential Administration. Illustration: Arve Hansen

Because October Square is empty of landmarks, there are few natural focal points. If one wants to address a crowd, the most central elevation point is a few steps up the stairs surrounding the palace, between the massive columns of the building. This vantage point not only excludes the audience on the square's right and left sides, it also puts the speaker symbolically in the shadow of Lukashenka's success. Probably because of this, the opposition decided to speak to the crowds from between the columns of the Palace of Culture instead (Khashchavatski 2007), with similar problems of lateral visibility.

The Soviet architects had considered this lack of a focal point, and in 1957 they built an elevated tribune in the wall on Aliaksandrawski Garden

Square, from which officials could address the people on October Square on official occasions. But the tribune is only accessible through locked gates and, as will soon become apparent, the authorities can easily block access to the entire park.

Communication on October Square is further hampered by a large screen, which faces into the square from one of its corners. The screen is usually showing one of the official news channels, and the loudspeakers are powerful enough to potentially drown out any challenge to the official propaganda. (Yaraslaw)

Figure 31: The Wall on Aliaksandrawski, Minsk

Photo: Anonymous

Milinkevich goes on to explain that the main reason for protesting at October Square was its proximity to the president. One might therefore expect that protesters occupying October Square would take the opportunity to demonstrate outside the presidential administration. However, such intentions face significant obstacles, the first being to cross the eight lanes of Independence Avenue. Next, the natural choice would be to walk straight through Aliaksandrawski Garden Square to the presidential administration. A convenient overflow location should a protest outgrow the space on October Square, Aliaksandrawski is, however, closed off by its surrounding stone fence, and the park's few entrances can easily be blocked by a handful of police officers. This effectively turns the park into an obstacle to the masses. There is an alternative route to the presidential administration on the right side of Aliaksandrawski, but this path runs up several flights of stairs to a narrow strip of space between the walls of Aliaksandrawski and the House of Officers. This means that it is also easy to control. The only remaining option is to go via Engels Street: a predictable route that can easily be blocked by law enforcement personnel, who would be well prepared to do so.

> One evening [in 2006] the organisers led the crowd in the direction of the presidential administration [...]. Just as we got to the theatre, they turned us back [...]. They were defending the administration well. Everybody felt the truncheons. [92] (Pawliuk)

Dzmitry (switching to Russian) recounts a similar situation in 2004: "We went there along Engels Street. We got to the corner of the administration, but buses with special forces had already arrived. They started to beat us, to detain us, to thrash us." [93]

On the other side of the Palace of the Republic, police are able to control movement by blocking the two ends of Internationalists' Street. This area is well suited for police manoeuvres such as 'kettling' (surrounding) the protesters, and limiting their movement to Independence Avenue. In 2006, police controlled all the sides surrounding the protests, and could stop and arrest people going to and from the protest camp. "They blocked the square quite successfully. They did not allow cars to stop, and they prevented people from bringing food."[94] (Piatro). During the night of March 24, riot police were deployed to the square, rapidly clearing the tents and arresting the protesters.

---

92 "Odin vecher [v 2006 g.] organizatory poveli tolpu v napravlenii administratsii prezydenta [...]. Kak tol'ko doshli do teatra, vsekh tam razvernuli [...]. Administratsiiu zashchishchali ochen' khorosho. Dubinkami poluchili vse."

93 "My khodili tuda [...] po Engel'sa. My doshli do ugla administratsii, no tuda uzhe pod'ekhali avtobusy so spetsnazovtsami. Oni nas nachali bit', zaderzhivat', molotit'."

94 "Dovol'no uspeshno blokirovali ploshchadi. Ne pozvoliali mashinam ostanavlivat'sia i zapretili liudiam prinosit' edu"

8.5.2 Independence Square and Ploshcha 2010

As a protest space, Independence Square has some assets worth mentioning. It is easy to get to, larger than October Square (approximately 40000 m²) and is surrounded by a few buildings of symbolic value to the protesters, such as the Red Church and the University. Still, the descriptions my respondents, as well as other observers, give of the square are less encouraging:

Figure 32: Independence Square, Minsk (map)

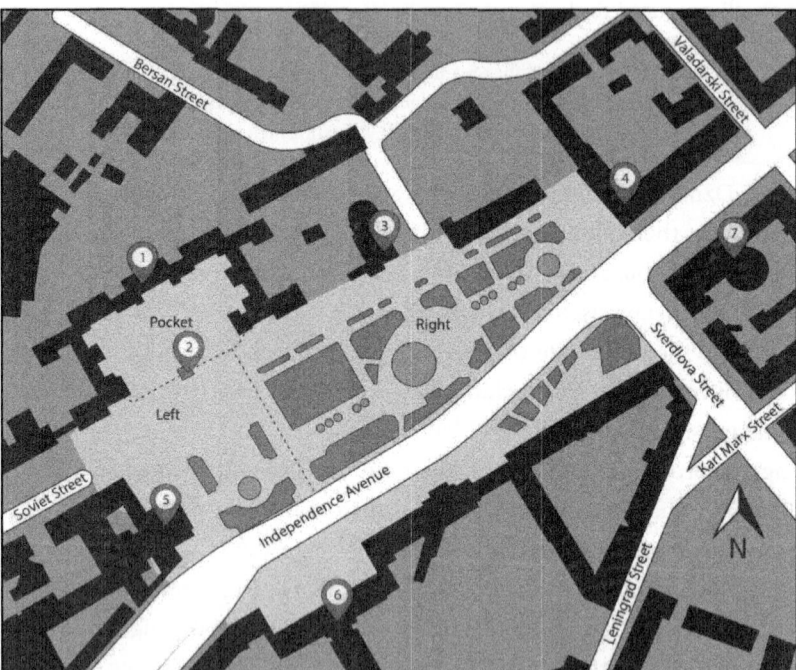

1: House of Government. 2: Lenin monument. 3: Church of Saints Simon and Helena. 4: Hotel Minsk. 5: Belarusian State Pedagogical University. 6: Belarusian State University. 7: Post Office. Illustration: Arve Hansen

> Independence Square in Minsk, Belarus's sad capital, is one of the most terrifying public spaces in Europe. It is nothing but concrete, steel, glass and fearsome horizons—no benches, shelter, or anything for people who might wish to do something so normal as to assemble and speak together. Where anything vertical rises from the

ground, it bears a video camera, ensuring that any gathering can be observed by the Belarusian KGB. (Snyder, 2010)

Although Snyder might be mistaken about the benches (the square has quite a few), Independence Square is indeed little more than hard surfaces and "fearsome horizons". Statkevich also talks about the practical problems with the square after the 2006 reconstruction:

> There is no single area there. There are separate places broken up by these domes. There are many of them, and citizens of Minsk jokingly call the square *the Industrial Greenhouse*. It is possible to fit tens of thousands of people there, but it's rather a disjointed space. [95] (Statkevich)

For the sake of clarity, in figure 8, I have divided the square into three main parts as follows. <u>Left</u>: The rectangular-shaped space between the Lenin statue and Independence Avenue. This is fairly open, apart from a few flowerbeds and a glass dome at one end. <u>Right</u>: the space between the Left and Hotel Minsk. This part is the biggest, but it is crowded with flowerbeds, glass domes, benches and fountains. <u>Pocket</u>: The small square behind Lenin, between the walls of the House of Government.

As Independence Square is a long space with numerous obstacles and virtually without elevations, the problem of the absence of a good focal point applies here, too. For people on the Left side, the Lenin statue is a natural place to look, but it is not as visible to those on the Right side. On the Right side, only the Church of Saints Simon and Helena offers a good focal point, but the many objects obstructing the view would divide the spectators into separate clusters.

In 2010, therefore, the opposition leaders chose the former option and spoke from the plinth of the Lenin statue—dwarfed by the giant Lenin and with the House of Government towering behind them.

After an alleged provocation, the riot police went in to clear the square. According to Vital', the square was cleared in seven minutes,

---

[95] "Edinogo bol'shogo prostranstva tam net, tam est' otdel'nye mesta, razbitye etimi kupolami tam. Ikh ochen' mnogo i minchane nazyvaiut v shutku etu ploshchad' parnikovyi kombinat. Tam mozhno razmestit' desiatki tysiach liudei, no eto budet nemnogo razbitoe prostranstvo."

despite the number of protesters assembled there; according to Pawliuk, it took only five. Perhaps less prone to exaggeration, Statkevich claims it took considerably longer, perhaps 30 or 40 minutes. Even so, this can hardly be described as a difficult or long-lasting police operation. The group of people gathered in the Pocket and on the Lenin statue's plinth were quickly cornered by police who came in from Soviet Street and blocked off the only exit. The rest of the protesters on the Left and the Right were also soon 'kettled in' by police between Independence Avenue and the buildings to the north:

> The first part cordoned off the whole square in a ring. They ran along the perimeter of the avenue [...]. We saw that everything up to Hotel Minsk was cordoned off. They simply chased us, encircled us, separated us into groups and threw us into buses.[96] (Katsiaryna)

The riot police used the architecture of the square to efficiently and brutally put an end to the second Belarusian Ploshcha. We can therefore see that both October and Independence Squares are easily surrounded and controlled, despite their differences in size and shape. In this way, the physical elements of Minsk themselves constitute a major challenge for public demonstrations and their organisers.

---

96 "Pershaia chastka wziala wsiu ploshchu v atsaplenne kal'tso. Iani behli pa perymetru praspektu [...]. My pabachali, shto da hatelia 'Minsk' usio atseplena. Nas prosta hnali i liudzei razbirali na hrupy w takiia kol'tsy, i zakidvali w awtobusy."

Figure 33: House of Government, Minsk

Photo: Alexander Groshev / <u>Wikimedia Commons.</u> Licensed under CC-BY-SA 3.0 (https://creativecommons.org/licenses/by/3.0/deed.en)

8.6 Conclusions

In the introduction, I stated that space is a potentially important condition for collective action. My aim in this chapter was to demonstrate this by applying a spatial perspective to mass protests in Minsk.

Belarus is an autocratic country, and the opposition is faced with many obstacles, such as state controlled media, a weak national identity and a large security apparatus willing to use force to repress protests. Still, people have on occasion ventured into the public space of Minsk in large numbers to protest against their current leadership. Notably, the opposition took to the streets in large numbers in 2006 and 2010. When analysing the success or failure of such collective actions, in addition to asking what external and internal conditions are present, I contend that we should also be looking at the protests from a spatial perspective: "What space are the protesters using?", "Why?" and "How are protests affected by this space?" By asking these questions, in the case of Minsk, we can see that the Belarusian opposition is faced with considerable spatial obstacles.

The opposition does not have much room to choose from when it comes to holding a protest in the city. Only two squares are large enough to contain tens of thousands of protesters while also being in proximity to the political centre. However, these two squares—October Square and Independence Square—both present obstacles to the opposition and reinforce the strategies used by Lukashenka to stay in power, as follows: 1) The perceived elements of Minsk, as well as the two protest squares themselves, are associated with the Soviet Union, Lukashenka's success and the disappointment of failed protests, and thus do not have a preferable symbolic value for the largely pro-European opposition. 2) Additionally, the social elements of the city divide the city into political space (on and in proximity to Independence Avenue) and public space (where the citizens' nodes are). In a society where the media is controlled by the state, protests might therefore go unnoticed by large segments of the population. 3) This latter point is especially important given that the physical elements of the squares make policing particularly quick and easy, reducing the duration of the protests and lessening the chances of people learning about them—not to mention reaching the city centre before the protests are over. The physical elements of the squares also limit the protesters' communication, movement and flexibility.

I therefore conclude that a spatial perspective should be included in research on collective actions, because it could—as in the case of Minsk—be an additional contributory condition for their success or failure.

The spatial perspective would benefit from being further tested on cases where mass protests have had a variety of outcomes. Preferably, the next step would be to analyse a city with a similar history, culture or architecture to Minsk, such as Moscow or Chișinău.

9 Main Study

Swamp Square, Moscow

This main test study of the spatial perspective on mass protest is based on the article "A Spatial Perspective on Mass Protests: Moscow's Swamp Square and the March of Millions" (Hansen n.d.).

Abstract

Urban public space is one of the places where politics and people meet and interact. What constitutes "the public" and what level of access it has to public space, is, however, contested. This contestation is particularly visible in the Russian capital city, in which numerous protests have been organised in a variety of locations since the 1980s. The existing research literature provides several perspectives on public space, important as it is for political life; but these are rather limited when it comes to assessing the practical utility of such space. In what ways does space inhibit and/or facilitate the emergence, realisation, and impact of grassroots politics in the form of mass protests? In this article, I suggest how such a generalised approach might be structured, based on theories from architecture, sociology and political science. I illustrate this approach by applying it to Swamp Square—the main location for the 2011–2012 protest wave in Moscow, and for the 6 May 2012 *March of Millions* in particular. I argue that the architecture of Swamp Square was one of the decisive factors in why the Russian protests failed to achieve much in terms of change.

Since the mid-1980s, urban mass protests have been one of the main catalysts for change in Eastern Europe. Discontent in the Soviet Union and in the Warsaw Pact countries led to protests and declarations of independence, and eventually to the 1991 collapse of the Soviet Union. Frustration with the remnants of the Soviet elites turned into new waves of mass protest in the central squares of numerous cities in the early 2000s, and what are referred to as *colour revolutions* brought regime change in Serbia and Montenegro (2000), Georgia (2003) and Ukraine (2004). More recently, mass protests in Kyiv toppled the regime of Ukrainian president Ianukovych in 2014; and, in 2018, mass protests in Yerevan forced the Armenian president Sargsyan to resign.

However, not all recent mass protests in the post-Soviet area have had this kind of outcome. Some have set themselves less ambitious goals than regime change, and have aimed to bring about—and sometimes achieved—changes in policy. At other times, masses of people have repeatedly taken to the streets and squares of Minsk, Riga, Chișinău, Bucharest and many other capital cities, and hardly achieved anything at all.

In December 2011, a wave of demonstrations hit the Russian capital Moscow. Starting with the protests *For Fair Elections*, against the official results of the 2011 Duma elections, the protests culminated in March 2012 with record numbers of people protesting against Vladimir Putin's return to the presidency. During this time, public space was a continual source of contention. One dispute in particular played out between the authorities and the protest organisers. The city administration sanctioned protests on Sakharov Avenue in the northeastern corner of the city centre—far from the country's political institutions—and on Swamp Square, a secluded space just south of the Kremlin, on an island between the Moskva River and the Water Bypass Canal (*Vodootvodny Kanal'*). The organisers, in contrast, preferred more symbolic and visible spaces, such as Triumph Square, Manège Square, and Revolution Square—all three in close proximity to the Kremlin.

The choice of location split the opposition. The majority of the protest organisers agreed to move to Swamp Square, while a sizable minority decided instead to protest on the more central, but officially unsanctioned, Revolution Square. The protests on Swamp Square turned out to be a veritable disaster for the opposition. On 6 May 2012, it was discovered that the area designated for protest was surrounded by fences, which radically limited the space available. The protesters were easily surrounded, blocked from view, kettled in, and—when violence erupted—the protest was brutally and efficiently suppressed. What followed were political repressions and legal sanctions (such as fines and imprisonment) for many of the organisers, which would weaken the opposition for several years to come.

At the time, I was following the situation from afar, from the Russian city of Murmansk, and did not give much thought to the locations of these protests. Like many other external observers, I attributed the effective suppression of the protests to factors such as an experienced and efficient police force, a fractured opposition, and limited nationwide support for the protesters' cause.

Two years later, I witnessed the Ukrainian *Euromaidan* revolution at first hand, and my opinion about space changed. Conducting fieldwork in Kyiv for my research project on the Ukrainian opposition, I was struck by how valuable the central Maidan Square appeared to be for the Ukrainian protesters. Everything from the square's history, architecture, and social uses to its shape and size seemed to reinforce the protesters' goals, their visibility, and ability to counteract the riot police's strategies. Therefore, it was surprising to find a notable lack of spatial perspective in the existing literature on mass protests.

The absence of geography in discussions of collective action is most clearly visible in frequently cited publications by political scientists, such as Michael McFaul (2005), Joshua Tucker (2007), and Erica Chenoweth and Maria Stephan (2011), which aim to explain the conditions for successful resistance campaigns.[97] In sociology, too, surprisingly little attention has been given to space. For instance, Karl-Dieter Opp's (2009) review of the major theoretical perspectives on protests and social movements within sociology discusses various concepts, definitions, and approaches. None of the theories under discussion examine the limitations and

---

97   McFaul (2005) provides a list of seven necessary conditions for color revolutions to occur: 1) The regime has to be semi-autocratic, rather than fully autocratic; 2) there has to be an unpopular incumbent; 3) the opposition needs to be united and organised; 4) there must be independent electoral-monitoring capabilities available; 5) there must be a modicum of independent media; 6) the opposition must have the capacity to mobilize significant numbers of protesters; 7) and there must be a split among the "guys with guns." In other words, the opposition must have some support in the state apparatus., especially the so-called "power ministries". Tucker (2007) directs his attention to internal conditions, arguing that election fraud is the key event capable of uniting and motivating a broad enough group to create a revolution. Erica Chenoweth and Maria J. Stephan have made a statistical analysis of 323 major resistance campaigns between 1900 and 2006, and found that nonviolent campaigns are nearly twice as likely to be successful as violent ones. The authors also emphasise the ability of campaign organisers to mobilise large and diverse segments of the population as a key condition for success. Part of the argument is that large and diverse groups have a higher probability of having connections with members of the authorities and within the security apparatus, and are also more likely to be strategically innovative. (Chenoweth and Stephan 2011) In a TEDx-talk, Chenoweth states that all campaigns that have managed to mobilise more than 3.5 percent of the population have reached 'critical mass' and become successful (Chenoweth 2013).

possibilities provided by space. This is somewhat puzzling, considering the long tradition of using geographical arguments in academic disciplines such as sociology, history, international relations and political sciences. Geography is used to explain the occurrence and results of voting, healthcare, wars, economy, colonisation and so forth—why, then, is it not applied on the comparably smaller scale of urban protest?

When the relationship between public space and protests *is* discussed, this is usually within the field of political philosophy, in debates centred around the question of why space is important for democracy or society in general. This is often mentioned in relation to Hannah Arendt's understanding of *public space* (e.g. Salikov and Zhavaronkov 2018), Jürgen Habermas' less concrete *public sphere* (Gillespie and Nguyen 2019; Oren 2019), or Henri Lefebvre's *right to the city* (Lefebvre et al. 1996; Harvey 2012; Mitchell 2014; Attoh 2011). Some scholars consider these theories in comparison (Howell 1993; Goodsell 2003; Parkinson 2012; Cassegård 2014).

Other academic disciplines, such as architecture, urban planning and urbanism, are naturally concerned with physical space and occasionally relate it to protests. This literature, however, is usually concerned with the importance of space in general (McCarthy and McPhail 2006; Bilgic 2016; Harvey 2012; Smith et al. 2018), the importance of some concrete space in particular (Cybriwsky 2015; Hershkovitz 1993; Lee 2009), or describing the various forms of contestation *over* space or *in* space (Mitchell 2017; Gillham, Edwards and Noakes 2013; Ramadan 2013; Brown and Feigenbaum 2017). This large body of literature shows that, although there is a growing interest in protest locations, and space is regarded as important for various reasons, its analysis is still under-developed. Even when it is suggested that space has some effects on crowds, it is less apparent how these effects might be measured, since none of the theorists listed above provide a systematic and generalised approach for assessing the potential use value and limitations of protest spaces.

In this chapter, I suggest how such a generalised approach might be structured. The chapter consists of two sections, one theoretical, one practical. In the first section (9.1), I discuss the variables involved in a spatial perspective on mass protests, and suggest how we might trace causal connections between the characteristics of the space and the outcome of the protest. In the second section (9.2), I apply this theoretical approach to Swamp Square—one of Moscow's many public spaces. I argue that the geography of Swamp Square was one of the main reasons for the failure of the 2011–2012 protests.

9.1 Towards a Spatial Perspective

Urban public space includes, in its simplest form, open spaces between buildings; but even then it is also a space where politics and people meet and interact, and politics happens. In this chapter, public space is defined as physical outdoor locations in cities, such as squares, parks, streets, pathways and similar areas open to the general public. For 'protest', I apply the definition of German sociologist Karl-Dieter Opp: '*Protest* is [a] joint (i.e. collective) action of individuals aimed at achieving their goal or goals by influencing decisions of a target' (Opp 2009, 38).

Intuitively, we understand that space is fundamental to crowds of people: A small square naturally limits the number of participants, while a large field may accommodate thousands. A crowd in the outskirts of a city will likely attract less attention than a crowd in the middle of its bustling downtown. Some spaces (e.g. October Square in Minsk) are surrounded by intimidating architecture, while others contain inspiring ideological symbols, such as monuments (e.g. Maidan Square in Kyiv). How can we, in a structured way, estimate the effects that the vast variety of urban spaces may have on mass protests? Spaces vary in size, layout, position, proximity to places of interest; different places are imbued with different meanings. These are sites where different traditions are played out, and which are put to various day-to-day use. They evoke different feelings and associations in the people who inhabit/use them. All this adds to the complexities of urban space.

The following approach is structured on the analytical principles of process tracing, which advocates the use of large data sets and a meticulous focus on every detail of a case study. Process tracing also promotes the thorough examination of every link in a causality relationship, whilst remaining open to—and paying due attention to—rival theories.[98] In the majority of the research literature on urbanism, public space is treated as something constantly undergoing change, either physically—through the actions of governments and architects—or mentally, through contestations over a location and through its ever-shifting day-to-day use. In the short period of time a protest occurs, however, the potentials and limitations of a given space rarely change. The protesters might put up tents and barricades in the space, but this does not change its basic geography. So, if the goal is to understand the dynamics of protests, space should be treated as the independent variable. Accordingly, the protests—which necessarily relate to space—should be regarded as the dependent variable.

By describing the components of a space, we can define certain spatial qualities. If these spatial qualities are placed in the context of the political environment, it is possible to map how space—alone or in combination with other factors—facilitates and/or inhibits the emergence, realization and impact of protests. In the following three sections, I will define three types of variable in this theoretical causality: the spatial elements (independent variables); spatial qualities and the political environment (intermediary variables); and the three main areas of protest (dependent variables).

---

98   For an in-depth explanation of process tracing, see Bennett and Checkel (2015).

Figure 34: Causality diagram, first version

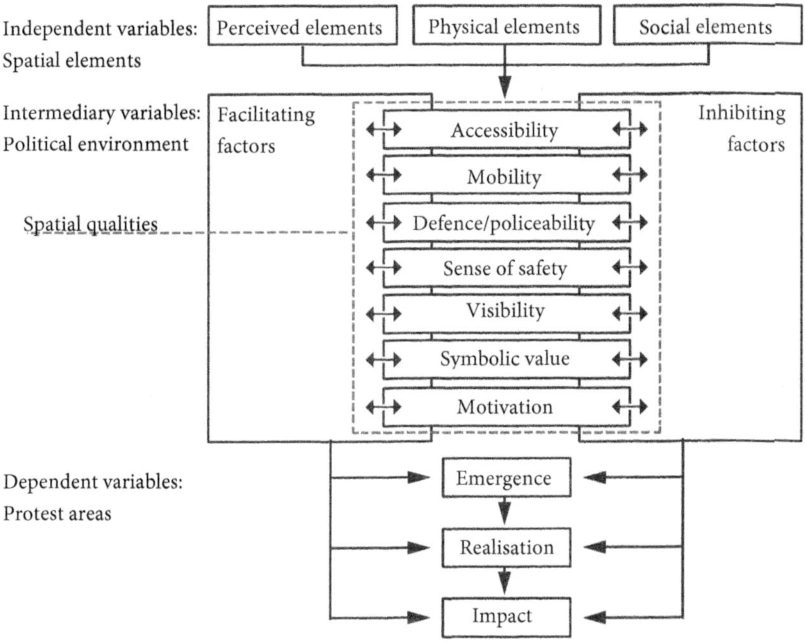

```
Independent variables:   | Perceived elements | Physical elements | Social elements |
Spatial elements

Intermediary variables:  Facilitating                                       Inhibiting
Political environment    factors      ↔  Accessibility  ↔                  factors
                                      ↔  Mobility       ↔
    Spatial qualities  ─ ─ ─ ─ ─ ─ ─  ↔  Defence/policeability ↔
                                      ↔  Sense of safety ↔
                                      ↔  Visibility      ↔
                                      ↔  Symbolic value  ↔
                                      ↔  Motivation      ↔

Dependent variables:              →  Emergence   ←
Protest areas                        ↓
                                  →  Realisation ←
                                     ↓
                                  →  Impact      ←
```

Arrows (→) signify effect

9.1.1 Spatial Elements

In order to facilitate the analysis, the independent variable (space) is broken down into smaller components, which can be identified using a modified version of urban planner Kevin Lynch's categorisation of city elements. In *The Image of the City* (1960), Lynch examines how cities are used in day-to-day life, and divides city spaces into five elements: paths, nodes (points where paths start, intersect, or branch), landmarks, edges, and districts. For the current study's focus on protest spaces, I have adapted Lynch's theory by adding new elements. These new elements have been identified empirically based on my observations of protests, and on conversations with protesters and organisers of protests. All the elements are then divided into three categories: perceived (symbolic) elements, physical elements, and social elements.

The majority of elements are concrete and measurable, and can therefore be described using maps, research literature and personal observations. However, some of the perceived elements are abstract and must be identified qualitatively in conversations and interviews with protesters and organisers, or in research literature based on qualitative sources.

Figure 35: Elements of the city, second version

Perceived (subjective) elements		Physical elements	Social elements
Measurable:	Abstract:	Measurable:	Measurable:
History	Emotions	Location	Traditional use
Ideological symbols	Feelings	Size	Official use
Buildings	Associations	Shape	Districts
Monuments		Entrances	Paths
History of protests		Exits	Nodes
Landmarks		Walls	
		Floor	
		Objects	
		Edges	
		Public works	
		Focal points	
		Open/empty space	

The spatial elements of Moscow were mapped during fieldwork in the city in June 2017, in the course of which I observed and analysed central public spaces (Swamp Square among them). These elements are also based on observations made using web mapping services such as Google Maps and Yandex Maps, research literature on specific elements of the city (e.g. Rezvin 2015, on the history of Moscow), and personal communication with previous and current Moscow inhabitants.

9.1.2 Spatial Qualities and the Political Environment

Protests occur within a given context, which can be defined as the political environment. However, the political environment consists of more than space alone, and many other factors affect collective actions. For this reason, it is crucial not only to describe the spatial dimension of the environment, but also to identify the remaining factors which, alone or in combination with space, have or may have a correlative effect on mass protests.

One theoretical framework concerned with the environment in which protests occur is called *political opportunity structures* (POS). The aim of this approach is systematically to identify factors that (individually or collectively) stimulate or oppose collective action, and apply these factors in order to measure the chances of protests occurring and/or succeeding. However, when the variations of spatial qualities are combined with people (let alone crowds), history, law enforcement, legislation, political systems and various other factors from a potentially vast number connected to the political environment, we are confronted with a near-infinite number of variables. Any attempt to gather such a large data set and break it down to an operable calculation of 'chances for success' is likely to fail.[99] Nevertheless, POS might be useful for identifying possible factors in the political environment, and for theorising about their effect on certain aspects of political protests (Opp 2009, 351).

The data presented here on the political environment in Russia are based both on my own experience from living in Russia (2011–2013) and in former Soviet republics (2006–2007, 2008–2017) and on research literature (e.g. Green 2014; Gabowitch 2017; Skillen 2017, on protests in Russia). I have divided the data into two categories: facilitating factors and inhibiting factors, using as a guideline McFaul's seven conditions for a colour revolution to occur. It might not be possible to identify all actual and potential factors in the political environment, but this does not mean that attempting to map these factors is futile. Here, the aim is to trace the causality between space and protests through intermediary variables, while discussing the relevance of other factors. In order to do this, it is not necessary to know all possible interrelations or the effects they have on each other.

---

99 One criticism aimed at the theory is that it is virtually impossible to identify all factors in the political environment (or find the "correct" ones), and thus hard to calculate the "chances of success"; Opp (2009) also argues that the theory is poorly defined, and not clearly distinct from other major sociological theories on collective action.

Understanding the spatial dimension of the environment requires a closer look at how the combined elements generate certain spatial qualities. From research literature, and from my own observations of and research on protests in Kyiv, Minsk, Chișinău, Moscow, and Paris, I have identified seven spatial qualities with the potential to affect protests: accessibility, mobility, defensibility/policeability, sense of safety, visibility, symbolic value, and motivation.

Accessibility affects several aspects of a protest, such as getting to a location, furnishing protesters with necessary supplies, and the opportunity for people to join the protest spontaneously.

Mobility is closely related to accessibility, but includes the protesters' ability to move and be flexible once in situ. Some tactics, such as demonstrations starting out from a space occupied by protesters, are harder to organise if the public space has few exits, many obstacles, or can be easily surrounded by police forces.

The level of difficulty in **defending** and/or **policing** a space is important for the realisation of protests in societies where protest is either unsanctioned or has a high probability of being met with hostility, provocations, violence, and/or arrests.

The **sense of safety** is shaped by the physical layout of a space (see for example Dosen and Oswald 2013, on prospect refuge theory), as well as the protesters' actual ability to defend themselves (for example against heavy-handed policing).

One aspect of **visibility** is the protesters' ability to be seen externally by the public, the authorities, and national and international observers and audiences (including media outlets). Visibility may therefore affect the number of people who notice the action. The other aspect of visibility is internal: the protesters' ability to see what is going on around them. This aspect affects their coordination and communication within the protest camp.

Several elements influence the **symbolic value** of a space, ranging from the physical (e.g. its proximity to the institutions targeted) and the social (whether the protesters are occupying a space commonly used by others) to the perceived (such as the history of the space and the outcome of previous collective actions held there).

Finally, **motivation** is perhaps the most important of the spatial qualities, since it has a direct impact on the number of participants in a collective action and their belief in the likelihood of achieving their goals (I will elaborate on the goals in the following section). This quality is shaped both by physical and perceived elements, as well as other spatial qualities (e.g. sense of safety—if it feels safe, the chances of going out to protest might be higher).

9.1.3 Protest Areas

Having described the spatial elements and identified the spatial qualities of a protest location, as well as other factors of the political environment, it is time to establish their combined impact on public protests. But, just as space is comprised of various elements, protests, too, are complex and consist of a wide range of actions. What variables make up a protest, and which of these might be influenced by the spatial qualities present in the political environment?

In several conversations and interviews with members of the Ukrainian, Belarusian, Russian, and Moldovan oppositions, conducted for the purposes of this and previous analyses (Hansen 2015; 2016; 2017), I presented the interviewees with ideas about the importance of space for the outcome of collective actions. The initial response was often a statement to the effect that people, i.e. the protesters and authorities, control and are responsible for the turn of events, not geography. But when asked why they chose particular locations for their protests, or why some events turned out the way they did, my respondents did often concede that space has affected their actions in a number of ways: 'We chose this square because it has a tradition of such actions', 'This is the most visible public space in the city', 'The police easily trapped us between the walls of this and that building', and so on.

In these conversations, we also discussed what the protesters wished to achieve. Unsurprisingly, the conversations confirm that the goal of virtually all protests is to change some aspect of society. Many protests aim to change the public discourse (in the Russian context, the 2014 protests against the war with Ukraine are a good example). Others press for policy change (e.g. the 2018 protests against the plans to raise the pensionable age in Russia). Other, more radical protests have the goal of forcing regime change (as we saw during the mass protests in Moscow in 2011–2012). A protest action might also change its goals while underway. Affected by external events or the shifting mentality in the protest camp, a collective action intended to change a particular policy might, for instance, turn into a movement against the ruling power. (For example, the Ukrainian Euromaidan revolution went from a small pro-European rally to a revolutionary movement against the president.) But the main idea of a protest is some form of change, and we could therefore assess the success or failure of a given protest by looking at the amount of change the protesters managed to achieve.[100]

The act of protesting could be divided into three *protest areas*, which follow one another in logical sequence. If the goal of a mass protest is to achieve change, protests need to 1) emerge in a public space, 2) realise their potential through action, and 3) attract attention. Therefore, spaces should be examined with a view to whether or not they affect the *emergence, realisation*, and *impact* of protests. "Emergence" is understood here as the protesters' ability to mobilise, organise and implement a protest action. "Realisation" is the protesters' ability to execute their planned action (their level of communication, coordination, and organisation, how and how well they resist aggressive policing, and so on). "Impact" is their ability to be seen, and to use this visibility effectively in order to change public discourse, policy, or leadership.

---

[100] This definition of success is more broad than that of Chenoweth and Stephan (2011), who consider a campaign successful only if all stated goals have been achieved "within a year of the peak of activities and a discernible effect on the outcome, such that the outcome was a direct result of the campaign's activities" (2011, 33). Chenoweth and Stephan focus solely on campaigns for regime change, antiooccupation, or secession, making their work more specific than research on mass protests in general. A mass protest might arguably be considered successful even if some of its goals are not reached.

The data on the three protest areas are based on research literature and on footage of collective actions found in documentary films (e.g. Srok 2014) and on YouTube. During my fieldwork in Moscow, I also observed a protest action on Tverskaia Street (*Tverskaia ulitsa*) and Pushkin Square on 22 June 2017. Watching the interactions between the people and the law enforcement agencies present gave me valuable insights into just how much control the Russian authorities have over the city's public spaces.

This section has established the theoretical framework for a spatial perspective. In the following section, I will apply this perspective to Swamp Square in Moscow—the main location of the 2011–2012 protests. It opens with an introduction to the political environment of the city, including a history of collective actions in Russia, and the reasons for the failed uprising in 2012 as identified in the research literature. Then follows a description of the spatial elements and spatial qualities of Swamp Square, and a discussion of their impact on the three protest areas: emergence, realisation and impact.

9.2 Moscow, Swamp Square and *the March of Millions*

On 7 May 2012, a motorcade escorted by police vehicles drove through a deserted Moscow city centre. The brand-new limousine at its heart carried Vladimir Putin, on his way to his third inauguration as president of the Russian Federation. The ceremonial drive to the Kremlin marked the transition from one presidency to another[101] whilst demonstrating the government's level of control over the capital and its public spaces.

Boris Nemtsov, one of the most prominent opposition leaders at the time, described the scene as 'deeply symbolic' (Nemtsov 2012); during the

---

101 Vladimir Putin was acting president of the Russian Federation from 31 December 1999, and was officially elected in 2000 and 2004. From 2004 to 2008, having exhausted the maximum of two terms as president, he served as prime minister. Notably, he made this shift only after first extending the prime minister's term in office by two years. During this period, the presidential term in office was similarly increased from 4 to 6 years. Putin was able to return to power and serve two more terms, since the Constitution only prohibits three consecutive terms (RF Const. art. 81, § 3).

previous five months, several mass protests had been held in the city, opening up a dispute around the question of who controlled the city's public space: the authorities, or the people. Starting with the December 2011 protests *For Fair Elections*, there had been constant negotiations with the city administration about where such collective actions should be held; and, in May, the protests culminated with the anti-Putin *March of Millions* to Swamp Square in downtown Moscow. In spite of record high numbers of demonstrators, this march was efficiently and brutally suppressed. In the battle for the control over public space, the government, for now, had demonstrated its victory.

Even though the massive wave of protests in 2011–2012 came as a surprise to some observers of Russian politics, neither the contestation of public space nor the voicing of public discontent were news to the city. Even if one disregards the most famous and violent events, such as the 1917 Bolshevik Revolution and the 1993 constitutional crisis, there have been numerous protests and demonstrations in the capital's modern history. In the late 1980s, people frequently protested against the scarcity of food and other consumables, and demanded more far-reaching political reforms in the Soviet Union. In August 1991, hundreds of thousands took to the streets of Moscow to protest against an attempted coup d'état by Soviet conservatives. With the fall of the Soviet Union the same year, protests against inflation, uncontrolled privatisation, social injustice, the wars in Chechnya, and rising crime became regular features on the squares of the capital (Katsva 2003; Bacon 2014).

Coinciding with Vladimir Putin's first presidency and a rise in oil revenues, the economy stabilised in the early 2000s, and much of the discontent disappeared. After a decade of political turmoil and economic hardship, a majority of Russians preferred the stability under the Putin administration to seeking change. Simultaneously, the authorities steadily increased their control over society: The political power vertical from the Soviet era was reintroduced; the oligarchy, legal system, parliamentary opposition, and regional power institutions were increasingly harnessed by the new central powers; and mass media (including a majority of TV broadcasters) were brought under state control. Demonstrators were more frequently subject to police harassment, their access to public space was limited by law, and formal parliamentary opposition was subdued. After a relatively free (if somewhat chaotic) period under the presidency of Boris Yeltsin (1991–1999), political dissent had once again become a dangerous business. (Bacon 2014). This development itself led to several mass protests in favour of political reform.[102]

Two years after the *For Fair Elections* and *March of Millions* protests (2011–2012), public discontent became less visible. Russia's military interventions in Ukraine (from February 2014) were popular at home, and Putin's support rose again to almost 90% (Voronin 2015). Since the Ukrainian *Orange Revolution* in 2004, the Russian authorities had successfully established a discourse according to which dissidents were regarded as unpatriotic people of dubious motives, working in the interest of foreign powers to weaken Russia. During and after *Euromaidan*—the Ukrainian revolution of 2013–2014—this media discourse was strengthened even further. Even though large-scale demonstrations against the war in Ukraine were organised in 2014,[103] the pre-2013 protest movement became less active during the years 2013–2016 as its popular support decreased.

As Russia's euphoria following the annexation of Crimea has died down and news from the war zone in Donbas (Eastern Ukraine) become less frequent, attention has slowly been returning to Russia's domestic scene, whose political, social, and economic problems have not gone away. Economic mismanagement—combined with lower oil prices, Western sanctions, Russian counter-sanctions, and widespread corruption—has hit the Russian economy hard, breeding discontent once more. In addition to

---

102 Notably, one group, in response to being systematically denied access to public space for protest, began demonstrating on the 31st day of every long month beginning from 31 July 2009. *Strategy-31* gathered to demand the right to assembly, guaranteed by Article 31 of the Russian Constitution (RF Const. art. 31), hence the choice of dates. The protest action was initiated by Eduard Limonov, the leader of the organization *Drugaia Rossiia* (Another Russia). (Previously, he was the leader of the National Bolshevik Party, until it was outlawed as an extremist organisation in 2007.)

103 Two mass demonstrations against the war were held on 2 and 15 March 2014. A third demonstration planned for 1 March 2015 effectively became a vigil, as the aforementioned opposition leader and peace march organiser, Boris Nemtsov, was murdered less than two days before it.

protests against corruption in the elite, there have been protests in favour of political reforms, against a raised retirement age (which was introduced as a solution to the country's economic problems), against Internet censorship, against certain city redevelopment plans,[104] and against the creation of numerous open-air landfills. Increasingly, much of the anger has been aimed at President Putin himself, especially since his announcement in December 2017 that he would continue in office for a fourth term—possibly extending his presidency to 20 years (RFE/RL 2017).

9.2.1 The Political Environment of Moscow

This brief chronology of protest events shows that mass protest is not new to the Russian capital. Discontent has come and gone in waves; the authorities have to a large extent controlled the events, with the help of an efficient police force, new legislation on public assembly and the right to protest, media control, and campaigns against most forms of actual and potential oppositional activity. The following is an overview of the factors mentioned above, put into the context of McFaul's (2005) seven conditions required for a colour revolution to occur:

1. A semi-autocratic rather than fully autocratic regime: It is difficult to assess whether Russia has a semi-autocratic or an autocratic regime. However, in the context of public protests, it should be noted that the legislature restricts virtually all demonstrations of discontent. Additionally, a majority of the religious (Papkova 2011), economic and political (Bacon 2014, 149) elites support the incumbent president, who has altered the country's constitution to remain in power for as long as possible. Additionally, law enforcement in Moscow appears especially well financed,

---

104 The project consists partly of tearing down about 5000 low-rise, concrete paneled buildings, known as *khrushchevki*, which were built in the 1960s, often in the areas of Moscow that have now become lucrative. Such buildings were nicknamed after the then Soviet leader, Nikita Khrushchev. Their current residents, who are being forcefully evicted, claim they are being offered neither market value for their apartments nor a desirable enough resettlement alternative, and refuse to move. (Inizan and Coudroy de Lille 2019; The Guardian 2017)

numerous, and experienced. Russia is thus tending towards the autocratic.
2. An unpopular incumbent: There is growing discontent in several demographic layers of the population (see Lanskoy and Myles-Primakoff 2018, 83–84). But there is still widespread popular support for Putin (Levada 2019).
3. A united opposition: In Russia, there is virtually no real formal parliamentary opposition (Bacon 2014, 121–122). The informal opposition is split between various ideological extra-parliamentary groups. (Gel'man 2015).
4. Independent electoral-monitoring capabilities: Although independent domestic monitoring organizations exist, they are frequently subject to crackdowns, and appear to be diminishing (Rossiiskaia gazeta 2016; HRW 2015). Additionally, independent foreign observers are no longer admitted to the Russian elections at the same level as before, and are being replaced with Kremlin-friendly individuals (Spiegel 2007; Shekhovtsov 2018).
5. A modicum of independent media: Traditional media (such as TV, radio, and newspapers) is controlled by the authorities (Herasimenka 2018). The opposition has become increasingly active on social media, but the authorities' control over media platforms is growing (Denisova 2017).
6. Mobilizing the masses: As demonstrated by several rallies organised by opposition leader Aleksei Naval'nyi, the opposition has the capacity to mobilise significant numbers of protesters. However, it has still not been able to mobilise enough people to force notable change to the system.
7. Splits among the 'guys with guns': There is a palpable internal rivalry between the so-called 'power ministries' (i.e. the police, the Federal Security Service, the National Guard, etc.). Although this has not yet translated into a weakening of the ruling authorities, it might in the future (Stanovaya 2019).

To summarise, the Russian opposition[105] is faced with considerable obstacles even before public space is taken into account. Despite growing discontent and an increasingly active and organised opposition—both on- and offline—the political environment is not contributing much to the emergence, realisation, or impact of public protests. The centralised authorities in Moscow are increasingly autocratic and dominate the political environment. They directly control the political and economic elite, mass media, religious and educational institutions, and all the law enforcement agencies. At the same time, public protests are represented in the media as unpatriotic and destructive; almost all demonstrations of public discontent are deemed illegal; and unsanctioned protests, defamation of public leaders, and statements not in line with the official policies are treated as punishable offences. Moscow's law enforcers are trained, experienced, and demonstrate advanced policing strategies and high levels of coordination with the city administration.

9.2.2 Public Spaces in Moscow

Several public spaces in the Russian capital qualify to be studied as protest locations. Starting from the centre of Russian power, Red Square is a natural space. The same goes for nearby squares, such as Manège Square, Revolution Square, Theatre Square, and Lubianka Square, all accessible and visible public spaces that have housed mass protests. Further interesting locations are situated along Moscow's main Tverskaia Street, which starts on Manège Square—right outside the Kremlin—and leads to Tver Outpost Square, outside Belarusian Train Station (*Belorusskii vokzal*). On the way, it crosses Tver Square, Pushkin Square and Triumph Square. More distant spaces, such as Sakharov Avenue and the space in front of the Russian House of Government, could also make interesting within-case studies.

---

105 "The opposition" refers in this chapter to the extra-parliamentary opposition in the country, as little real opposition to the current leadership can be identified in parliament.

Figure 36: Public spaces in Moscow (map)

1: Red Square; 2: Manege Square; 3: Theatre Square; 4: Revolution Square; 5: Lubianka Square; 6: Tver Square; 7: Pushkin Square; 8: Triumph Square; 9: Tver Outpost Square; 10: Sakharov Avenue; 11: House of Government; 12: Swamp Square; 13: October Square. Centre: Kremlin. Illustration: Arve Hansen

However, in the current chapter, space limitations force me to concentrate on Swamp Square for the purpose of illustrating the spatial perspective. Swamp Square has been both transition point and main location for several mass protests throughout the 1990s and 2000s. Notably, three mass protest actions called *For Fair Elections* were held there during the winter of 2011–2012, on 10 December, 17 December, and 4 February; and a fourth protest, the *March of Millions*, was permitted to take place there on 6 May of the same year. Deemed undesirable by some of the political opposition, Swamp Square became the failed (and hidden) focal point for the protesters, as most of the perceived, physical, and social elements hindered the protests' emergence, realization and impact. This is partly because many of the existing obstacles to the opposition identified in the political environment (see above) were enhanced by the spatial elements.

9.2.3 The Elements

Perceived Elements

Swamp Square is a large, green, park-like public space next to the Water Bypass Canal. It is situated right outside the political centre, on an island in the middle of the Moskva River, in an area frequently used by tourists.

The name *Bolotnaia ploshchad'*, translates as the 'swamp' or 'marsh' square and derives from Swamp Region (*Boloto*) on the southern side of the river Moskva, which until the late eighteenth century was frequently flooded. To combat the flooding, a water bypass canal was built from the 1780s, and Swamp Region became Swamp Island (*Bolotnyi ostrov*). Between the fifteenth and seventeenth centuries, the space was used for public executions, including the hanging and quartering of Emelian Pugachev—the leader of the eighteenth-century Cossack rebellion against Catherine II (Evtuhov et al. 2004, 288). Since then the area was used as a marketplace, until the 1938 Iofan architectural project turned it into a square for recreation. In 1962 the public space was renamed Repin Square (*Ploshchad' Repina*) after the realist painter, Il'ia Repin, before being once again given its original name of Swamp (*Bolotnaia*) in 1994 (Moskva 24 2017). Today, the square is colloquially known in Moscow both as Repin Garden Square (*Repin skver*) and Swamp Square (*Bolotnaia*).

Figure 37: Swamp Square, Moscow (map)

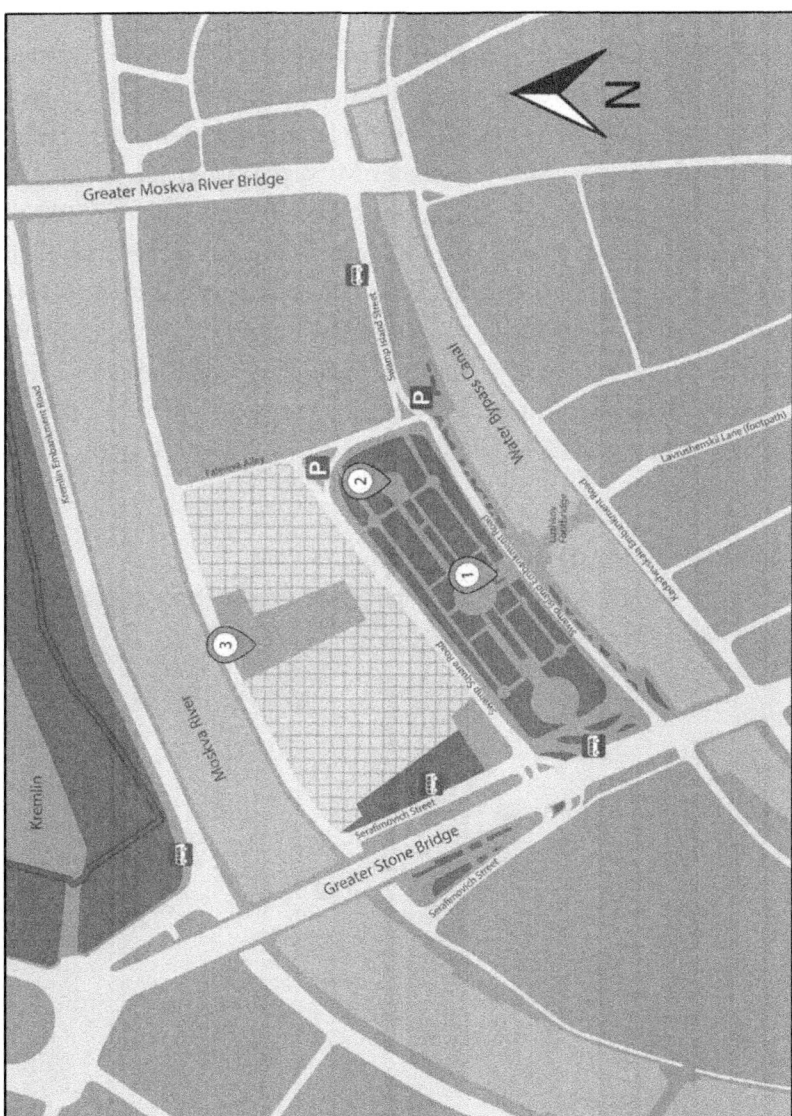

1: Repin Monument; 2: Children are the Victims of Adult Vices; 3: British Embassy.
Illustration: Arve Hansen

The space contains two monuments: a statue to the memory of Il'ia Repin, and a monument named Children are the Victims of Adult Vices (*Deti – zhertvy porokov vzroslykh*). The former is a traditional granite statue of the standing realist painter, holding a palette and brushes. Repin is about twice life size, and he is further enlarged by a 3.5-metre pedestal. This monument was made by sculptor Matvei Manizer and unveiled in 1958 (Mosprogulka n.d.). The latter monument, by sculptor Mikhail Shemiakin, was commissioned by the Mayor of Moscow at the time, Yurii Luzhkov. It portrays two blindfolded children, surrounded by 13 figures that represent vices (alcoholism, prostitution, thievery …). It is girded by a tall fence, and on two of its sides are small playgrounds. After its 2001 unveiling, the monument was heavily criticised for its ominous and grotesque look and accused of seeming to glorify the 13 vices (Shishova 2001; Mos-Holidays n.d.).

Figure 38: Swamp Square, Moscow, June 2017a

Photo: Arve Hansen

As a part of a large-scale Moscow beautification project called My Street (*Moia ulitsa*), much of the city's public space was renovated between 2015–2018. Parking spaces were removed, façades renovated, sidewalks, parks, squares and other pedestrian zones upgraded and made greener, and several new fountains were built. This coincided with other large-scale gentrification projects in the centre of Moscow, such as the 2014–2017 construction of a huge, 13-hectare green area next to Red Square (Zariad'e Park).[106] In 2017, gentrification reached Swamp Square, which received, amongst other things, two dry-deck fountains and freshly planted trees along Swamp Island Embankment Road; however, the layout of the square itself was largely left intact.

Several of the abandoned historic buildings north of the square have decayed and been demolished since the 1990s, and the surrounding area was closed off to the public for a number of years. The reconstruction of the area was announced in 2003, but started only in 2015 (Contact Real Estate 2014; StroiMos 2015). According to the developer, the ongoing construction will include high-end apartment blocks with '[…] an exclusive set of luxurious services […], restaurants […], a spa- and wellness centre […] and flagship stores of world fashion brands.' (CG n.d.) Whether or not this was the intention of the authorities from the start, this project might well change people's associations with the square, from the location of the anti-authoritarian protest movements of 2011–2012 to a green and gentrified area with high-end shops.

Physical Elements

Swamp Square is located in central Moscow, on the southern side of Swamp Island, across the river Moskva from the political centre. As the crow flies, the square is only 370 meters from the Kremlin walls; however, as I explain below, the actual walking distance is much longer.

There are few means of public transportation on the island, no metro stations, and few bus stops. Two roads cross the island in proximity to

---

106 See Makarova (2010) or Badyina and Golubchikov (2005) for more on the general gentrification processes of the centre of Moscow.

Swamp Square: the heavily trafficked Greater Stone Bridge (*Bol'shoi Kamennyi most*), one of the main thoroughfares from southern Moscow to the city centre; and, approximately 300 metres to the east of Swamp Square, the Greater Moskva River Bridge (*Bol'shoi Moskvoretskii most*).

On all four sides, Swamp Square is surrounded by roads: Swamp Island Embankment Road (*Bolotnaia naberezhnaia*) to the southeast; Swamp Square Road (*Bolotnaia ploshchad'*) to the northwest; Faleieva Alley (*Faleievskii pereulok*) to the east; and Serafimovich Street (*ulitsa Serafimovicha*), which runs on both sides of Greater Stone Bridge to the west. The buildings across the roads on the northern and eastern sides are massive, without paths or passages open to the public. The number of entrances to the square is further limited by the river canal, which follows the square along its southern side.

There are two main entrances to Swamp Square. The first and most obvious is from the west, crossing a large open space next to Serafimovich Street. The second is from the south, which is accessed via a short (75 meter) footbridge (*Luzhkov most*). The bridge is a natural prolongment of an urban footpath leading from the Tret'iakov Gallery (*Tret'iakovskaia galereia*) about 450 meters to the south. Other possible entrances are along the river from the east, through a parking lot, or from the northeast, through the narrow Faleieva Alley. However, the long buildings to the north and east of the square block movement in these directions.

Swamp Square is a rectangular space of approximately 38 000 m^2 (360–70 metres long, and 110–120 metres wide) with rounded corners. It is symmetrical, with a 20-metre-wide central path from the southwestern to the northeastern end of the square, and is divided into two parallel parts by a flower bed. Two 5-metre-wide alleys run parallel to the central path, and five alleys cross the square from northwest to southeast, perpendicular to the main paths. The main alley has three open, circular spaces: one by the entrance in the southwest, another by the footbridge, and a third in the northeastern end. Eight smaller circular spaces are located along the two parallel alleys. The alleys and circles are equipped with benches. Between the alleys, the square is covered by lawn, small hedges and a large number of tall trees (mainly hardwoods and pine). Around the square is a low fence, probably intended to prevent people from stepping on the grass.

Social Elements

The primary everyday use of Swamp Square is as a place for recreation. The trees and fountains give some protection from the often-sweltering summers in the Russian capital, although the square might seem cold and uninviting at other times of year. The trees, which provide shelter from the sun, offer no protection from snow or rain, and there are few cafes, shops or facilities in the vicinity to attract people to the area. Visitors do come to see the Estrada Theatre, the Centre for Contemporary Culture, the Museum of Culture, and the Church of St. Nicholas at Bersenevka, but these are located on the western side of the Greater Stone Bridge, which is elevated over most of the island and acts as a great stone barrier between Swamp Square and the buildings mentioned.

Tourists use the area as a transition node, coming in by buses that stop on the parking lots along Swamp Island Embankment Road, near the footbridge. Here, one of Moscow's many river cruise sightseeing ports is located. However, tourists do not usually make their way on to the square itself. Seven metal 'trees of love' were erected along the middle of the footbridge in 2016, and couples are encouraged to leave padlocks on these to profess their unbreakable love for one another. For this reason, the bridge is one of many spots in the city that attracts newlyweds (Msmap n.d.).

In daytime, Swamp Square is used as a place for strolling by mothers with small children and business workers on a lunch break. Wanderers usually enter from the footpath to the south, which offers the only pleasant path to the square. The Greater Stone Bridge and the streets leading to Swamp Island Embankment Road are too heavily trafficked and noisy for recreation. In the evenings, some people use the public space for walks, but the square is rarely brimming with people. Jugglers and flame throwers also use the square in the evenings to practice their skills, and, according to one study, it has become an attractive space for subcultures including '[…] Moscow left- (anti-fascist) and right-wing (football fans) informal groups, poi performers, goths and reenactors' (Abramova 2015, 10). My walks in the square in June 2017 confirm this varied use by subcultures. At night, the sparse artificial lighting often attracts groups of young people who consume alcohol and listen to music from portable loudspeakers. Their presence makes the square a less desirable destination for other potential night-time visitors.[107]

9.2.4 Spatial Qualities

A prominent feature of Swamp Square is its lack of *visibility*, both internal and external. The square's location makes it virtually unnoticeable from the political centre, although in close proximity to it. Furthermore, trees surround the square on all sides, and it is rendered even less visible from the outside by a fountain in the centre of the first circle. Few nodes are located on the square, and virtually no paths cross it, thus greatly limiting its visibility to casual observers. Masses of people gathered in the square would be noticed from the southern side of the river (even though a second line of trees was planted along the river bank in 2017), but would be completely invisible from the northern (political) side of the river. Moreover, in the event of a demonstration, tourists in the area could easily be redirected to less sensitive spaces. Because the majority of media outlets are directly or indirectly controlled by the government, protesters rely on foreign media outlets and social media to notice their discontent and relay their messages to the outside world.

Internal visibility is obstructed by the same obstacles that hinder external visibility. In the midst of chaotic confrontations between protesters and police, this lack of visibility might well intensify the feeling of being trapped. It also makes it difficult to see what moves the police are preparing

---

107 This reputation as a "space for alcoholics" has attracted the attention from the vigilante anti-alcohol, anti-profanity, clean-streets initiative, Lev Protiv. The group is particularly concerned with the state of Swamp Square and go there often to "stop criminal acts", which consists of provoking people by taking their alcohol and pouring it out while broadcasting the action (and the often violent altercations that follow) on YouTube (Lev Protiv n.d.). This increased negative attention has worsened the square's image even further.

to make. The perception of being in a vulnerable position is enhanced by not being able to see approaching threats. The Repin monument is the only tall shape on the square, but, since it is situated between the second circular space and the footbridge, it is mainly visible from the central parts of the square. Moreover, Repin faces southeastwards, away from the square. Since there are no other significant elevations or places rising above the square, it lacks a natural focal point or elevated area that might serve as a podium.

The small number of entrances and lack of public transportation makes *accessibility* largely reliant on what the authorities allow the protesters to do. If the authorities shut down public transportation and close the bridges, the protesters have little chance of entering the square. This means that, even though Swamp Square is physically close to the political centre, it is also quite secluded from it.

Swamp Square could be used as a node where demonstrators gather before moving towards the Kremlin. But the same elements that reduce the square's accessibility also affect *mobility*. Only two routes connect the square to the political centre. The shorter one goes through Swamp Island Street eastwards and over Greater Moskva River Bridge, which leads directly to Red Square; while the longer one goes over Greater Stone Bridge and around the Kremlin to Manège Square. The authorities, should they choose, can simply block a few choke points in order to limit, stop or completely surround the event. Even though the space comprises 38 hectares, the amount of people the square can hold is greatly limited. Most of the square is occupied by trees and other fixed objects that also restrict movement.

Figure 39: Swamp Square, Moscow, 2017b

Photo: Arve Hansen

Accessibility and *mobility* also affect policing of the square. Surrounded on all sides by water and tall buildings, with few exits and reduced motion, the protesters on Swamp Square are easy to control. If kettling[108] is the preferred police strategy, protesters on Swamp Square are effectively already kettled by the choice of space. Conversely, the police can open up one or more exits to vent the protesters (and possibly arrest them as they attempt to leave).

The low *sense of safety* induced by the square is largely an effect of ease of policing, the claustrophobic lack of visibility and factors such as the

---

108 Sociologist Hilary Pilkington describes kettling as "a police strategy of surrounding demonstrators at a protest in order to contain them in a particular place. The police argue it is necessary as a preventative measure to avoid violence or disorder during demonstrations, but it is increasingly being used for long periods of time and protest groups have argued that it is deployed to deliberately frustrate demonstrators or as a means of ascertaining personal details and photographs of protestors." (Pilkington 2012). Kettling can also be used to provoke the outbreak of violence, thus justifying violent countermeasures on the part of the police.

high risk of facing arrest and, usually, retributions for political dissent. On top of this comes the memory of previous, unsuccessful mass protests on the square, including the March of Millions, which also turned violent (see below).

The square's *symbolic value* is greatly limited by its almost complete invisibility to the country's political institutions. Additionally, the name connotes something undesirable, a kind of immobility and a feeling of being stuck, further reducing the space's appeal to protesters.

The combination of largely negative spatial qualities also affect *motivation*, which is further diminished by the perceived elements of the square. Going to a swamp populated by drunkards[109] to protest against a fortified elite out of sight across the river in the Kremlin is a discouraging prospect for many. Add in the space's history as a place for executing political dissidents, and the memory of recent failed protest actions, and it becomes clear why a protester might think twice about joining a demonstration there. Why should they risk protesting in a space from which no past calls for change have been answered, where few people will see their action, and where the chances of being beaten up, arrested, and fined are high?

---

109 Conversely, I met one man in his early thirties in Moscow (June 2017), who claimed that opposition leaders preferred to protest on Swamp Square in 2011-2012 because "it is easy to pay alcoholics to protest [...] you could get them to do anything for a few roubles".

Figure 40: Swamp Square Road, Moscow, June 2017

Photo: Arve Hansen

9.2.5 Emergence, Realization, Impact

The problems with Swamp Square were already evident during the planning of the first protest action there, *For Fair Elections*, on 10 December 2011. Reduced motivation, lack of symbolic value, and the prospect of arranging protests on the authorities' terms (effectively at their mercy) were all factors that discouraged parts of the opposition from joining the protest. The opposition leaders wanted their action to be held at Revolution Square, but were denied access by the Moscow city administration. After lengthy negotiations with the administration, during the night of 8–9 December 2011, the liberal opposition agreed to move their action to Swamp Square, while Eduard Limonov, leader of the illiberal nationalist anti-Putin organization The Other Russia (*Drugaia Rossiia*), insisted on protesting at Revolution Square.

Limonov's preference for Revolution Square was probably due to its more positive spatial qualities. The square is close to the Kremlin and easily accessible through many nodes of transportation in the area; it is larger than Swamp Square, has many exits, and is therefore harder to police. Revolution Square also has a much higher visibility and a more symbolically powerful name. Limonov argued that Swamp Square was '[…] a dangerous trap, where all the conditions are created not only for [a stampede], but also for dropping people into [the river and canal].' (Limonov 2012b).

The disagreement about location caused a deep rift in the opposition. As the spatial qualities of Swamp Square became more and more apparent during the winter of 2011–2012, the opposition sometimes sought other, often unsanctioned spaces for their actions (such as Triumph Square, Revolution Square, Pushkin Square and Lubianka Square).

As part of the realisation of the *For Fair Elections* and *March of Millions* protests on Swamp Square, their organisers applied some of the same strategies as those used during the colour revolutions in neighbouring Georgia in 2003 and Ukraine in 2004. The colour of choice for the Russian protests was white, and a white ribbon became a symbol of discontent. Similarly to the colour revolutions of the 2000s, the demonstrations often had a carnivalesque atmosphere, and the protesters brought humorous signs and inflatable figures painted with symbols and political messages. Some protesters sported fancy dress. But the reduced accessibility and mobility turned the actions on Swamp Square into introvert events. All the spatial qualities discussed above had a negative effect on the realisation of the protests, but those relating to accessibility, mobility, and policing/defensibility were especially negative. As expected, the protesters had little room for movement and were easy to control.

The *March of Millions* event on 6 May serves to illustrate the level of control the authorities exerted over the space. The protesters and authorities had agreed that the march would start from October Square and move northwards to Swamp Square over Greater Stone Bridge. Protesters would also have the option to go directly to the square over the bridge from the north. To maintain security, Greater Moskva River Bridge would be closed off in both directions.

As it turned out, however, the only entrance offered to Swamp Island was from the southwest, and the square itself was fenced off by the police. This forced the masses into the narrow strip of land between the square and the canal (see figure 42) on Swamp Island Embankment Road/Swamp Island Street. The limited space led to thousands being unable to enter the island, as well as to scuffles with the police. At one point, people broke through the police barriers by sheer strength of numbers and started to walk towards the Kremlin, which resulted in clashes with the police, numerous injuries and eventually the police systematically clearing Swamp Square (Mvru 2012). The whole action, from the moment the first protesters entered the area until the protest was suppressed, took less than four hours. In retrospect, one Russian blogger highlighted the problematic spatial qualities of the square by calling it 'a mousetrap' (Vishka 2009).

The 2011–2012 protests on Swamp Square received some international attention. International media recorded the events and, following the legal proceedings against protesters and organisers, Russia received much criticism from organisations such as the European Parliament, the European Court of Human Rights, and Amnesty International. Yet neither the media attention, nor the critique from European organisations were likely to have been generated by the spatial qualities of Swamp Square.

MAIN STUDY 221

Figure 41: March of Millions, Agreed upon rally (map)

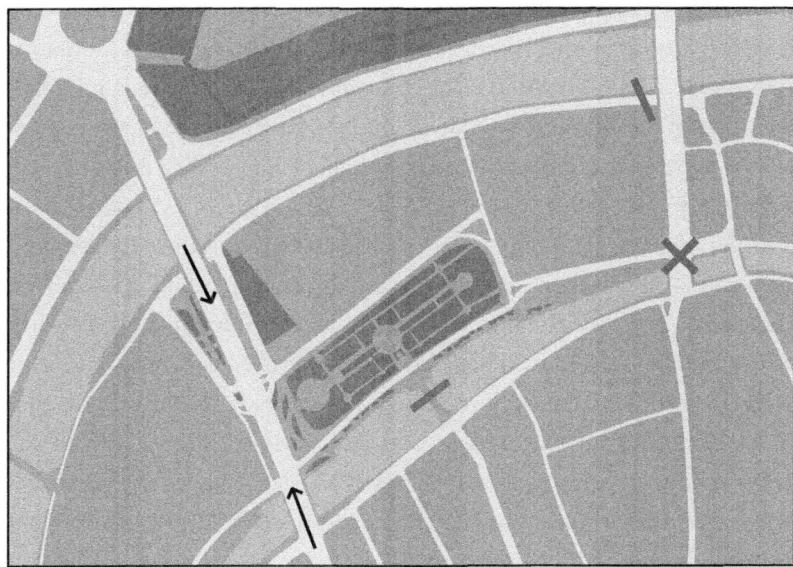

Figure 42: Actual rally (map)

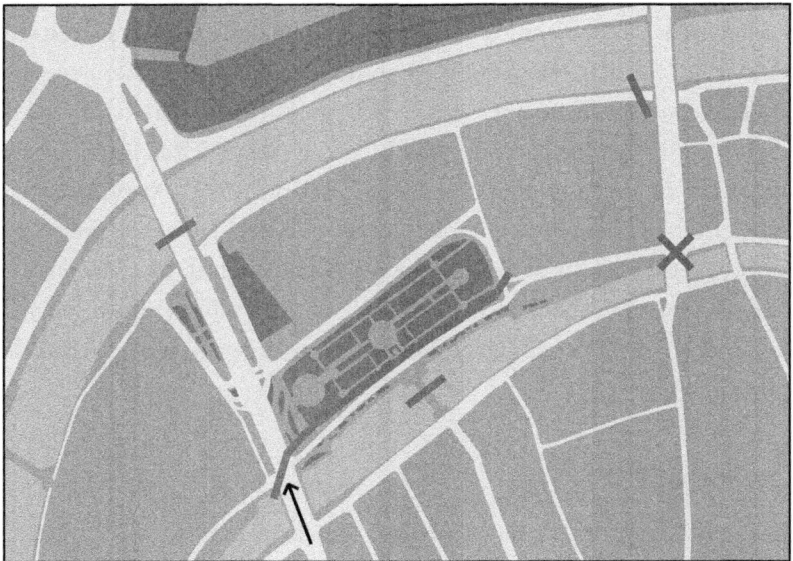

Illustrations: Arve Hansen

Nationally, the protests did little to change the situation in the country. Even though the opposition at the time united a broad group of people from a variety of political backgrounds, and consisted of tens of thousands of protesters, they did not manage to occupy more than a small, insignificant part of the city; and even then, once the police decided to intervene, they were forced into a small pocket of that area, provoked into violence, and swiftly and efficiently removed.

In addition to being hidden from the political centre, the external constraints on mobility prevented the protesters from changing the public discourse. The visibility of demonstrations is paramount, particularly when a majority of news outlets are state controlled and not inclined to cover the protests in the first place. The little coverage of the protests that did reach the national news focused mostly on violent clashes with police, consistently representing the protesters in a negative light. More than 400 protesters were detained that day (Barry and Schwirtz 2012), and criminal proceedings were initiated against the opposition leaders, some of whom were sentenced to prison or house arrest (RFE/RL 2016).

Today, because Swamp Square is associated with failure and (literally and figuratively) being stuck in a swamp, few advocate holding protests in this square. Rarely if ever does the opposition apply for permission to stage collective actions at Swamp Square, and opposition leaders have voiced their distaste for this particular public space. Notably, Eduard Limonov called the square 'a symbol of defeat' (Limonov 2012a). At present, the most prominent opposition leader in Russia, Aleksei Naval'nyi, prefers to arrange legal protests at Sakharov Avenue (although it, too, has several negative spatial qualities such as reduced internal visibility and little symbolic value) or on one of the unsanctioned public spaces along Tverskaia Street.

9.3 Conclusions

In countries with little political freedom, public space is highly significant. When the media and most political institutions are closed to society, discontented people can only resort to city streets and squares in order to express their opinions. But not all spaces are available, practical, significant or visible to the general public.

The spatial perspective on mass protests described in this chapter gives us a way to understand how people and space interact, and how these interactions are perceived. It provides a strategic view of protesting and policing, and helps us understand why protesters and police prefer certain spaces over others. For these reasons, this perspective should be of value to a range of academic disciplines such as sociology, group psychology, urbanism, political science, social movement theory, jurisprudence, and area studies.

This perspective is not, however, an attempt to undermine the existing arguments in political sciences or sociology. The conditions, identified by the likes of McFaul (2005) and Tucker (2007), briefly mentioned in the introduction, are undoubtedly important, but they become particularly so when combined with the conditions space provides. The authorities' privilege in choosing the protesters' space, the generous amounts of time available to the authorities to prepare before a protest, and their ability to keep protesters out of the public discourse have all, to a great degree, dictated the outcome of previous mass protests; and they continue to do so.

Rather than offer an exhaustive analysis of the urban public space in Moscow, I have focused on the theoretical approach and confined my case study to one geographically limited area. I have argued that the spatial elements of Moscow's Swamp Square produce spatial qualities that greatly inhibit its potential use for collective action. The combined effect of these qualities and the other factors present in the political environment negatively affects the potential emergence, realisation, and impact of protests.

I selected Swamp Square as a case study partly because it was the main location of one of the largest post-Soviet protest waves in Russia, and partly because its spatial qualities are almost universally negative. It demonstrates just how unfavourable space can be for a protest movement in a repressive political environment, even despite high numbers of protesters. This negative case study implies, but does not in itself demonstrate, that the reverse is also true: some spaces can be of great value for mass protest. The spatial perspective might therefore benefit from being applied to other spaces of interest to the Russian opposition in Moscow (such as Pushkin Square or Revolution Square) to identify which spatial qualities make these spaces attractive. A comparison of different case studies in Moscow also has the potential to create a fuller picture of the spatial conditions the city offers.

Even though my focus has been on largely peaceful protests—or, at least, protests that initially aimed to be peaceful—it might also be possible to adapt the spatial perspective to research on violent collective actions such as riots, uprisings and revolutions. Moreover, not all spatial analyses necessarily deal with spaces used by the masses who are critical of a regime. A spatial perspective could also be used to explore the potential impact of government-arranged demonstrations and celebrations, illustrating the effect of space on the emergence, practical realisation, and impact of public parades and festivities.

In this study, I have aimed to turn the spatial perspective on mass protests into a general approach. However, it has been developed within a certain geographical and cultural sphere, and this context has naturally influenced my results. The post-Soviet East-Slavic region probably has a myriad of urban characteristics and protest cultures that differ from those in other cities in the world. Thus, the spatial perspective would benefit from being tested on other locations. New spatial elements, spatial qualities, and protest areas might be identified by applying this approach to other public spaces, such as Civic Square in Hong Kong, Revolution Square in Paris, or France Square in Caracas.

Part III

Figure 43: Khreshchatyk Avenue, Kyiv, November 2013

Photo: Arve Hansen

10 To Paris and Beyond

> Found the protesters on [*Place de la République*…]. Police [try to] control the streets [leading] to [Champs-Élysées] [,] separate the protesters in groups. Protesters [still] managed to communicate and regroup […]. Getting closer and closer to the city centre.
> Paris, 6th January 2019

Urban public space is not just open areas between buildings. It is where interactions, recreation, deliberations, and contention occur, and these are vital for the functioning of our political systems. How these spaces are shaped, what they contain, how they are used, and how they are subjectively perceived—by the people, by the authorities, and by observers—affect our political systems and influence society in several ways.

This project is not the first to highlight geography as important for mass protest. A long history of urban contention bears witness to the power of space, and a range of academic disciplines explains this importance from different points of view. But what effects exactly do urban spaces have on mass protests? And how can these effects be measured? The aim of this book has been to develop a theoretical model for assessing the limitations and possibilities urban public spaces provide, for the first time, in a structured and generalised way. The three articles, which supply case studies from the East Slavic region, illustrate and contribute to the development of this model:

The prestudy of Kyiv was written to open up the field and establish the effects Maidan—a space with a history of successful mass protests—has on contention in the city and country. Maidan supplies protesters with visibility, room enough for tens of thousands of protesters, and a powerful symbolic significance—whether the protest is against corruption, election fraud, or against a Russian-leaning president. The square is easily accessible and creates flexibility and mobility. If there is a sufficient number of protesters, Maidan provides them with a sense of safety, since it is difficult for the police to control, clear, or hinder movement to the square. To put the findings of the first article in terms of my current theoretical framework, Maidan's spatial elements produce favourable conditions for the protesters, and these, despite some unfavourable conditions in the political environment, laid the foundation for the success of Euromaidan and other protests before it. (Chapter 7)

The transitional study adds a new dimension to the understanding of how and why demonstrations might fail, as it investigates the widely different space of Minsk. The already marginalised opposition in Belarus is affected negatively by the capital's urban space. The architecture of the city symbolises the greatness and success of the Soviet Union and President Lukashenka, and the only two squares near the political centre with enough room for thousands of protesters are not much frequented, easy to police, and hard to defend. They do not offer much in terms of accessibility, communication, or movement. These aspects are limiting in an already autocratic society in which law enforcement agencies and the media are directly controlled from the top down. Minsk is thus a negative case study, which shows that the elements of the city's two main squares produce spatial conditions that, combined with the repressive factors in the political environment, greatly limit the possibilities for the opposition in the city to express itself in the form of mass protests. (Chapter 8)

The main test-study takes the theoretical model a step further and explicates the structure of the causal mechanisms between urban space and mass protests in Moscow, followed by a case study of Swamp Square, to which the spatial perspective is applied in its current form. While Moscow has many urban public spaces, several of which provide room for thousands of people and are located in the middle of, and in proximity to, the political centre, the Russian authorities have chosen a different tactic than their Belarusian colleagues to diminish the emergence, realisation, and impact of urban protests. Protests critical of the regime are permitted to manifest in urban spaces with poor spatial qualities, such as the distant Sakharov Avenue or the secluded Swamp Square. Swamp Square provides the police with full control over the protesters, which are effectively at the authorities' mercy. Protests here are largely invisible and have little room for movement and a very negative symbolic value. The third article thus shows that the spatial elements of Swamp Square in Moscow produce negative spatial qualities that hinder protests from emerging, realising their potential, and having an impact. (Chapter 9)

In sum, urban public space can affect mass protests in a variety of ways.

For reasons explained in chapter 2 (2.2), this study has been limited to a single geographic and cultural region. How does the model fare when it is applied to a case study in another political environment? In the following section, the primary and secondary research questions outlined in chapter 4 (4.3) are presented in the form of a pilot study, in order to show how the theory can be practically applied to a case study outside the former Soviet Union. This pilot study is not intended to be a full study, but to demonstrate the potential of the spatial perspective for further studies in different and wider contexts. Therefore, some of the methods have not been fully applied and others only in a limited extent.

After this practical demonstration, I provide a summary of the contents of this book and its findings, followed by a discussion of the utility of the spatial perspective model and a few suggestions for how it can be developed further.

10.1 Republic Square and the Yellow Vests

As outlined in chapter 2, the urban conditions of late-eighteenth-century Paris fostered discontent, and gave the revolutionaries of the time the chance to gain upper hand in their struggle against the monarchy by barricading the narrow streets (2.1.1). Several troublesome decades later, after many upheavals, insurgencies, riots, and revolutions, Paris was radically renovated in a grandiose reform project (1853–1870), supervised by the prefect Georges-Eugène Haussmann. One consequence of Hausmann's project was that several conditions for urban discontent disappeared, along with many opportunities supplied to insurgents by the previous shape of the city. A new underground sewer system and large, illuminated open spaces were effective means to battle disease and criminality, while plenty of new open squares and straight wide avenues provided troops with enough room for manoeuvre and made new weaponry such as muskets and cannons effective against crowds of urban rioters.

A century and a half later, in November 2018, contention arose in the city once more. A social movement known as the Yellow Vests (Fr.: *Mouvement des gilets jaunes*) organised several mass actions against the government in urban centres in France, and new protests were planned in the capital for 5 and 6 January 2019. This provided a good opportunity for me to visit the city to see how the spatial environment of this "birthplace" of urban contention affects protests in the twenty-first century.

10.1.1 Applying the Model

In chapter four (4.3) the primary research question for this book is stated as follows:

> How are mass protests affected by urban public space?

In order to analyse the spatial conditions of Paris, this question can be adjusted and narrowed down significantly by focusing only on Republic Square (Fr.: *Place de la République*) and the collective action by the Yellow Vests I observed there on 6 January 2019. This should provide sufficient data for testing the spatial perspective by asking:

> How was the French Yellow Vests' action of 6 January 2019 affected by the spatial features of Republic Square, Paris?

To answer such a question, a theoretical framework is needed, which leads to the following secondary research question:

1. What should a theoretical model exploring the causal connections between urban public space and mass protests look like?

A spatial perspective on protest in Paris needs to explore the causal links between space (the independent variable) and protest (the dependent variable). As discussed in chapter 5, there are pitfalls in geographical determination that should be avoided (5.3). For this reason, other factors in the political environment in Paris and France must also be identified and analysed in order to establish their effects on protest. (A more thorough answer to this secondary research question is elaborated in chapter 5). This proposed model leads to four new secondary questions:

2. What variables does Republic Square include?

First of all, Republic Square has symbolic and historic value, and it produces various feelings, emotions, memories, and associations, which people can relate to and may be affected by. (For a detailed description of perceived elements, see chapter 6, 6.1.1) This specific urban space contains several symbols related to the French Republic, including its name, history, and central monument.

Republic Square was given its current name during Hausmann's post-revolutionary and radical city development in 1879, which included this particular square. The Monument to the French Republic (Fr.: *Le monument à la République*), the centrepiece of the square, consists of a 9.5-metre-tall figure of a woman in bronze standing on a 15.5-metre-high pedestal in marble (Didier n.d.). The woman is Marianne, the symbolic figure used by revolutionaries during the French Revolution, who is seen as a symbol and an embodiment of the French Republic (Gouvernement 2014). Other notable symbols are the national motto—Liberty, Equality, Fraternity (Fr.: *Liberté, égalité, fraternité*)—represented in three smaller statues, along with a bronze lion symbolising universal suffrage; a bronze ballot box for democracy; and a series of bronze reliefs from important events in the history of the revolution and in the life of the French Republic (Didier n.d.). Thus, the monument evokes a wide range of associations, most of which are directly or indirectly revolutionary and related to women.

The actions of protesters, police, and commercial interests (in the form of a pink van, see below) on 5 and 6 January bear witness to a strong sense of repertoires of contention in Paris. One of these ROCs includes Republic Square itself, which has been used for numerous mass actions in its history of protest (6.1.1). Demonstrations in Paris often start at the symbolic Bastille Square (Fr.: *Place de la Bastille*) and march up to the larger (and no less symbolic) Republic Square.[110]

Secondly, Republic Square consists of a range of physical elements. (For a detailed description of physical elements, see 6.1.2) It is located on the intersection between several main avenues, about 2 km from the Louvre Museum. After a major redesign in 2013, it went from a heavily trafficked roundabout to Paris' largest pedestrian square (it is approximately 120 by 300 metres) (Frearson 2014). It is rectangular, surrounded by roads on all four sides (although the traffic on its north-eastern side is regulated to low levels), and with entrances and exits in all directions. Except for the monument as the focal point in the middle, a few lines of trees—generously spaced—a café in the north-western corner and an abundance of benches, there are few objects on the square, which generally feels open. The central monument is the square's only massive structure.

---

110 Notably during the mass protests on the verge of revolution in May 1968 (Keller 2018), as well several more recent actions. For instance, the protests against the Israeli offensive in Gaza in 2014 (Rose 2014); it was here the "I am Charlie" (Fr.: *Je suis Charlie*) demonstrations occurred in 2015 (Fage 2015), and the Standing Up All Night (Fr.: *Nuit Debout*) protests in 2016 (Harsin 2018); etc.

Figure 44: Republic Square, Paris (map)

Photo: Google Maps

Thirdly, Republic Square has daily, official, and traditional uses. (For a detailed description of social elements, see 6.1.3) Although I have not observed or researched the space at great length, the square seems to be popular amongst Parisians, including people out strolling, young skateboarders, and tourists. The latter group is probably attracted by the points of interest in the vicinity of the public space.[111] It is situated along several paths for pedestrians, cars, and public transportation, and five metro lines stop underneath at Republic Metro Station (Fr.: *Republique*).

3. What variables does the Yellow Vests' action of 6 January 2019 include?

Any protest consists of a context, set of actors, and three protest areas: emergence (6.3.1), realisation (6.3.2), and impact (6.3.3). The protest in Republic Square on 6 January 2019 must be viewed in the wider context of the Yellow Vests movement (ongoing at the time of writing). When they first erupted in November 2018, the protests were mostly rural and involved people with lower education levels and low-paying jobs, but they quickly turned into a broader movement against unwanted taxation, unpopular laws, the French establishment, globalism, and President Emmanuel Macron. The protesters wore yellow emergency reflective vests, which are required in all cars in France, and usually occupied central, affluent areas of urban centres in the country (Chamorel 2019, 50–52).

The demonstration in question was held the day after violent clashes between protesters and police during the Yellow Vests' ACT VIII.[112] It was the movement's first women's march, intended to show a human face to

---

111 In the words of a local guide: "Three neighbourhoods converge [on the square] – the youthful Canal Saint-Martin, the historic yet hip Upper Marais and the trendy 11th arrondissement [administrative district], which is brimming with some of Paris's best restaurants [...]" (Monaco 2019).
112 I observed the Yellow Vests on 5 January outside Musée d'Orsay where they were stopped by echelons of riot police on their way to the National Assembly, as well as the clashes that ensued. This was the eighth mass protest in Paris since the social movement against economic inequality began seven weeks earlier (although numerous supportive protests, such as the one of 6 January, were organised throughout urban centres in France).

the inequalities of French society and demonstrate that the violent events of the previous day were not representative of the whole movement ("Hundreds" 2019). The protesters had gathered earlier that day on Bastille Square, from where they marched to Republic Square, where I caught up with them. When I arrived, speeches and appeals were being directed against the French establishment. After a while, the women marched, singing and playing drums, towards Champs-Élysées (one of the main shopping streets). The protests were followed closely by the police and a pink van, which specialised in selling food, snacks, beverages, and other necessities to the protesters, perhaps responding to the regularity of such contentious actions in the city.[113]

Figure 45: The pink van, Paris, January 2019

Photo: Arve Hansen

Since their initial action, the women's marches have become a regular occurrence in Paris and other cities. Judging by the media coverage of

---

113 I had observed the same van several times during the street fighting the previous day, usually located right behind the protesters and often dangerously close to the clashes. The people operating the van seemed, however, unfazed and familiar with working in such an environment.

the protests, the women's march 6 January received far more positive coverage that the other acts by the movement. Cf. *France 24*'s coverage of the actions of 5 (France 24 2019) and 6 January 2019 (Clifford 2019). Therefore, the protest had some level of impact.

4. What other variables can be identified in the causal chain between Republic Square and the Yellow Vests' action of 6 January 2019?

A monument, tree, or node does not have a great effect on mass protests when considered individually. It is when they are combined their qualities appear and influence protests. We can identify seven such spatial qualities: accessibility, mobility, defensibility/policeability, sense of safety, visibility, symbolic value, and motivation (see chapter 6, <u>6.2.</u>1).

Considering the travel nodes on and under the square, and its many entrances and exits, we can safely assume that the square has high levels of accessibility and mobility. These qualities improve the square's already high visibility due to its openness and central location in Paris, nearby travel nodes and paths, and the much-frequented districts in the area. The only hindrance to visibility is the monument, which is so wide and massive that speakers who use it as a platform for addressing the crowds can only be visible to the people on one side of the square at a time.

In situations of confrontation, the square will probably have some of the same qualities as Independence Square in Minsk, which benefits the Belarusian law enforcement agencies (<u>8.5.2</u>). The main roads encircling Republic square on three sides naturally concentrate people in the area around the monument, which leaves the protesters open to policing manoeuvres from three sides. Nonetheless, in contrast to Independence Square, there is enough mobility in Republic Square that the sense of safety remains high. There is virtually always an exit available, so it is relatively easy to avoid being kettled by the police.

The symbolic value of Republic Square is difficult to overestimate. As a large open square in the city centre, with historical and allegorical symbols that most French can relate to—including a history of protest — the square is associated with a feeling of "people power". It is likely that the square has an even a stronger symbolic value for women, as their role in demanding and achieving revolutionary change is emphasised by the monument to Marianne (some of the women on 6 January 2019 wore red Phrygian caps, related to the French Revolution, apparently to reinforce this association). The mainly positive qualities of Republic Square probably have a motivating effect on prospective protesters.

Protests may also be affected by other micro, meso, and macro factors in the political environment, as well as by events and external influences. Therefore, non-spatial independent and intermediary variables (i.e. combined with space) should also be identified. (For a detailed description of intermediary variables, see chapter 6, 6.2.)

A quick investigation into the research literature has resulted in some examples of macro factors, such as economic inequalities, a non-inclusive establishment (Baulaigue 2018), and an increase in anti-protest legislation in the wake of the January 2015 terrorist attacks (Harsin 2018, 1822–1823); meso factors, such as a nationwide network of protest groups, and media outlets critical to the protests (Chamorel 2019, 54–55); and micro factors, such as the goal of the protesters to oust President Emmanuel Macron ("Yellow Vests plan" 2019), or the lack of a shared purpose and direction (Chamorel 2019, 55). Taxation on diesel and Macron's "blunt and provocative public statements" (Chamorel 2019, 50–51) have been identified as some of the main triggering events that started the protests and kept them going. Regarding external influences, the protesters may have been inspired by global protest waves, such as the Arab Spring, Occupy, and others. Even Russian interference has been suggested by the French government as a possible factor in the emergence of the Yellow Vests (Matlack and Williams 2018), a claim routinely denied by the Kremlin (News Trotteur 2018).

5. How can these variables be mapped and measured?

The best way to identify the effects a given space has on protest is by observing protests in the space first-hand (see chapter 5, 5.1.1). Although my time in the square was limited, I had the opportunity to observe the protesters and their interactions with the urban space and law enforcement agencies, as well as to write a few notes about the square and its most prominent elements.

Interviews with participants, organisers, and other observers (see chapter 5, 5.1.2), as well as the use of research literature and other sources (such as video footage and news articles), can provide detailed and alternative descriptions of the space. For this demonstration of the spatial perspective model, I did not conduct any interviews and have consulted only a limited amount of research literature and news articles.

To facilitate analysis, mapping should be utilised at all four stages of development (preparation, field work, analysis, presentation—see chapter 5, 5.1.3). Mapping was done in preparation for the study of Paris and during field work, but not as a part of the analysis or of this presentation. A satellite photo of the square is provided to compensate for the lack of maps (fig. 44).

Based on the data collected using these methods, the above spatial qualities have been induced by logical reasoning. Three types of hypotheses can then be made: 1) the effect of the spatial qualities on the emergence, realisation and impact of protests; 2) the correlation between spatial qualities and non-spatial variables; and 3) their cumulative effect on protests. These hypotheses can be confirmed or disproved by interviews and observations. To control for spatial determinism, the effect of other independent variables in the political environment should also be examined. See chapter 5 (5.1.1, 5.1.2, 5.1.3, 5.6) and chapter 6 for more on the model's methodology.

The high level of motivation as a spatial quality probably encourages the emergence of protests on Republic Square. It is, at the very least, hard to imagine a situation in which people might be discouraged by the thought of protesting in this location, least of all women protesting for inclusivity and social change. Additionally, as far as I have been able to detect, the realisation of the women's march was not hampered by holding their action at this square, either. They were able to enter the urban space, hold their action, and leave, despite the police attempting to impede their movement towards the city centre (more on this below, 7.3). Moreover, the impact of the protesters, visible as they were on a square symbolising the French people and the power of women and at an intersection of paths, roads, and districts, did not diminish the effect of the protests.

Regarding the second and third types of hypothesis, some can be made on the basis of the limited data set available. Here are a few examples:

1. The protesters' choice of space, in the form of a highly affluent urban area, is in contrast to the poor and (initially) rural protest movement, thus highlighting the inequalities they are fighting against.
2. If the media, as the protesters have implied (Chamorel 2019, 54–55), has a negative attitude to the movement and regularly focuses too much on violence, it might be harder to create this type of impression of protests that take place in the middle of the city where more people can see what is (really) going on.
3. Several recent protests and revolutions have been started on central squares across the world, in Baghdad, Cairo, Istanbul, Tehran, and Tripoli—therefore, if a protest is held on one of the largest squares in Paris, the threat of revolution might seem more plausible (and thus result in concessions and/or increased violence).

This account is first and foremost intended as an illustration. Since it is based on limited data and only selected parts of the method are applied, it remains speculative in its current form. It could be researched further in a full analysis, including maps and detailed descriptions of the variables of the urban space and in the political environment. It could include more hypotheses, and interviews with protesters, organisers, experts, and observers. Nonetheless, even at this initial level it generates discussion of overall key issues and, if compared to other sources of information and used actively in interviews, it might be possible to attain a detailed understanding of the square and the possibilities and limitations it provides.

10.2 Summary and Conclusions

The ten chapters of this book have traced the development of a theoretical model that provides a spatial perspective on mass protests. It started with the initial question that motivated me to study the potentials of Maidan (see chapter 1, and chapter 5, 5.4), and viewed the recent Ukrainian revolution in the context of other contemporary and historic tendencies of urban contention (chapter 2). A mapping of research literature on protest and space showed that there is no systematic approach available to analyse protest spaces (chapter 3). After defining key concepts, such as mass protests and urban public space, the aim of developing such a theory in this book was clarified (chapter 4). This was followed by a description of the theorising processes; the methods and considerations used in the development; how causal inference between space and protest can be made; and the testing of the theory (chapter 5). The variables in the spatial perspective model, along with the methods used for identifying them, were then explicated (chapter 6). Finally, key elements of the spatial perspective were applied to a pilot study of Paris (chapter 10).

Let us return to the full research question stated in chapter 4 (4.3):

> How are mass collective actions by pedestrians, engaged in static occupation of an urban public space and aimed at changing society by influencing the decisions of a target by nonviolent means, affected by this urban public space (i.e. outdoor open areas between buildings in a city environment, which in its ideal form is equally accessible and open to everyone in the general population)?

When factors and conditions in the political environment produce discontent to such an extent that people are prepared to protest, these protests might be affected by urban space in a number of ways.

Initially, prospective protesters and organisers look to the urban public space available to them and, whether consciously or not, assess spaces by: their proximity to the political centre or other target institutions; how visible protests located there would be; whether protesters would be safe or vulnerable; whether there would be room to move; and what symbolic value that space might supply to the protesters. They would ask one key question: will our protest in this space have an impact? And the answer to this question might motivate them to or discourage them from protest.

When discontent starts to manifest itself in an urban space, protesters are affected by the square or park into which they have ventured. The walls and entrances, landmarks and monuments, and the people passing and crossing the urban space, all might have an effect on the people congregated there. Protesters have practical needs, such as communication within the camp and getting necessary supplies to it; they want to be seen and heard by the public and by those against whom their protest is aimed. They would want to keep motivation up, and hinder attempts to stop them from carrying out their protest. At the same time, they would be affected by instincts, such as the need for safety; by memories of past events; and by thoughts about the symbolic value of their action.

Once the demonstration of discontent has ended, the goal or goals of the protesters may or may not have been achieved. And this result may have been affected by the length of time the protesters managed to stay in their space of contention; how visible their protest was to the general public and to the authorities; and whether their action was enhanced by the symbolic value of the space.

To conclude, the three areas of protest—emergence, realisation, and impact—might be considerably affected by the spatial qualities produced by urban public space.

10.2.1 "So what?"

After presenting my research project and preliminary results from Kyiv and Minsk to a group of scholars at the Kyiv-Mohyla Academy in November 2016, one established researcher in the audience commented (paraphrased):

> You might very well be right that space has affected such actions. Space might, as you say, have an influence on protests […] but so might weather [long pause…]. So what?

The answer to such a blunt question is that in order to analyse an event, all aspects of it need to be examined for their potential effect. Urban public space has greatly affected protests in Kyiv, had a considerable impact on protests in Minsk and Moscow, and the pilot study above (10.1) indicates that protests in Paris are also affected to a large extent by public space. If we omit space from analyses of collective actions, we do not acquire a full picture, and this reductionism entails a risk of misinterpretation—even if only potentially.

The questioner might have been aware of such instances, however; and, yes, it is not difficult to find examples of protesters being stopped or helped by space, but the researcher probably wanted to know whether the spatial perspective could be put into practical use. What could a spatial perspective be used for? Is it just an interesting thought experiment, or can it be used as a tool for researchers, protesters, or police?

I firmly believe that the spatial perspective model can be of assistance to researchers within sociology, political science, urbanism, jurisprudence, and more. It contributes to our general understanding of protest: a complex issue that should be analysed from all perspectives, including the spatial one. The model can be used as a tool for assessing one of many factors that may or may not be significant in the occurrence and outcome of a collective action. Considering the many static protests that have occurred and made an impact on world politics in the last two decades alone, the importance of a spatial perspective becomes even more evident.

The pilot study, used as an illustration above, shows that the model does not have to be applied in its most detailed form in order to contribute to our understanding of a given location. It could be developed further to produce a more accurate picture of why this space is chosen, what it means to the protesters and to Parisians, and what effect it has on the emergence, realisation, and impact of protests. Conversely, the analysis could be kept to a minimum, and the results included in a larger study of the Yellow Vests. It could also be part of a study of the city (because any study of Paris should, in one form or another, include urban contention).

In other words, the model can be applied in its entirety or selectively. It contributes a language that can be used to discuss space by researchers, who may not necessarily focus on the spatial features of protests, but may need to describe the scene of an action or some important spatial quality. The model can also have some utility for protesters and police, although I doubt that the perspective itself will teach them anything new. Local inhabitants tend to have more intimate knowledge of their cities and its potentials than any generalised theoretical model ever will. But the language this model supplies to researchers may help protesters, police, and observers to more adequately discuss unfolding events and their consequences.

Finally, much can be learned about a society, its level of democracy, and relations between power holders and ordinary people by looking at the contention in, and the control of, city space. We do not inhibit space randomly, and space is not arbitrary. Understanding the social line of space is necessary in order to describe society and its ongoing processes. The model can thus be used as a framework in order to establish whether there is space available for protesters. Or, put another way, whether the ideal form of urban public space as described in chapter 4 exists in the city (4.2).

Take for instance Kyiv, which has Maidan, a symbolic and accessible urban public space with an important role as a safety valve in Ukrainian society. If, after two popular revolutions and a number of mass protests, people still feel the need to use this safety value—to demonstrate, to make demands, and to repeat the threat of "a new Maidan" (i.e. mass protest, 7.1)—it shows that the Ukrainian democratic system is far from perfect.

The urban spaces of Minsk and how they are governed bear witness to fundamental problems in the Belarusian political system. An oft-repeated label for Belarus is "Europe's last dictatorship", coined by former US Secretary of State Condoleezza Rice. Whether this label is correct or not, looking at the empty but clean streets and monumental buildings of Minsk and its absence of public protest, one might be led to think that Rice was right.

In Moscow, too, urban space bears witness to the authoritarian nature of the regime. Although protests do occur in the Russian capital and often attract thousands of people, they are usually repressed with violence and arrests. Nothing demonstrates the Russian authorities' power over the capital city more effectively than their ability to empty the city centre of people in celebration of Putin's third re-election as president in 2012.

10.2.2 Limitations

The causal model proposed in these chapters still has room for development. More empirical tests can be applied, and the variables in the model can probably be elaborated and expanded. It might also benefit from being applied to urban public spaces with clear positive *and* negative spatial qualities, as this would demonstrate that spatial elements can produce different qualities with various effects on various areas of protest.

Except for the work done in Chișinău and Paris, the book has been limited geographically to the East Slavic region, and would thus benefit from being applied to more case studies in other regions of the world, where new variables and causal connections might be identified.

The theory would probably also benefit from further exploring the relationship between actors, events, and space. Whereas this book has focused mainly on the viewpoints of single groups of protesters, limited to one or two collective actions, interesting results might be found by a spatial perspective applied to a variety of urban protests in a single urban space over a long period of time. For instance, an analysis of how Republic Square has affected protests between 1968 and 2019.

10.3 Moving On

When the women's march in Paris moved away from Republic Square on their way to the city centre, my observations were technically finished. The limitations I had set for this study dictated that I focus on static demonstrations and occupations. Moving marches such as this were not part of my study (4.1). But, spurred by curiosity, I decided to move along with the protesters.

The epigraph in the introduction to this chapter is from my field notes made when observing the protesters that day. The police obviously had orders to stop or delay the women marching to the city centre, and they repeatedly attempted to block the demonstrators' movement. Despite a large police presence—possibly as large as the protest group itself—the authorities had a hard time trying to keep the protesters out of the area around Champs-Élysées. Their strategy was to have two police forces: one in the rear, following the protesters, and one more mobile, which attempted to predict where the women would go and quickly block the streets before they got there. Sometimes, if they saw fit, they would run through the protesters at a weak spot in the crowd and divide them into separate groups. But the protesters would always locate their co-protesters, regroup somewhere, and continue their march.

Figure 46: Yellow Vests, Paris, January 2019

Photo: Arve Hansen

Moving protests are a bigger part of the repertoire of contention in Paris than in Kyiv, Minsk, and Moscow. Why? By looking at the women's march of 6 January 2019, we can create an hypothesis that the avenues of Paris, which lack the common European grid street plan (see fig. 44), made the protesters' movement unpredictable and difficult to control. However, in order to check this hypothesis, a greater study is needed that maps all the ways urban space affects mobile protests. But the events in Paris show that the spatial perspective model can (and should) be developed further to include mobile protests, too. What, then, about violent protests? Or protests in vehicles? Or, conversely, non-contentious actions such as public celebrations? Perhaps the perspective can teach us something about events far back in history, too?

There are several possibilities, but one thing is certain: urban contention is not going to disappear any time soon.

References

100 realty. 2019. "Naselennia Kyivs'koi ahlomeratsii dosiahlo 7,5 mil'ioniv meshkantsiv." *100 realty*, 21.2., https://100realty.ua/uk/news/naselenna-kiiv skoi-aglomeracii-dosaglo-75-milioniv-meskanciv (accessed 14.10.2020).

Abramova, Evgeniya. 2015. "The Bolotnaya Square: Urban Design in Moscow Between Social Activities and Political Protests." *Widok. Teorie i praktyki kultury wizualnej*, 3, 9. http://widok.hmfactory.com/index.php/one/article/view/272/554 (accessed 15.10.2020).

Ackerman, Peter, and Christopher Kruegler. 1994. *Strategic Nonviolent Conflict: The Dynamics of People Power in the Twentieth Century*. Westport, CT: Praeger Publishers.

Afitsyinyi sait Respubliki Belarus'. 2016. "Lukashenka: Pry narmal'nykh umovakh zhytstsia niiakikh kaliarovykh revaliutsyi ne budze." *Afitsyinyi sait Respubliki Belarus'*, 17.11., https://www.belarus.by/by/government/events/lukashenka-pry-narmalnyx-umovax-zhytstsja-njakx-kaljarovyx-revaljutsyj-ne-budze_i_0000048897.html (accessed 14.10.2020).

Agnew, John A, and Luca Muscarà. 2012. *Making Political Geography*. 2 ed. Lanham, MD: Rowman and Littlefield.

Andretta, Massimiliano, Gianni Piazza, and Anna Subirats. 2015. "Urban dynamics and social movements." In *The Oxford Handbook of Social Movements*, edited by Donatella della Porta and Mario Diani, 200–218. Oxford: Oxford University Press.

Appleton, Jay. 1975. "Landscape evaluation: The Theoretical Vacuum." *Transactions of the Institute of British Geographers,* (66), 120–123. https://doi.org/10.2307/621625.

Arendt, Hannah. 1958/1998. *The Human Condition*. 2 ed. Chicago, IL: University of Chicago Press.

Attoh, Kafui A. 2011. "What kind of right is the right to the city?" *Progress in Human Geography,* 35(5), 669–685. https://doi.org/10.1177%2F0309132510394706.

Atwal, Maya, and Bacon, Edwin. 2012. "The youth movement Nashi: contentious politics, civil society, and party politics." *East European Politics*, 28(3), 256–266. https://doi.org/10.1080/21599165.2012.691424.

Bacon, Edwin. 2014. *Contemporary Russia*. Basingstoke: Palgrave Macmillan.

Badyina, Anna, and Oleg Golubchikov. 2005. "Gentrification in central Moscow – a market process or a deliberate policy? Money, power and people in housing regeneration in Ostozhenka." *Geografiska Annaler: Series B, Human Geography, 87*(2), 113–129. https://doi.org/10.1111/j.0435-3684.2005.00186.x.

Barrington, Lowell W., and Erik S. Herron. 2004. "One Ukraine or many? Regionalism in Ukraine and its political consequences." *Nationalities Papers, 32*(1), 53–86. https://doi.org/10.1080/0090599042000186179.

Barry, E and Schwirtz, M. 2012. "Arrests and Violence at Overflowing Rally in Moscow." *The New York Times*, 6.5, https://www.nytimes.com/2012/05/07/world/europe/at-moscow-rally-arrests-and-violence.html (accessed 15.10.2020).

Barsamov, Vladimir Aleksandrovich. 2006. "'Tsvetnye revolutsii': teoreticheskii i prikladnoi aspekty." *Sotsiologicheskie issledovaniia*, (8), 57–66. http://ecsocman.hse.ru/data/163/785/1219/Sotsis_08_06_p57-66.pdf.

Baulaigue, Michel. 2018. "Tensions à l'île de la Réunion: la puissance populaire des gilets jaunes." *Sociétés*, (3), 133–139. https://doi.org/10.3917/soc.141.0133.

BBC Russian Service. 2014. "Putin poobeshchal ne dopustit' 'tsvetnoi revolutsii' v Rossii." *BBC*, 20.11., https://www.bbc.com/russian/russia/2014/11/141120_russia_putin_extremism (accessed 14.10.2020).

BBC Russian Service. 2020a. "Aktsii solidarnosti s Xabarovskom: politsiia razognala mitingi v Moskve i Peterburge." *BBC*, 1.8., https://www.bbc.com/russian/news-53622228 (accessed 14.10.2020).

BBC Russian Service. 2020b. "V Xabarovske politsiia zhestko razognala miting v podderzhku Furgala. Dva cheloveka - v bol'nitse." *BBC*, 10.10., https://www.bbc.com/russian/news-54492059 (accessed 14.10.2020).

BBC. 2009. "Ukraine's Economy 'to Shrink 9%'." *BBC*, 7.4., http://news.bbc.co.uk/2/hi/business/7988196.stm (accessed 14.10.2020).

Beach, Derek, and Rasmus Brun Pedersen. 2013. *Process-Tracing Methods: Foundations and Guidelines*. Ann Arbor, MI: University of Michigan Press.

Beacháin, Donnacha Ó., and Abel Polese, eds. 2010. The Colour Revolutions in the Former Soviet Republics: Successes and Failures. Routledge.

Bellwood, Peter, and Marc Oxenham. 2008. "The Expansions of Farming Societies and the Role of the Neolithic Demographic Transition." In *The Neolithic Demographic Transition and its Consequences*, edited by Jean-Pierre Bocquet-Appel, and Ofer Bar-Yosef, 13–34. https://doi.org/10.1007/978-1-4020-8539-0_2.

Bennett Andrew, and Jeffrey T. Checkel. 2015. *Process Tracing: From Metaphor to Analytic Tool*. Cambridge: Cambridge University Press.

Bennett, Brian. 2011. *The last dictatorship in Europe: Belarus under Lukashenko*. London: Hurst & Co.

Bichof, Günter, Stefan Karner, and Peter Ruggenthaler, eds. 2010. *The Prague Spring and the Warsaw Pact Invasion of Czechoslovakia in 1968*. Plymouth: Lexington Books.

Bilgiç, Ali. 2016. "'Sofa and Facebook or tent and Syntagma': understanding global resistance movements from Syntagma to Tahrir." *Global Affairs, 2*(1), 79–90. https://doi.org/10.1080/23340460.2016.1154350.

Biroul național de statistică. n.d. "Populația și procesele demografice." *Biroul național de statistică*, http://statistica.gov.md/category.php?l=ro&idc=103& (accessed 14.10.2020).

Bismarck, Pedro Levi. 2014. "Architecture and the Aestheticization of Politics." *Places Journal*. https://placesjournal.org/article/architecture-and-the-aestheticization-of-politics/.

Boguslavskaia, Aleksandra. 2020. "Ploshchad' peremen: kak zhiteli Minska srazhaiutsia za svoĭ dvor i peremeny v strane (11.09.2020)." *DW*, 11.9., https://p.dw.com/p/3iMIq (accessed 14.10.2020).

Bohn, Thomas. M. 2013. *Minskii fenomen. Gorodskoie planirovanie i urbanizatsiia v Sovetskom Soiuze posle Vtoroi mirovoi voiny* (E. Slepovich, Trans.). Moscow: Rossiiskaia politicheskaia entsiklopediia.

Boldyrev, Iurii. 2018. "Razbor poleta." *Echo Moskvy*, 25.6., https://echo.msk.ru/programs/razbor_poleta/2227432-ech/ (accessed 14.10.2020).

Brown, Gavin, Anna Feigenbaum, Fabian Frenzel, and Patrick McCurdy, eds. 2017. *Protest Camps in International Context: Spaces, Infrastructures and Media of Resistance*. Chicago: Policy Press.

Brunt, Peter Astbury. 1966. "The Roman Mob." *Past and Present*, (35), 3–27. http://www.jstor.org/stable/649964.

Bunce, Valerie J., and Sharon L. Wolchik. 2010. "Defeating Dictators: Electoral Change and Stability in Competitive Authoritarian Regimes." *World Politics, 62*(1), 43–86. http://www.jstor.org/stable/40646191.

Bylina, Vadzim. 2017. "Covering Protests: A New Epoch For The Belarusian Media." *BelarusDigest*, 4.5., https://belarusdigest.com/story/covering-protests-a-new-epoch-for-the-belarusian-media/ (accessed 14.10.2020).

Călugăreanu, Vitalie. 2015. "'Maidan' pașnic la Chișinău: demonstrație de amploare împotriva guvernanților." *Deutsche Welle*, 7.7., https://p.dw.com/p/1GRzp (accessed 14.10.2020).

Całus, Kamil. 2016. "Moldova: from oligarchic pluralism to Plahotniuc's hegemony." *Centre for Eastern Studies, 208*, 1–9. https://www.files.ethz.ch/isn/1967 28/commentary_208.pdf.

Cassegård, Carl. 2014. "Contestation and Bracketing: The Relation between Public Space and the Public Sphere." *Environment and Planning D: Society and Space, 32*(4), 689–703. https://doi.org/10.1068%2Fd13011p.

CG. n.d. "Sokrovishche naprotiv Kremlya." *Capital Group*, http://capitalgroup.ru/objects/residential/the-residences-mandarin-oriental-moscow (accessed 15.10.2020).

Chamorel, Patrick. 2019. "Macron Versus the Yellow Vests." *Journal of Democracy, 30*(4), 48–62. https://doi.org/10.1353/jod.2019.0068.

Chan, Sue. 2003. "Massive Anti-War Outpouring." *CBS News*, 16.2., https://www.cbsnews.com/news/massive-anti-war-outpouring/ (accessed 14.10.2020).

Chenoweth, Erica, and Maria Stephan. 2011. *Why civil resistance works: The Strategic Logic of Nonviolent Conflict*. New York: Columbia University Press.

Chenoweth, Erica. 2013. "The success of nonviolent civil resistance." *TEDx Boulder*, 4.11., https://tedxboulder.com/speakers/erica-chenoweth.

Chivers, Christopher John. 2005. "Crowd Protests Fraud in Azerbaijan Vote." *The New York Times*, 10.11., https://www.nytimes.com/2005/11/10/world/asia/crowd-protests-fraud-in-azerbaijan-vote.html (accessed 14.10.2020).

Clifford, Catherine. 2019. "Hundreds of female 'Yellow Vests' protestors hold peaceful French demo." *France 24*, 6.1., https://www.france24.com/en/2019 0106-hundreds-female-yellow-vests-peaceful-protest (accessed 14.10.2020).

Contact Real Estate. 2014. "Stroyashchiesya i budushchie elitnye zilye kompleksy na beregakh Moskvy-reki." *Contact Real Estate*, 5.11., http://www.kre.ru/news/8596/ (accessed 15.10.2020).

Cordesman, Anthony H. 2014. "Russia and the 'color revolution'. A Russian military view of a world destabilized by the US and the West." *Center for Strategic and International Studies*. http://csis.org/files/publication/140529_Russia_Color_Revolution_Summary.pdf.

Cross, Samuel Hazzard, and Olgerd P. Sherbowitz-Wetzor. 1953. *The Russian primary chronicle: Laurentian text*. Cambridge, MA: Mediaeval Academy of America. https://www.mgh-bibliothek.de/dokumente/a/a011458.pdf.

Cybriwsky, Roman A. 2014a. *Kyiv, Ukraine*. Amsterdam: University Press.

Cybriwsky, Roman A. 2014b. "Kyiv's Maidan: from Duma Square to Sacred Space." *Eurasian Geography and Economics, 55*(3), 270–285. https://doi.org/10.10 80/15387216.2014.991341.

d'Entrèves, Maurizio Passerin, and Ursula Vogel. 2005. Public and Private: Legal, Political and Philosophical Perspectives. New York: Routledge.

DeCesare, Micahel. 2013. "Understanding Social Movements: Theories from the Classical Era to the Present." *Social Movement Studies*, *13*(4), 519–523. https://doi.org/10.1080/14742837.2013.844062.

della Porta, Donatella, Abby Peterson, and Herbert Reiter, eds. 2006. *The Policing of Transnational Protest*. Ashgate Publishing.

della Porta, Donatella, and Herbert Reiter, eds. 1998. *Policing Protest: The Control of Mass Demonstrations in Western Democracies* (Vol. 6). University of Minnesota Press.

della Porta, Donatella, and Mario Diani, eds. 2015. *The Oxford Handbook of Social Movements*. Oxford: Oxford University Press.

della Porta, Donatella, and Mario Diani. 2006. *Social Movements: An Introduction*, 2 ed. Malden, MA: Blackwell.

della Porta, Donatella. 2013. *Clandestine Political Violence*. Cambridge: Cambridge University Press.

Dembiński, Mirosław. (Director). 2006. *Lekcja Białoruskiego*. Belarus/Poland: Studio Filmowe Everest/Telewizja Polska. https://youtu.be/cgqJ5t36Mwc.

DeMichele, Matthew. 2008. "Policing protest events: The Great Strike of 1877 and WTO protests of 1999." *American Journal of Criminal Justice*, *33*(1), 1–18.

Denisova, Anastasia. 2017. "Democracy, protest and public sphere in Russia after the 2011–2012 anti-government protests: digital media at stake." *Media, Culture & Society*, *39*(7), 976–994. https://doi.org/10.1177/0163443716682075.

Didier, Cyrielle. n.d. "La leçon d'histoire de la statue de la République." *Paris Zig Zag*. https://www.pariszigzag.fr/secret/histoire-insolite-paris/la-lecon-dhistoire-de-la-statue-de-la-republique (accessed 14.10.2020).

Divaki production. 2011. "16 dniv. Revolutsiia na hraniti. (povna versiia)." *YouTube*. https://youtu.be/7NY_icyX2Tg (added by DivakiProduction, 15.3.2011; accessed 14.10.2020).

Dosen, Annemarie S., and Michael J. Ostwald. 2013. "Prospect and refuge theory: Constructing a critical definition for architecture and design." *The International Journal of Design in Society*, *6*(1), 9–24. https://doi.org/10.18848/2325-1328/CGP/v06i01/38559.

Dosen, Annemarie. S., and Michael J. Ostwald. 2016. "Evidence for prospect-refuge theory: a meta-analysis of the findings of environmental preference research." *City, Territory and Architecture*, *3*(1), 4.

Doyle, William. 1989. *Origins of the French Revolution*. New York: Oxford University Press.

Dyczok, Marta. 2006. "Was Kuchma's Censorship Effective? Mass Media in Ukraine Before 2004." *Europe-Asia Studies*, 58(2), 215–238. https://doi.org/10.1080/09668130500481386.

Eisinger, Peter. 1973. "The Conditions of Protest Behavior in American Cities." *The American Political Science Review*, 67(1), 11–28. https://doi.org/10.2307/1958525.

Evtuhov, Catherine, David M. Goldfrank, Lindsey Hughes, and Richard Stites. 2004. *A History of Russia: Peoples, Legends, Events, Forces*. Belmont: Wadsworth.

Fage, Luc Henri. 2015. "Je suis Charlie, place de la République, 7 janvier 2015." *YouTube*. https://youtu.be/RinbknbfWRk (added by Luc Henri Fage, 9.1.2015; accessed 14.10.2020).

Fisher, Bonnie S., and Jack L. Nasar. 1992. "Fear of Crime in Relation to Three Exterior Site Features: Prospect, Refuge, and Escape." *Environment and Behavior*, 24(1), 35–65. https://doi.org/10.1177/0013916592241002.

Flikke, Geir. 2020. *Russlands rebeller*. Oslo: Cappelen Damm.

Flippen, J. Brooks. 2011. *Jimmy Carter, the Politics of Family, and the Rise of the Religious Right*. Athens GA: University of Georgia Press.

Focus. n.d. *Merriam-Webster's collegiate dictionary*. https://www.merriam-webster.com/dictionary/focus.

Fokus. 2007. "Stilnyi biznesmen Harri Korogodskii stroit torgovye tsentry v Kieve, no odezhdu i ochki pokupaet za granitsei." *Fokus*, 14.12., https://focus.ua/news/13931 (accessed 14.10.2020).

France 24. 2019. "Quelques accrochages durant l'Acte VIII des Gilets jaunes." *France 24*, 5.1., https://www.france24.com/fr/20190105-france-manifestation-gilets-jaunes-acte-viii (accessed 14.10.2020).

Frearson, Amy. 2014. "TVK transforms Place de la République into Paris' largest pedestrian square." *De Zeen*, 4.1., https://www.dezeen.com/2014/01/04/tvk-place-de-la-republique-paris/ (accessed 14.10.2020).

Frenzel, Fabian, Anna Feigenbaum, and Patrick McCurdy. 2014. "Protest camps: An emerging field of social movement research." *The Sociological Review*, 62(3), 457-474. https://doi.org/10.1111/1467-954X.12111.

Gabowitsch, Mischa. 2017. *Protest in Putin's Russia*. Cambridge: Polity.

Gel'man, Vladimir. 2015. "Political Opposition in Russia: A Troubled Transformation." *Europe-Asia Studies*, 67(2), 177–191. https://doi.org/10.1080/09668136.2014.1001577.

Gillespie, John, and Quang Hung Nguyen. 2019. "Between authoritarian governance and urban citizenship: Tree-felling protests in Hanoi." *Urban Studies, 56*(5), 977–991. https://doi.org/10.1177/0042098018784865.

Gillham, Patrick F., Bob Edwards, and John A. Noakes. 2013. "Strategic incapacitation and the policing of Occupy Wall Street protests in New York City, 2011." *Policing and Society, 23*(1), 81–102. https://doi.org/10.1080/10439463.2012.727607.

Gladkikh, Tatiana and Iekaterina Ievstafieva. 2020. "Na ploshchadi Lenina novosibirtsy ustroili aktsiio v podderzhku zaderzhannogo gubernatora Khabarovskogo kraia." *NGS*, 18.07., https://ngs.ru/text/politics/2020/07/18/69373786/ (accessed 14.10.2020).

Godin, Iu. F. 2014. "Ukraina i 'Slavianskii treugol'nik'." *Rossiia i novye gosudarstva Evrazii*, (2), 9–27.

Göle, Nilüfer. 2013a. Public Space Democracy. *Transit, 44*. https://www.eurozine.com/public-space-democracy/.

Göle, Nilüfer. 2013b. "'Gezi' – Anatomy of a Public Square Movement." *Insight Turkey, 15*(3), 7–14. http://www.jstor.org/stable/26299481.

Goodsell, Charles T. 2003. "The Concept of Public Space and Its Democratic Manifestations." *The American Review of Public Administration, 33*(4), 361–383. https://doi.org/10.1177/0275074003254469.

Gouvernement. 2014. "Marianne and the motto of the Republic." *Gouvernement*, 11.7., https://www.gouvernement.fr/en/marianne-and-the-motto-of-the-republic (accessed 14.10.2020).

Gowlett, John A. 2016. "The discovery of fire by humans: a long and convoluted process." *Philosophical Transactions of the Royal Society B: Biological Sciences, 371*(1696). https://doi.org/10.1098/rstb.2015.0164.

Grzelczak, Piotr. n.d. "Plac Adama Mickiewicza w Poznaniu w latach 1945-1989. Historia polityczna." *Odkryj Dzielnicę Zamkową: Wydawnictwo Pokonferencyjne*, 94–107.

Gunning, Jeroen, and Ilan Zvi Baron. 2014. Why Occupy a Square?: People, Protests and Movements in the Egyptian Revolution. Oxford University Press.

Habermas, Jürgen. 1962/1989. The Structural Transformation of the Public Sphere: An Inquiry into a Category of Bourgeois Society (T. Burger, Trans.). MIT press.

Hammond, John L. 2013. "The Significance of Space in Occupy Wall Street." *Interface, 5*(2), 499–524.

Hansen, Arve, Andrei Rogatchevski, Yngvar Steinholt, and David-Emil Wickström. 2019. *A War of Songs: Popular Music and Recent Russia-Ukraine Relations*. Stuttgart: ibidem Verlag.

Hansen, Arve. 2015. *Majdan 2013–2014: Plassen, protestene, drivkreftene*. Master's thesis, Faculty of Humanities, Social Sciences, and Education, UiT – the Arctic University of Norway, Tromsø. http://hdl.handle.net/10037/7700.

Hansen, Arve. 2016. "Majdan Nezalezjnosti: symbolikk og funksjon." *Nordisk Østforum*, 30(2). https://doi.org/10.17585/nof.v30.424.

Hansen, Arve. 2017. "Public space in the Soviet city: A spatial perspective on mass protests in Minsk." *Nordlit*, (39), 33–57. http://doi.org/10.7557/13.4202.

Hansen, Arve. 2020. *Mass Protests from a Spatial Perspective: Discontent and Urban Public Space in Kyiv, Minsk, and Moscow*. Doctoral thesis, Faculty of Humanities, Social Sciences, and Education, UiT – the Arctic University of Norway, Tromsø. https://hdl.handle.net/10037/17417.

Hansen, Arve. n.d. A Spatial Perspective on Mass Protests: Moscow's Swamp Square and the March of Millions. Unpublished.

Hansen, Arve. n.d. Home. *YouTube*, https://www.youtube.com/arvehansen (accessed 15.10.2020).

Harsin, Jayson. 2018. "The Nuit Debout Movement: Communication, Politics, and the Counter-Production of 'Everynight Life'." *International Journal Of Communication*, 12, 1819–1839. https://ijoc.org/index.php/ijoc/article/view/9339.

Harvey, David. 1989. *The Urban Experience*. Baltimore: Johns Hopkins University Press.

Harvey, David. 2008. "The Right to the City." *NLR*, 53. https://newleftreview.org/issues/II53/articles/david-harvey-the-right-to-the-city.

Harvey, David. 2012. *Rebel Cities: From the Right to the City to the Urban Revolution*. Verso books.

Hatuka, Tali, and Rachel Kallus. 2008. "The Architecture of Repeated Rituals: Tel Aviv's Rabin Square." *Journal of Architectural Education*, 61(4), 85–94. https://doi.org/10.1111/j.1531-314X.2008.00192.x.

Hemment, Julie. 2012. "Nashi, Youth Voluntarism, and Potemkin NGOs: Making Sense of Civil Society in Post-Soviet Russia." *Slavic Review*, 71(2), 234–260. https://doi.org/10.5612/slavicreview.71.2.0234.

Herasimenka, Aliaksandr. 2016. "Information and Communication Technologies and new Possibilities of Political Participation in Belarus." *Piaty mizhnarodny kanhres dasledchykau Belarusi – Pratsounyia materyialy*, 5. http://icbs.palityka.org/wp-content/uploads/2016/10/01_herasimenka.pdf.

Herasimenka, Aliaksandr. 2018. "What's behind Alexei Navalny's digital challenge to Vladimir Putin's regime? Five things to know." *The Washington Post*, 23.2., http://wapo.st/2oluLTc?tid=ss_mail (accessed 4.9.2019).

Hershkovitz, Linda. 1993. "Tiananmen Square and the politics of place." *Political Geography*, 12(5), 395-420. https://doi.org/10.1016/0962-6298(93)90010-5.

History.com. 2019. "Vietnam Veterans Against the War demonstrate." History.com, 28.7., http://www.history.com/this-day-in-history/vietnam-veterans-against-the-war-demonstrate (accessed 14.10.2020).

Hoensch, Jorg K. 1984. *A History of Modern Hungary*. Longman.

Holovne upravlinnia statystyky. 2019. "Chysel'nist' naselennia (za otsinkoiu) na 1 serpnia 2019 roku ta serednia chysel'nist u sichni-lypni 2019 roku." *Holovne upravlinnia statystyky u M. Kyievi*, http://www.kiev.ukrstat.gov.ua/p.php3?c=1123&lang=1 (accessed 14.10.2020).

Hou, Jeffrey, and Sabine Knierbein, eds. 2017. *City Unsilenced: Urban Resistance and Public Space in the Age of Shrinking Democracy*. Routledge.

Hou, Jeffrey, ed. 2010. *Insurgent Public Space: Guerrilla Urbanism and the Remaking of Contemporary Cities*. Routledge.

Howell, P. 1993. "Public Space and the Public Sphere: Political Theory and the Historical Geography of Modernity." *Environment and Planning D: Society and Space*, 11(3), 303–322. https://doi.org/10.1068/d110303.

HRW. 2015. "Russia cracks down on Moscow election monitors." *Newsweek*, 9.7., https://www.newsweek.com/russia-cracks-down-moscow-election-monitors-352039 (accessed 15.10.2020).

Hryshchenko, M. V. 2013. "Publichnyi prostir Kyeva jak seredovyshche proiavu postkomunistychnykh transformatsii ukrainskoho suspilstva." In *Psikholohia v Ukraiini ta za kordonom. Materialy mizhnarodnoii naukovo-praktychnoii konferentsii (m. Chernihiv, 8–9 lystopada 2013 roku)*, 82–88. Kherson: Vidavnichii dim «Helvetika». http://molodyvcheny.in.ua/files/conf/psy/01nov2013/01nov2013.pdf.

Huntington, Samuel P. 1991. "Democracy's third wave." *Journal of democracy*, 2(2), 12–34. https://doi.org/10.1353/jod.1991.0016.

Iel'chaninov, Mikhail Semenovich. 2007. "Eshche raz o vozmozhnosti revolutsii v sovremennoi Rossii." *Sotsiologicheskie issledovaniia*, (12), 50–57. http://ecsocman.hse.ru/data/007/636/1219/Elchaninov_6.pdf.

Inceoglu, Irem. 2014. "The Gezi Resistance and its Aftermath: A Radical Democratic Opportunity?" *Soundings: A Journal of Politics and Culture*, 57(1), 23–34. https://muse.jhu.edu/article/554024/pdf.

Inceoglu, Irem. 2015. "Encountering Difference and Radical Democratic Trajectory: An Analysis of Gezi Park as Public Space." *City, 19*(4), 534–544. https://doi.org/10.1080/13604813.2015.1051743.

Inizan, Guénola, and Lydia Coudroy de Lille. 2019. "The last of the Soviets' Home: Urban demolition in Moscow." *Geographia Polonica, 92*(1), 37–56. https://doi.org/10.7163/GPol.0135.

International Business Times. 2015. "Moldova\'s [sic] Maidan: Echoes of Ukraine crisis amid anti-corruption protest movement." *International Business Times*, 10.10., https://www.ibtimes.co.uk/moldovas-maidan-echoes-ukraine-crisis-amid-anti-corruption-protest-movement-1523124 (accessed 14.10.2020).

Jones, Martin, Rhys Jones, Michael Woods, and Mike Woods. 2014. *An Introduction to Political Geography: Space, Place and Politics.* Routledge.

Kanet, Roger E. 2006. "The Superpower Quest for Empire: The Cold War and Soviet Support for 'Wars of National Liberation'." *Cold War History*, 6(3), 331–352. https://doi.org/10.1080/14682740600795469.

Karduni, Alireza. 2017. *Anatomy of a Protest: Activism, People, Social Media, and Urban Space.* Master's thesis, the University of North Carolina at Charlotte. https://search.proquest.com/docview/1899863322?pq-origsite=gscholar.

Katsva, Aleksandr. 2003. "Rossiya 1990-x: Protestnoe dvizhenie." *Otechestvennye zapiski, 3.* http://magazines.russ.ru/oz/2003/3/2003_3_31.html (accessed 15.10.2020).

Keller Kate. 2018. "Fifty Years Later, France Is Still Debating the Legacy of Its 1968 Protests." *Smithsonian*, 4.5., https://www.smithsonianmag.com/history/fifty-years-later-france-still-debating-legacy-its-1968-protests-180968963/ (accessed 14.10.2020).

Khashchavatski, Iuryi. (Director). 1996. *Obyknovennyi prezident.* Belarus: Kinokompaniia L.O.N. https://youtu.be/gmb5ZMBItrE (accessed 15.10.2020).

Khashchavatski, Iuryi. 2007. *Ploshcha.* Estonia: Baltic Film Production. https://youtu.be/GlKfWl_6Q8Y (accessed 15.10.2020).

Kibal'chich, E. (Director). 2011. *Belarusskaia mechta.* Belarus: Belarus in Focus. https://youtu.be/R2IjKa-Gi9A (accessed 15.10.2020).

Kireev, Alex. 2007. "Ukraina. Prezidentskie vybory 2010." *Elektoralnaia geografiia 2.0.* www.electoralgeography.com/new/ru/countries/u/ukraine/ukraina-prezidentskie-vybory-2010.html (accessed 14.10.2020).

Knox, Paul L. 2011. *Cities and Design.* Routledge.

Kohn, Margaret. 2013. "Privatization and Protest: Occupy Wall Street, Occupy Toronto, and the occupation of public space in a democracy." *Perspectives on Politics, 11*(01), 99-110. https://doi.org/10.1017/S1537592712003623.

Köksal, Isabelle. 2012. "Walking in the City of London." *Social Movement Studies, 11*(3-4), 446-453. https://doi.org/10.1080/14742837.2012.704356.

Kondrashova, Natal'ia. 2018. "Potomki semerykh. Kak zhivut sem'i tekh, kto v 1968-m vyshel na Krasnuiu ploshchad'." *Radio Svoboda*, 19.8., https://www.svoboda.org/a/29404471.html (accessed 14.10.2020).

Krasovskaia, Nataliia. 2019. "'Im nuzhen vash mozg': kak vliiaiut na chelovechestvo informatsionnye voiny." *Rambler*, 15.8., https://news.rambler.ru/other/42666295-im-nuzhen-vash-mozg-kak-vliyayut-na-chelovechestvo-informatsionnye-voyny/ (accessed 14.10.2020).

Kuhn, Betsy. 2011. *Gay Power!: The Stonewall Riots and the Gay Rights Movement, 1969.* Minneapolis, MN: Twenty-First Century Books.

Kurlansky, Mark. 2005. *1968. De gränslösa drömmarnas år* (F. Sjögren, Trans.). Stockholm: Ordfront.

Kuzik, Lilia. 2014. " L'vivs'kyi Avtomaidan piketuvav restoran rodyny Sala." *Zakhid.net*, 2.2., https://zaxid.net/lvivskiy_avtomaydan_piketuvav_restoran_rodini_sala_n1301844 (accessed 14.10.2020).

Kuzio, Taras. 2005. "From Kuchma to Yushchenko Ukraine's 2004 Presidential Elections and the Orange Revolution." *Problems of Post-Communism, 52*(2), 29–44. https://doi.org/10.1080/10758216.2005.11052197.

Kuzio, Taras. 2007. "Oligarchs, Tapes and Oranges: 'Kuchmagate' to the Orange Revolution." *Journal of Communist Studies and Transition Politics, 23*(1), 30–56. https://doi.org/10.1080/13523270701194839.

Kuzio, Taras. 2008. "Democratic Breakthroughs and Revolutions in Five Postcommunist Countries: Comparative Perspectives on the Fourth Wave." *Demokratizatsiya, 16*(1).

Kuzio, Taras. 2012. "2012 Parliamentary Elections in Ukraine." *Center for Strategic and International Studies* [podcast]. https://itunes.apple.com/no/podcast/2012-parliamentary-%20elections/id383698245?i=123419448&l=nb&mt=2@.

Lanskoy, Miriam, and Dylan Myles-Primakoff. 2018. "Power and Plunder in Putin's Russia." *Journal of Democracy, 29*(1), 76–85. http://doi.org/10.1353/jod.2018.0006.

Lee, Nelson K. 2009. "How is a political public space made? – The birth of Tiananmen Square and the May Fourth Movement." *Political Geography, 28*(1), 32–43. https://doi.org/10.1016/j.polgeo.2008.05.003.

Lefebvre, Henri. 1970/2003. *The Urban Revolution* (R. Bononno, Trans.). Minneapolis, MN: University of Minnesota Press.

Lefebvre, Henri. 1974/1991. *The Production of Space* (D. Nicholson-Smith, Trans.). Oxford: Blackwell Publishers.

Lefebvre, Henri. 1996. *Writings on Cities* (E. Kofman and E. Lebas, Trans.). Oxford: Blackwell Publishers.

Lev Protiv. n.d. Home. *YouTube*, https://www.youtube.com/user/lionversusSmoking (accessed 15.10.2020).

Levada. 2019. "Approval ratings." *Levada*, 14.1., https://www.levada.ru/en/2019/01/14/approval-ratings-6/ (accessed 15.10.2020).

Limonov Eduard. 2012a. "'Dnevnaya propoved' v chetverg'." *Livejournal*, 26.1., https://limonov-eduard.livejournal.com/187316.html (accessed 15.10.2019.

Limonov Eduard. 2012b. "Kak oni vas predavali." *Livejournal*, 4.12., https://limonov-eduard.livejournal.com/274344.html (accessed 15.10.2019.

Lopes de Souza, Marcelo, and Barbara Lipietz. 2011. "The 'Arab Spring' and the City: Hopes, Contradictions and Spatiality." *City*, *15*(6), 618–624. https://doi.org/10.1080/13604813.2011.632900.

Lumsden, Linda J. 2000. "Beauty and the Beasts: Significance of Press Coverage of the 1913 National Suffrage Parade." *Journalism & Mass Communication Quarterly*, *77*(3), 593–611. https://doi.org/10.1177%2F107769900007700309.

Lynch, Kevin. 1960. *The Image of the City*. Cambridge, MA: MIT press.

maidan. 1989. O.S. Melnychuk, V.T. Kolomiets, V.H. Skliarenko, T.B Lukinova and O.B. Tkachenko, eds. *Etymolohichnyi slovnyk ukraiinskoi movy*, Vol. 3. Kyiv: Naukova dumka.

Makarova, Katia. 2010. "Postindustriyalizm, dzhentrifikatsiya i transformatsiya gorodskogo prostranstva v sovremennoi Moskve." *Neprikosnovennyi zapas*, *2*, 279–296.

Manoilo, Andrei Viktorovich. 2014. "Ukrainskii krizis i 'upravliaemyi khaos': sled 'tsvetnykh revoliutsii' Arabskoi vesny." *Vlast'* (4). https://cyberleninka.ru/article/n/ukrainskiy-krizis-i-upravlyaemyy-haos-sled-tsvetnyh-revolyutsiy-arabskoy-vesny.

Manoilo, Andrei Viktorovich. 2015. "Tsvetnye revolutsii i tekhnologii demontazha politicheskikh rezhimov." *Mirovaia politika* (1), 1–19. http://e-notabene.ru/wi/article_12614.html.

Marples, David R. 1994. "Kuropaty: The Investigation of a Stalinist Historical Controversy." *Slavic Review*, *53*(2), 513-523. https://doi.org/10.2307/2501303.

Marples, David R. 2004. *The Collapse of the Soviet Union, 1985–1991*. Harlow: Pearson Longman.

Marples, David R. 2006. "Color revolutions: The Belarus case." *Communist and Post- Communist Studies, 39*(3), 351–364. https://doi.org/10.1016/j.postcomstud.2006.06.004.

Marshall, Tim. 2015. *Prisoners of Geography: Ten Maps That Tell You Everything You Need to Know About Global Politics*. London: Elliot and Thompson.

Mass. n.d. *Merriam-Webster's collegiate dictionary*. https://www.merriam-webster.com/dictionary/mass.

Matchanka, Anastasiya. 2014. "Substitution of Civil Society in Belarus: Government-Organised Non-Governmental Organisations." *Journal of Belarusian Studies, 7*(2), 67–94. http://belarusjournal.com/sites/default/files/Matchanka-upload.pdf.

Matlack, Carol, and Robert Williams. 2018. "France to Probe Possible Russian Influence on Yellow Vest Riots." *Bloomberg*, 8.12., https://www.bloomberg.com/news/articles/2018-12-08/pro-russia-social-media-takes-aim-at-macron-as-yellow-vests-rage.

Matuszak, Sławomir. 2012. "The Oligarchic Democracy: The Influence of Business Groups on Ukrainian Politics." *OSW Studies, 42*. http://aei.pitt.edu/58394/.

McCann, Eugene J. 1999. Race, Protest, and Public Space: Contextualizing Lefebvre in the US City. *Antipode, 31*(2), 163–184. https://doi.org/10.1111/1467-8330.00098.

McCarthy, John D., and Clark McPhail. 2006. Places of Protest: The Public Forum in Principle and Practice. *Mobilization: An International Quarterly, 11*(2), 229–247. https://doi.org/10.17813/maiq.11.2.45054350171u704q.

McFaul, Michael. 2002. "The Fourth Wave of Democracy and Dictatorship: Noncooperative Transitions in the Postcommunist World." *World Politics, 54*(2), 212–244. www.jstor.org/stable/25054183.

McFaul, Michael. 2005. "Transitions from Postcommunism." *Journal of Democracy, 16*(3), 5–19. https://doi.org/10.1353/jod.2005.0049.

Mikhailowskaia, R. (Director). 2015. *Banda*. Belarus: Belarusian Documentation Center. https://youtu.be/lhdCfXilD4o (accessed 15.10.2020).

Miller, George A. 2003. "The cognitive revolution: a historical perspective." *Trends in Cognitive Sciences, 7*(3), 141–144. https://doi.org/10.1016/S1364-6613(03)00029-9.

Mitchell, Don. 1995. "The end of public space? People's Park, definitions of the public, and democracy." *Annals of the association of american geographers, 85*(1), 108-133.

Mitchell, Don. 1998. "Anti-Homeless Laws and Public Space: I. Begging and the First Amendment." *Urban Geography*, *19*(1), 6–11. https://doi.org/10.2747/0272-3638.19.1.6.

Mitchell, Don. 2011. "Homelessness, American Style." *Urban Geography*, *32*(7), 933–956. https://doi.org/10.2747/0272-3638.32.7.933.

Mitchell, Don. 2014. *The Right to the City: Social Justice and the Fight for Public Space*. New York: Guilford.

Mitchell, Don. 2016. "Tent Cities: Interstitial Spaces of Survival." In *Urban Interstices: The Aesthetics and the Politics of the In-between*, edited by A. M. Brighenti, 65–85. London: Routledge.

Mitchell, Don. 2017. "People's Park again: on the end and ends of public space." Environment and Planning A, 49, no. 3 (2017): 503-518. https://doi.org/10.1177/0308518X15611557.

Monaco, Emily. 2019. "Local's Guide to the Best Things To Do in République, Paris." *Culture Trip*, 10.10., https://theculturetrip.com/europe/france/articles/the-top-10-things-to-do-and-see-in-republique-paris/ (accessed 14.10.2020).

Morrison, John. 1993. "Pereyaslav and After: the Russian-Ukrainian Relationship." International Affairs 69(4), 677–703. https://www.jstor.org/stable/2620592.

Mos-Holidays. n.d. "Pamyatnik 'Deti – zhertvy porokov vzroslykh'." *Mos-Holidays*, https://mos-holidays.ru/pamyatnik-deti-zhertvy-porokov-vzroslyx/ (accessed 15.10.2020).

Moskva 24. 2017. "Udivitel'naya istoriya Bolotnoi ploshchadi." *Moskva 24*, 23.6., https://tv.m24.ru/videos/132672 (accessed 15.10.2020).

Mosprogulka. n.d. "Pamyatnik Il'e Repinu." *Mosprogulka*, http://mosprogulka.ru/places/pamjatnik_repinu (accessed 15.10.2020).

Msmap. n.d. "Luzhkov most (Potseluev most)." *Msmap*, https://www.msmap.ru/bridges/2041 (accessed 15.10.2020).

Mvru. 2012. "Miting na Bolotnoi Proryv kol'tsa otsepleniya – 6 Maya 2012." *YouTube*. https://youtu.be/SI0S2VKE91g (aded by Mvru, 6.5.2012; accessed 15.10.2020).

Naumov, Aleksandr Olehovich. 2016. "'Tsvetnye revolutsii' kak ugroza gosudarstvennomu suverenitetu. Opyt Kyrgyzstana." *Mirovaia politika*, (2), 36–45. http://e-notabene.ru/wi/article_17599.html.

Naviny. "2015 Piataia inauguratsiia Aleksandra Lukashenko. Onlain-reportazh." *Naviny*, 6.11., http://naviny.by/rubrics/elections/2015/11/06/ic_articles_623_190205 (accessed 15.10.2020).

Nemtsov, Boris. 2012. "Novaya real'nost." *Livejournal*, 7.5., https://echo.msk.ru/blog/nemtsov_boris/886129-echo/ (accessed 15.10.2019).

Nersesov, Dmitrii. 2017. "V Belorussii zamaiachil prizrak Maidana." *Pravda*, 22.3., https://www.pravda.ru/world/1328186-belarus/ (accessed 14.10.2020).

NESH. 2016. "Guidelines for research ethics in the social sciences, humanities, law and theology." *Norwegian National Research Ethics Committees*. https://www.etikkom.no/globalassets/documents/english-publications/60127_fek_guidelines_nesh_digital_corr.pdf.

News Trotteur. 2018. "La Russie nie toute implication dans le mouvement de protestation des 'Gilets jaunes'." *News Trotteur*, 10.12., https://newstrotteur.fr/2018/12/10/la-russie-nie-toute-implication-dans-le-mouvement-de-protestation-des-gilets-jaunes/ (accessed 2019).

Nielsen, Emma. 2017. "The feeling of a place: A psychogeographic exploration in Walworth." *Social Life*. http://www.social-life.co/media/files/The_feeling_of_a_place_2017_mLaowqZ.pdf.

Nielsen, Nikolaj. 2012. "Belarus: a look inside Europe's 'last dictatorship'." *EU observer*, 20.3., https://euobserver.com/belarus/115635 (accessed 15.10.2020).

Noakes, John, and Patrick F. Gillham. 2006. "Aspects of the 'New Penology' in the Police Response to Major Political Protests in the United States, 1999–2000." In *The Policing of Transnational Protest*, edited by D. della Porta, A. Peterson, and H. Reiter, 97–115. London: Routledge.

NTV. 2019. "Na Ukraine vorovali amerikanskie granty 'na demokratiu'." *NTV*, 29.3., https://www.ntv.ru/novosti/2172880/ (accessed 14.10.2020).

Núñez, Rafael, and Kensy Cooperrider. 2013. "The tangle of space and time in human cognition." *Trends in Cognitive Sciences*, 17(5), 220-229. https://doi.org/10.1016/j.tics.2013.03.008.

Obshchaia gazeta. 2017. "Dal'noboishchiki 27 marta nachnut bessrochnuiu aktsiiu protesta protiv sistemy 'Platon'." *Obshchaia gazeta*, 1.3., https://og.ru/society/2017/03/01/87067 (accessed 14.10.2020).

Olzak, Susan. 1989. "Analysis of Events in the Study of Collective Action." *Annual review of sociology*, 15(1), 119-141. https://doi.org/10.1146/annurev.so.15.080189.001003.

Olzak, Susan. 1990. "The Political Context of Competition: Lynching and Urban Racial Violence, 1882-1914." *Social Forces*, 69(2), 395–421. https://doi.org/10.2307/2579665.

Onliner. 2016. "Kakim budet kompleks ot Dana Holdings na Oktiabr'skoi ploshchadi? Poiavilsia vozmozhnyi variant." *Onliner*, https://realt.onliner.by/2016/12/30/dana-3 (accessed 15.10.2020).

Onuch, Olga, and Henry E. Hale. 2018. "Capturing ethnicity: the case of Ukraine." *Post-Soviet Affairs*, 34(2-3), 84–106. https://doi.org/10.1080/1060586X.2018.1452247.

Opp, Karl-Dieter. 2009. *Theories of Political Protest and Social Movements: A multidisciplinary introduction, critique, and synthesis*. Routledge.

Oren, Michel. 2019. "Reconfiguring the Turkish Cultural Public Sphere." *Cultural Critique, 102*, 90–116. https://doi.org/10.5749/culturalcritique.102.2019.0090.

Örs, İlay Romain. 2014. "Genie in the bottle: Gezi Park, Taksim Square, and the realignment of democracy and space in Turkey." *Philosophy & Social Criticism*, 40(4–5), 489–498. https://doi.org/10.1177/0191453714525390.

Osipov-Gipsh, Yegór. 2019. "Conversations Not Finished: Memory Narratives of the 1990s in Contemporary Russia." *Russian Space RSCPR research group guest lecture series* [Guest lecture], 4.10., https://en.uit.no/tavla/artikkel/645932/yeg_r_osipov-gipsh_conversations_not_finished.

Ostermann, Christian F., and Malcolm Byrne, eds. 2001. *Uprising in East Germany, 1953: the Cold War, the German question, and the first major upheaval behind the Iron Curtain*. Budapest: Central European University Press.

Papkova, Irina. 2011. *The Orthodox Church and Russian Politics*. New York: Oxford University Press.

Parkinson, John R. 2012. *Democracy and Public Space: the Physical Sites of Democratic Performance*. New York, NY: Oxford University Press. https://doi.org/10.1093/acprof:osobl/9780199214563.001.0001.

Paul, Michael C. 2008. "Was The Prince of Novgorod a 'Third-Rate Bureaucrat' after 1136?" *Jahrbücher für Geschichte Osteuropas*, 56(1), 72. http://www.jstor.org/stable/41052013.

Peoples Dispatch. 2019. "Yellow Vests plan future course of action ahead of first anniversary." *Peoples Dispatch*, 6.11., https://peoplesdispatch.org/2019/11/06/yellow-vests-plan-future-course-of-action-ahead-of-first-anniversary/ (accessed 14.11.2020).

Pikulicka-Wilczewska, Agnieszka. 2020. "Kyrgyzstan prime minister resigns amid election protests." *Al Jazeera*, 6.10., https://www.aljazeera.com/news/2020/10/6/kyrgyzstan-pm-resign-amid-election-protests (accessed 14.10.2020).

Pilkington, Hilary. 2012. "When is a kettle not a kettle? When it is on slow boil…" *British Politics and Policy at LSE*. http://eprints.lse.ac.uk/48722/1/blogs.lse.ac.uk-When_is_a_kettle_not_a_kettle_When_it_is_on_slow_boil.pdf.

Popovic, Srdja, and Matthew Miller. 2015. *Blueprint for Revolution: How to Use Rice Pudding, Lego Men, and Other Nonviolent Techniques to Galvanize Communities, Overthrow Dictators, or Simply Change The World*. New York, NY: Spiegel & Grau.

Popovic, Srdja, Andrej Milivojevic, and Slobodan Djinovic. 2006. *Nonviolent Struggle: 50 Crucial Points. A Strategic Approach to Everyday Tactics*. Belgrade: Center for Applied NonViolent Action and Strategies.

Powelson, Michael. 2003. "US Support for Anti-Soviet and Anti-Russian Guerrilla Movements and the Undermining of Democracy." *Demokratizatsiya, 11*(2), 297–304.

Project for Public Spaces. 2005. "10 principles for successful squares." *Project for Public Spaces*, https://www.pps.org/article/squaresprinciples (accessed 14.10.2020).

Public works. n.d. *Merriam-Webster's collegiate dictionary*. https://www.merriam-webster.com/dictionary/public%20works.

Public. n.d. *Merriam-Webster's collegiate dictionary*. https://www.merriam-webster.com/dictionary/public.

Radnitz, Scott. 2010. "The Color of Money: Privatization, Economic Dispersion, and the Post-Soviet 'Revolutions'." *Comparative Politics, 42*(2), 127–146. www.jstor.org/stable/27822300.

Ramadan, Adam. 2013. "From Tahrir to the world: The camp as a political public space." *European Urban and Regional Studies, 20*(1), 145–149. https://doi.org/10.1177/0969776412459863.

Ramanujam, Priti. 2007. *Prospect-refuge theory revisited: A search for safety in dynamic public spaces with a reference to design*. Master's thesis, the University of Texas at Arlington. https://rc.library.uta.edu/uta-ir/bitstream/handle/10106/67/umi-uta-1277.pdf?sequence=1&isAllowed=y.

Rezvin, Vladimir Aleksandrovicha. 2015. *Moskva i ee glavnyie arkhitektory. Ot F'oravanti do Posokhina*. Moscow: Iskusstvo-XXI vek.

RFE/RL. 2016. "Russia Releases One Bolotnaya Prisoner." *RFE/RL*, 15.7., https://www.rferl.org/a/russia-bolotnaya-prisoner-krivov-released/27860146.html (accessed 15.10.2020).

RFE/RL. 2017. "Putin Announces He Will Run For Reelection In March." *RFE/RL*, 6.12., https://www.rferl.org/a/russia-putin-hints-president-reelection-doesnt-announce/28900426.html (accessed 15.10.2020).

Romanchuk, Iaroslav. 2011. "Iaroslav Romanchuk. KRIZIS. Chetyre aisberga dlia belorusskogo "Titanika". *Naviny*, 27.4., http://naviny.by/rubrics/opinion/2011/04/27/ic_articles_410_173414 (accessed 15.10.2020).

Romaniuk, Oleksandr. 2005. "Postkomunistychni revoliutsii." *Polytychnyi menedzhment, 4*, 16–28. http://dspace.nbuv.gov.ua/handle/123456789/8881.

Rose, Michel. 2014. "Thousands ignore ban in Paris to protest Israeli offensive in Gaza." *Reuters*, 26.7., https://www.reuters.com/article/us-mideast-gaza-france-protests/thousands-ignore-ban-in-paris-to-protest-israeli-offensive-in-gaza-idUSKBN0FV0MR20140726 (accessed 14.10.2020).

Rossiiskaia gazeta. 2016. "Federal'nyj zakon ot 15 fevralja 2016 g. N 29-FZ 'O vnesenii izmenenii v Federal'nyj zakon 'Ob osnovnykh garantiyakh izbiratel'nykh prav i prava na uchastie v referendume grazhdan Rossiiskoi Federacii' i stat'yu 33 Federal'nogo zakona 'O vyborakh deputatov Gosudarstvennoi Dumy Federal'nogo Sobraniya Rossiiskoi Federacii' v chasti deyatel'nosti nablyudatelei'." *Rossiiskaia gazeta*, 17.2., https://rg.ru/2016/02/17/vybori-dok.html (accessed 15.10.2020).

Routledge, Paul. 2015. "Geography and Social Movements." In *The Oxford Handbook of Social Movements*, edited by Donatella della Porta and Mario Diani, 383–398. Oxford: Oxford University Press.

Routledge, Paul. 2017. *Space Invaders: Radical Geographies of Protest*. London: Pluto Press.

Rudling, Per. 2008. "'For a Heroic Belarus!': The Great Patriotic War as Identity Marker in the Lukashenka and Soviet Belarusian Discourses." *Sprawy Narodowościowe, 32*, 43–62.

Rusin, Aleksandr Olegovich. 2016. "Kto polozhil konets 'likhim 90-m'?" *Tsentr Sulakshina*, 6.12., http://rusrand.ru/replika/kto-polozhil-konets-lihim-90-m.

Russian Ministry of Defence. 2014. "O voennykh aspektakh 'tsvetnykh' revolutsii 'na poliakh' III Moskovskoi konferentsii vystupil nachal'nik Glavnogo operativnogo upravleniia Genshtaba Vooruzhennykh Sil RF general-polkovnik Vladimir Zarudnitskii." *Russian Ministry of Defence*, 23.5., https://function.mil.ru/news_page/country/more.htm?id=11929774@egNews (accessed 14.10.2020).

Salikov, Aleksei, and Aleksei Zhavaronkov. 2018. "Transformatsiya publichnogo prostranstva v usloviyakh revolutsii: vzgliad iz perspektivy Khanny Arendt." *Sotsiologicheskoie obozreniie, 17*(1).

Salmenkari, Taru. 2009. "Geography of Protest: Places of Demonstration in Buenos Aires and Seoul." *Urban Geography, 30*(3), 239–260. https://doi.org/10.2747/0272-3638.30.3.239.

Sarna, Aleksandr. 2008. "Minsk – gorod pobedivshego glamura." *Elektronnaia Biblioteka BGU*, 334–353. http://elib.bsu.by/handle/123456789/11332.

Schlögel, Karl. 2012. *Moscow, 1937* (R. Livingstone, Trans.). Cambridge: Polity Press.

Sharp, Gene. 1973. *The politics of nonviolent action* (Vol. 3). Boston, MA: Porter Sargent Publisher.

Shekhovtsov, Anton. 2018. "Politically Biased Foreign Electoral Observation at the Russian 2018 Presidential Election." *European Platform for Democratic Elections*, 16.4., https://www.epde.org/en/news/details/politically-biased-foreign-electoral-observation-at-the-russian-2018-presidential-election.html (accessed 15.10.2020).

Shishova, T. 2001. "'Pamyatnik porokam' Shemiakina s tochki zreniya psikhologa'," *Provoslavie.ru*, 5.12., http://www.pravoslavie.ru/guest/abramenkova.htm (accessed 4.9.2019).

Skillen, Daphne. 2017. *Freedom of Speech in Russia: Politics and media from Gorbachev to Putin*. London: Routledge.

Smidchens, Guntis. 2014. *The Power of Song: Nonviolent National Culture in the Baltic Singing Revolution*. Seattle, WA: University of Washington Press.

Smith, Neil, and Mitchell, Don. 2018. *Revolting New York: How 400 Years of Riot, Rebellion, Uprising, and Revolution Shaped a City*. Athens, GA: Georgia Press.

Snyder, Timothy. 2010. "Brutality in Belarus." *The New York Review of Books*. http://www.nybooks.com/daily/2010/12/21/brutality-in-belarus/ (accessed 15.10.2020).

Snyder, Timothy. 2014. "Fascism, Russia, and Ukraine." *The New York Review of Books*. https://www.nybooks.com/articles/2014/03/20/fascism-russia-and-ukraine/ (accessed 14.10.2020).

Soja, Edward. 2010. "Writing the city spatially." *City*, 7(3), 269–280. https://doi.org/10.1080/1360481032000157478.

Solovei, Valerii Dmitriievich. 2016. *Revolution!: Osnovy revolutsionnoi bor'by v sovremennuiu epokhu*. Moscow: Eksmo.

Space. n.d. *Merriam-Webster's collegiate dictionary*. https://www.merriam-webster.com/dictionary/space.

Spain, Daphne. 2016. *Constructive Feminism: Women's Spaces and Women's Rights in the American City*. Ithaca, NY: Cornell University Press.

Spiegel. 2007. "The Russian Vote. Election Observers Unwelcome." *Spiegel Online*, 16.11., https://www.spiegel.de/international/world/the-russian-vote-election-observers-unwelcome-a-517879.html (accessed 15.10.2020).

Staeheli, Lynn, and Don Mitchell. 2008. *The People's Property?: Power, Politics, and the Public*. Routledge.

StroiMos. 2015. "Mezhdunarodnyi arhitekturnyi konkurs na razrabotku kontseptsii mnogofunktsional'nogo kompleksa na Sofiiskoi naberezhnoi v Moskve." *StroiMos*, 22.6., https://stroi.mos.ru/arhitekturnye-konkursy/mezhdunarodnyi-arhitekturnyi-konkurs-na-razrabotku-koncepcii-mnogofunkcionalnogo-kompleksa-na-sofiiskoi-naberezhnoi-v-moskve (accessed 15.10.2020).

Swedberg, Richard. 2012. "Theorizing in sociology and social science: Turning to the context of discovery." *Theory and society, 41*(1), 1–40.

Taiga.net. 2020. "'Ot Amura do Baikala vystupaem za Frugala': nesoglasovannyie aktsii v podderzhku protestov v Khabarovske proshli v Sibiri." *Taiga.info*, 25.07., https://tayga.info/157503 (accessed 14.10.2020).

Tarrow, Sidney. 1993. "Cycles of Collective Action: Between Moments of Madness and the Repertoire of Contention." *Social Science History, 17*(2), 281–307. https://doi.org/10.2307/1171283.

Tass. 2019. "Nurgaliev zaiavil, chto NATO gotovit 'tsvetnye revolutsii' v riade stran ODKB." *TASS*, 2.7., https://tass.ru/politika/6622680 (accessed 14.10.2020).

Terra Dignitas. 2015. "Pro konkurs." *Terra Dignitas*. https://terradignitas.kga.gov.ua/pro-konkurs (accessed 20.7.2015).

Thagard, Paul. 2018. "Cognitive Science." *Stanford Encyclopedia of Philosophy*. https://plato.stanford.edu/entries/cognitive-science/.

The Guardian. 2017. "Protests in Moscow at plan to tear down Soviet-era housing in affluent areas." *The Guardian*, 14.5., https://www.theguardian.com/world/2017/may/14/people-protest-moscow-plans-to-tear-down-housing (accessed 15.10.2020).

Thornton, Kevin. 1996. "The Confederate Flag and the Meaning of Southern History." *Southern Cultures, 2*(2), 233–245. https://www.jstor.org/stable/26235412.

Titarenko, Larissa, and Anna Shirokanova. 2011. "The Phenomenon of Minsk: the City Space and the Cultural Narrative." *LIMES: Borderland Studies, 4*(1), 21-35. https://doi.org/10.3846/20290187.2011.577197.

Titarenko, Larissa. 2008. "Historical Memory, Embodied in the Social Space of Minsk, and Its Influence on the Formation of National and European Identity of Belarusians." *LIMES: Cultural Regionalistics*, (1), 32-45. https://doi.org/10.3846/2029-0187.2008.1.32-45.

Törnquist-Plewa, Barbara. 2001. *Vitryssland: språk och nationalism i ett kulturellt gränsland*. Lund: Studentlitteratur AB.

Törnquist-Plewa, Barbara. 2001. *Vitryssland: språk och nationalism i ett kulturellt gränsland*. Lund: Studentlitteratur AB.

Traugott, Mark. 1993. "Barricades as Repertoire: Continuities and Discontinuities in the History of French Contention." *Social Science History*, 17(2), 309–323. https://doi.org/10.2307/1171284.

Tucker, Joshua A. 2007. "Enough! Electoral Fraud, Collective Action Problems, and Post-Communist Colored Revolutions." *Perspectives on Politics*, 5(3), 535–551. https://doi.org/10.1017/S1537592707071538.

Twomey, Terrence. 2014. "How domesticating fire facilitated the evolution of human cooperation." *Biology & Philosophy*, 29(1), 89–99. https://doi.org/10.1007/s10539-013-9402-2.

UiT. n.d. "Russian Space: Concepts, Practices, Representations (RSCPR)." *UiT*, https://en.uit.no/forskning/forskningsgrupper/gruppe?p_document_id=408709 (accessed 14.11.2020).

Ukrainian Ministry of Health. 2014. "Informatsiia pro postrazhdalykh u sutychkakh v tsentri Kyieva stanom na 06.00 hod. 23 lutoho 2014 roku." *Ukrainian Ministry of Health*, 23.2., www.moz.gov.ua/ua/portal/pre_20140223_b.html (accessed 10.10.2015).

UN News Centre. 2015. "Despite Less Fighting, Eastern Ukraine Still 'Highly Flammable,' UN Reports, as Death Toll Tops 9,000." *UN*, 9.12., https://news.un.org/en/story/2015/12/517672-despite-less-fighting-eastern-ukraine-still-highly-flammable-un-reports-death (accessed 14.10.2020).

UNHCR. 2015a. "Ukraine: 2015 UNHCR Subregional Operations Profile – Eastern Europe." *UNHCR*. http://www.unhcr.org/cgi-bin/texis/vtx/page?page=49e48d4d6&submit=GO# (accessed 18.1.2016).

UNHCR. 2015b. "Ukraine Situation: UNHCR Operational Update. 2–24 December 2015." *UNHCR*. https://www.unhcr.org/5614d3fb9.html (accessed 14.10.2020).

Urban. n.d. *Merriam-Webster's collegiate dictionary*. https://www.merriam-webster.com/dictionary/urban.

Van Deusen, Richard. 2002. "Public space design as class warfare: Urban design, the right to the city and the production of Clinton Square, Syracuse, NY." *GeoJournal*, 58(2–3), 149–158. https://doi.org/10.1023/B:GEJO.0000010834.17907.5e

Van Deusen, Richard. 2004. "The state, culture and *rights*: a response to Sallie Marston's 'Space, culture, state: uneven developments in political geography'." *Political Geography*, 23(1), 27-34. https://doi.org/10.1016/j.polgeo.2003.09.008.

Vardomatskii, Andrei Petrovich. 1995. "Vybory pervogo prezidenta Belorussii." *Sotsiologicheskie issledovaniia*, (9), 45-49.

Vasianovych, Anatolii. 2011. "'Ploshcha' i 'maidan'." *FirstUA*, 18.2., http://firstua.com/uk/video/program/zapamjatay/2011/02/18/2149 (accessed 18.10.2015).

Vishka. 2009. "Kak u nas ukrali revolutsiyu. Sobytiya glazami ochevidtsa." *Livejournal*, 9.12., https://vishka.livejournal.com/221501.html (accessed 15.10.2020).

Voronin, Nikolai. 2015. "Reiting Putina – 90%: uroki istorii." *BBC Russian Service*, 22.10., https://www.bbc.com/russian/international/2015/10/151022_putin_highest_approval_rating_list (accessed 15.10.2020).

Wasserstrom, Jeffrey N. 2005. "Chinese Students and Anti-Japanese Protests, Past and Present." *World Policy Journal*, 22(2), 59–65. www.jstor.org/stable/40209964.

Way, Lucan. 2008. "The Real Causes of the Color Revolutions." *Journal of Democracy* 19(3), 55–69. https://doi.org/10.1353/jod.0.0010.

Whelan, Chad, and Adam Molnar. 2018. *Securing Mega-Events: Networks, Strategies and Tensions*. London: Palgrave Macmillan Limited.

Wilde, Robert. 2018. "Pre-Revolutionary France." *ThoughtCo*, 30.6., https://www.thoughtco.com/french-revolution-pre-revolutionary-france-1221877 (accessed 14.10.2020).

Wilson, Andrew. 2005. *Ukraine's Orange Revolution*. New Haven: Yale University Press.

Wilson, Andrew. 2011. "'Political Technology': Why Is It Alive and Flourishing in the Former USSR?" *Open Democracy: Russia and Beyond*, 17.6., https://www.opendemocracy.net/en/odr/political-technology-why-is-it-alive-and-flourishing-in-former-ussr/ (accessed 14.10.2020).

Wilson, Andrew. 2011. *Belarus: The last dictatorship in Europe*. New Haven & London: Yale University Press.

Wojnowski, Zbigniew. 2018. "The Impact of the Prague Spring on the USSR." In *Eastern Europe in 1968: Responses to the Prague Spring and Warsaw Pact Invasion*, edited by Kevin McDermott and Matthew Stibbe, 71–96. Palgrave Macmillan, Cham.

Yacobi, Haim. 2004. "In-Between Surveillance and Spatial Protest: the Production of Space of the 'Mixed City' of Lod?" *Surveillance & Society*, 2(1). https://doi.org/10.24908/ss.v2i1.3327.

Zaazaa, Ahmed. 2009. "Cairo: The Multi-Schizophrenic City Alqahrt: madinat al-shakhsiat almutaeadida." *Blogspot*, 1.11., http://cairomsc.blogspot.com/2009/11/el-tahrir-square-multi-layered-history.html.

Zakharov, Yevhen, ed. 2014. "Human Rights in Ukraine – 2013." *Ukrainian Helsinki Human Rights Union*. Kharkiv: Prava Ludyny.

Zik. 2010. "1932–1933 Genocide in Ukraine was Invented by Foreign Historians, Tabachnyk Says." *Zik*, 1.9., http://zik.ua/en/news/2010/09/01/243009 (accessed 14.10.2020).

Zolotoriov, Volodymyr. 2013. "O polze majdanov." *Kontrakty.ua*, 28.11., http://kontrakty.ua/article/70358 (accessed 14.10.2020).

Personal communication

Name / *pseudonym*	Date	Communication	Language
"The major"	Jan 2014	Face-to-face	Russian
Bohdan	Mar 2014	Face-to-face	Ukrainian
Dzmitry	Oct 2016	Skype	Belarussian
East-European political scientist	Mar 2016	E-mail	English
Hanna	Apr 2014	Face-to-face	Ukrainian
Hoff, Harald	Dec 2013– Jan 2014	Several conv.	Norwegian
Katsiaryna	Oct 2016	Skype	Belarussian
Kis, Zorjan	Mar 2015	E-mail	Ukrainian
Klymenko, Oleksandr	Jan, Jun 2014	Face-to-face	Russian
Løken, Håkon	Apr 2014	Face-to-face	Norwegian
Milinkevich, Aliaksandr	Oct 2016	E-mail	Belarussian
Moldovan political scientist	Aug 2016	Face-to-face	English
Nadia	Jun 2014	Face-to-face	Russian
Natasha	Oct 2016	Telephone	Russian
Nordbø, Arnfinn	Dec 2013	Skype	Norwegian
Oleksii	Jan–Jun 2014	Several conv.	Ukrainian
Pawliuk	Nov 2016	Skype	Russian
Piatro	Sep 2016	Skype	Russian
Plingau, Dinu	Aug 2016	Face-to-face	Russian
Scandinavian observer	Aug 2016	Face-to-face	Scandinavian
Scandinavian political scientist	Mar 2016	Telephone	Scandinavian
Scandinavian political scientist	Jul 2016	Telephone	Norwegian
Serhii	Mar 2014	Face-to-face	Russian
Shushkevich, Stanislaw	Oct 2016	Telephone	Russian
Stanislaw	Jun 2014	Face-to-face	Russian
Statkevich, Mikola	Nov 2016	Skype	Russian
Vital	Mar 2016	Skype	Russian
Yaraslaw	Nov, Dec 2016	Skype	Russian

Index

0-km sign, Minsk 161, 179, 181
1968, protests of 37, 232, 244
Abkhazia 38
Academician Sakharov Avenue, Moscow 87, 111, 190, 206, 207, 222, 228
Adam Mickiewicz Square, Poznań 37
Afghanistan 145
Africa 58
agora 32, 150, 151, 155
Akayev, Askar 39
Ala-Too Square, Bishkek 21, 39
Albania 36
Aleksandrovskii Garden, Moscow 87
Aliaksandrawski Garden Square, Minsk 179, 181, 182, 183
Ancient Roman Republic 34
Another Russia 203
anthropology 31
Antimaidan 49, 99
Appleton, Jay 68
Arab Spring 43, 68, 133, 237
Arbat district, Moscow 87
architecture 25, 27, 61, 65, 66, 67, 68, 83, 98, 100, 101, 102, 106, 115, 116, 118, 129, 130, 137, 145, 158, 160, 164, 166, 173, 181, 186, 188, 189, 191, 192, 193, 194, 208, 228,
Arendt, Hannah 61, 62, 100, 157, 192

Armenia 39, 54
Art Centre, Kyiv 145
Asia 38, 58
Automaidan 76
Azerbaijan 39, 53, 54
Baku 39
Balkans 38
Baltics 37, 57
Baseina Street, Kyiv 141
Bastille, Paris 26, 35, 93, 115, 232, 235
Beijing 35
Belarus, Republic of 15, 16, 17, 21, 38, 39, 40, 41, 42, 43, 53, 54, 56, 58, 99, 100, 101, 107, 108, 109, 125, 133, 158, 159, 160, 161, 162, 165, 172, 173, 177, 184, 187, 228, 243
Belarusian State Pedagogical University, Minsk 177, 184
Belarusian State University, Minsk 177, 184
Bennett, Andrew 84, 108, 161, 175, 194
Berlin 37
Berlin Wall 37
Bishkek 21, 39
Black Lives Matter 35
Black Sea 97
Black Sea Fleet 97
Bolshevik Revolution 135, 168, 170, 202
Bolsheviks 135

Borovitskaia Square, Moscow 87
Borys Hrinchenka Street, Kyiv 134, 136
Boulevard Ring, Moscow 87, 207
Bucharest 190
Budapest 37
Buenos Aires 70
Bulgaria 36
Bulldozer Revolution 38, 51
Cairo 71, 239
capitalism 53, 63, 139, 146, 168
Cassette Scandal 146
Castle Hill, Minsk 165
Catherine II 208
Catholic Christianity 134, 171, 172
Caucasus 38
causality 80, 101, 107, 108, 110, 112, 120, 194, 195, 197
Central Asia 38, 52
Central Bank, Kyiv 134, 136, 147
Central Post Office, Kyiv 137
Centre for Contemporary Culture, Moscow 213
Champs-Élysées, Paris 88, 93, 227, 235, 244
Charviakova Street, Minsk 21
Chechnya 38, 202
Chenoweth, Erica 51, 52, 156, 191, 200
Chernobyl Catastrophe 145, 160
Children are the Victims of Adult Vices, Moscow 209, 210
Chinatown, Moscow 87
Chişinău 39, 84, 86, 93, 104, 105, 106, 188, 190, 198, 244
Church of Saints Simon and Helena, Minsk 171, 172, 178, 184, 185. See also *Red Church*
Church of St. Nicholas at Bersenevka, Moscow 213
Civic Square, Hong Kong 224
Clinton Square 70
cognitive turn 31
Cold War 58
collective action theory 45, 54
colour revolution 38, 39, 42, 43, 50, 52, 53, 54, 55, 56, 57, 58, 59, 60, 105, 107, 109, 124, 156, 161, 169, 189, 197, 204, 219
Conservatoire, Kyiv 136, 137, 145
Cossack Rebellion 208
counteractivities. See *countermovement*
countermovement 49, 50, 99
counterrevolutionaries. See *countermovement*
coup d'état 37, 42, 56, 202
Crimea 42, 97, 129, 133, 203
criminology 108
critical mass 51, 191
Czechoslovakia 36, 37
Dagestan 38
della Porta, Donatella 48, 72
democracy 52, 53, 54, 59, 62, 64, 68, 70, 98, 99, 103, 133, 151, 155, 157, 192, 231, 243
districts 66, 104, 114, 119, 132, 158, 159, 195, 196, 236, 239
Dnipro 133, 134, 141, 145

Donbas 15, 42, 129, 130, 133, 145, 203
Donii, Oleksandr 145
Duma Square, Kyiv 135. See also *Maidan*
Duma, Kyiv 135, 137
Duma, Moscow 87, 190
dynamics of contention 45
Dzerzhinsky, Felix 165
East Germany 36
East Slavic Area Studies 15, 25
East Slavic region 15, 27, 40, 76, 224, 227, 244
Eastern Bloc 36, 37, 38, 58
Eastern Ukraine 15, 42, 163, 203
edges 66, 104, 114, 117, 118, 120, 121, 132, 158, 159, 195, 196
Egypt 68, 158
Egyptian Revolution 70
Eisinger, Peter 46, 123
election fraud 21, 38, 54, 59, 60, 124, 146, 147, 161, 169, 171, 191, 227
Engels Street, Minsk 180, 181, 183
Estonia 57
Estrada Theatre, Moscow 213
EU 21, 25, 42, 53, 58, 95, 97, 106
Euromaidan 49, 56, 57, 76, 89, 98, 99, 102, 105, 129, 130, 131, 132, 133, 139, 142, 143, 148, 150, 151, 154, 191, 200, 203, 228
European Square, Kyiv 134, 136
Faleieva Alley, Moscow 209, 212
Far East 20

Fatherland (Ukrainian political party) 98
Federal Security Service, Russia 205
feminism 35
For Fair Elections 111, 190, 202, 203, 208, 218, 219
framing perspective 45
France 95, 224, 230, 234, 236
France Square, Caracas 224
Freedom for Iuliia demonstrations 148, 151
Freedom Square, Minsk 175, 176, 181
Freedom Square, Yerevan 39
French Revolution 35, 36, 231, 237
Frugal, Sergei 20
Gagauzia 106
gated community 64, 78
Gay Rights Movement 35. See also *LGBT*
Gelebe/Galaba Square 39
geography 27, 61, 62, 65, 68, 72, 97, 98, 157, 191, 193, 194, 199, 227
Georgia 39, 52, 53, 54, 58, 189, 219
Gezi park 133. See also *Taksim Square*
glasnost 37, 145, 160
Golden Gate Station, Kyiv 136, 141
Gongadze, Heorhii 146, 147
Goodsell, Charles 64, 65, 79, 157, 192
Gorbachev, Mikhail 145, 160
Great Britain 83

Great National Assembly Square, Chișinău 39, 86, 89, 90, 105, 106
Great Patriotic War 162, 164, 166, 179. See also *Second World War*
Great Railroad Strike 35
Greater Glade Street, Moscow 87
Greater Iakimanka Street, Moscow 87
Greater Moskva River Bridge, Moscow 209, 212, 215, 220
Greater Ordynka Street, Moscow 87
Greater River Mouth Bridge, Moscow 87
Greater Stone Bridge, Moscow 209, 212, 213, 215, 220
GUM warehouse, Minsk 167, 176
Habermas, Jürgen 61, 62, 78, 99, 157, 192
Harvey, David 63, 67, 72, 157, 192
Heavenly Hundred 148, 149
Hotel Minsk, Minsk 177, 184, 185, 186
Hotel Ukraine, Kyiv 136, 137, 139
House of Government, Kyiv 134
House of Government, Minsk 168, 171, 172, 173, 174, 177, 184, 185, 187
House of Government, Moscow 87, 206, 207
House of Officers, Minsk 179, 181, 183
Hrodna 15
Hungary 36
Huntington, Samuel 52
Ianka Kupala National Theatre, Minsk 179
identity theory 45, 46
Independence Avenue, Minsk 165, 171, 174, 175, 177, 178, 179, 180, 181, 182, 183, 185, 186, 188
Independence Monument, Kyiv 116, 118, 138, 139, 141, 143
Independence Square Station, Kyiv 141
Independence Square, Kyiv 16, 25, 101, 126, 130, 131, 132, 133, 134, 137, 139, 140, 141, 142, 143, 144, 146, 147, 148, 149, 152, 158. See also *Maidan*
Independence Square, Minsk 28, 85, 89, 107, 111, 126, 155, 165, 166, 167, 170, 171, 172, 173, 174, 175, 176, 177, 178, 179, 184, 186, 188
inequality 36, 64, 68, 72, 234, 235, 237, 239
Ingushetia 38
Internet actions. See *social media*
invasion 33, 37, 42, 97, 129, 203
Irkutsk 20
Israel 70, 232
Istanbul 133, 157, 239
Iushchenko, Viktor 147
Jeans Revolution. See *Ploshcha*
Kalinin Square, Kyiv 135, 137
Kalinin Square, Minsk 165, 167, 175
Kalinin, Mikhail 135, 165

Kalinowskyi Square. See *Ploshcha*
Kalinowskyi, Kastus 169
Karl Marx Street, Minsk 176, 178, 181, 184
Kazakhstan 53, 54
kettling 49, 50, 183, 216
Khabarovsk Krai 20
Khreshchatyk Avenue, Kyiv 134, 136, 137, 141, 143, 152, 225
Khreshchatyk Square, Kyiv 135
Khreshchatyk Station, Kyiv 141
Khrushchev, Nikita 36, 137, 204
khrushchevki 204
Kievan Rus' 16, 40, 133, 135
Kontraktova Square, Kyiv 140, 142
Kossuth Lajos Square, Budapest 37
Krasnoyarsk 20
Kremlin, Moscow 20, 37, 55, 87, 190, 201, 205, 206, 207, 209, 211, 215, 217, 219, 220, 237
Kuchma, Leonid 139, 146, 147
Kuropaty Forest 160
Kyievo-Pechers'ka lavra, Kyiv 134, 140
Kyiv 15, 16, 17, 19, 25, 26, 27, 28, 29, 39, 40, 42, 84, 85, 86, 95, 98, 99, 100, 101, 102, 104, 105, 106, 110, 116, 118, 122, 126, 129, 130, 131, 132, 133, 134, 138, 139, 140, 141, 142, 144, 145, 146, 148, 149, 153, 154, 156, 158, 160, 162, 168, 176, 189, 191, 193, 198, 225, 227, 241, 243, 245
Kyrgyzstan 21, 39, 53, 54, 59

landmarks 66, 102, 104, 114, 116, 118, 122, 129, 132, 153, 157, 158, 159, 165, 177, 181, 195, 196, 241
law enforcement agencies 21, 76, 96, 143, 183, 197, 201, 204, 206, 228, 236, 238. See also *policing*
Lefebvre, Henri 63, 157, 192
Leipziger Straße, Berlin 37
Lenin 137, 165, 172, 173, 185
Lenin Monument, Kyiv 137, 145
Lenin Monument, Minsk 172, 177, 184, 185, 186
Lenin Square Station, Minsk 172
Lenin Square, Minsk 172, 177
Lenin Square, Khabarovsk 20
Lesia Ukrainka Boulevard, Kyiv 140, 141
LGBT 158
Likhie devianostye 38, 146, 160
Limonov, Eduard 203, 219, 222
linguistics 31
Lithuania 160
living standard 36, 56, 59, 124
London 37, 66
Lukashenka, Aliaksandr 15, 16, 21, 56, 107, 156, 160, 161, 162, 163, 165, 168, 169, 170, 171, 172, 173, 174, 178, 181, 188, 228
Luzhkov footbridge, Moscow 212, 213, 215
Luzhkov, Yurii 210
Lynch, Kevin 65, 89, 100, 101, 103, 116, 117, 119, 132, 158, 195
Madrid 37

Maidan Nezalezhnosti. See *Independence Square, Kyiv*

Maidan 16, 25, 26, 28, 29, 39, 42, 50, 78, 85, 89, 90, 98, 99, 100, 101, 102, 103, 105, 110, 115, 122, 126, 129, 130, 131, 132, 133, 136, 139, 140, 141, 142, 143, 144, 145, 146, 147, 148, 149, 150, 151, 152, 153, 154, 163, 170, 191, 193, 227, 228, 240, 243. See also *Independence Square, Kyiv*

Mala Zhytomyrs'ka Street, Kyiv 134, 136

Manège Square, Moscow 87, 111, 119, 126, 190, 206, 207, 215

Manoilo, Andrei 56, 57, 59

March of Millions 50, 111, 189, 201, 202, 203, 208, 217, 219, 220, 221

Marshall, Tim 97, 98

May Fourth Movement 35, 70

McFaul, Michael 52, 53, 54, 55, 123, 124, 156, 161, 191, 197, 204, 223

Mexico 37

Middle East 56

Milinkevich, Aliaksandr 158, 159, 168, 169, 170, 171, 175, 180, 182

military intervention 35, 37, 38, 57, 203

Milošević, Slobodan 38, 51

Minsk 17, 19, 21, 23, 27, 28, 39, 40, 42, 84, 85, 89, 90, 93, 95, 100, 101, 104, 106, 107, 110, 111, 114, 118, 124, 126, 155, 156, 158, 159, 160, 162, 164, 165, 167, 168, 169, 170, 171, 172, 173, 174, 175, 176, 177, 178, 179, 181, 182, 184, 185, 186, 187, 188, 190,193, 198, 228, 236, 241, 243, 245

Mitchell, Don 63, 64, 67, 70, 72, 78, 84, 157, 192

Moldova 38, 39, 54, 86, 95, 105, 106, 108, 125

Montenegro 189

Moscow 17, 19, 20, 27, 28, 37, 38, 39, 40, 42, 43, 58, 69, 79, 84, 87, 90, 93, 95, 101, 110, 111, 112, 119, 126, 127, 134, 188, 189, 190, 193, 196, 198, 200, 201, 202, 204, 206, 207, 208, 209, 210, 211, 212, 213, 216, 217, 218, 219, 223, 224, 228, 241, 243, 245

Moskva River, Moscow 190, 208, 209

Musée d'Orsay, Paris 88, 234

Museum of Culture, Moscow 213

music 37, 47, 49, 141, 214

Music Academy, Minsk 179, 181

Naberezhne Highway, Kyiv 140, 141

Nagorno-Karabakh 38, 145

National Assembly, Paris 88, 234

National Bolshevik Party (Russian political party) 203

National Guard, Russia 205
National Library, Minsk 166
nationalism 53
NATO 36, 58, 97
Nazi Germany 135
Near Abroad 54
Nemtsov, Boris 201, 203
Neolithic revolution 63
New York City 49, 70
NGO 55, 60, 147
Niamiha, Minsk 165, 167, 176
nodes 65, 104, 114, 117, 119, 120, 132, 158, 159, 179, 188, 195, 196, 214, 219, 236
Norway 19, 83
Novgorod 35
Novgorod Republic 35
Novosibirsk 20
Occupy Movement 43, 133
October Revolution Square, Kyiv 102, 137, 144, 145, 148
October Square, Minsk 16, 28, 39, 85, 89, 96, 107, 111, 155, 156, 159, 160, 165, 167, 168, 169, 170, 171, 173, 174, 175, 176, 177, 178, 179, 180, 181, 182, 183, 184, 186, 188, 193
October Square, Moscow 207, 220
oligarch 34, 105, 146, 147, 202
Olzak, Susan 36, 156
Omsk 20
Opp, Karl-Dieter 45, 46, 75, 191, 193, 197
Orange Revolution 39, 42, 57, 142, 143, 147, 148, 152, 203
Orthodox Christianity 133, 134
Oslo 22, 78, 84

Other Russia (political party) 219
Palace of Culture, Minsk 178, 179, 181
Palace of the Republic, Minsk 118, 165, 168, 169, 178, 179, 180, 181, 183
Paris 28, 35, 37, 84, 88, 91, 93, 198, 224, 227, 229, 230, 231, 232, 233, 234, 235, 236, 238, 239, 240, 241, 242, 244, 245
Parkinson, John R. 62, 71, 133, 157, 192
Parliament Square, Kyiv 149
paths 65, 67, 104, 114, 117, 119, 120, 132, 158, 159, 177, 178, 179, 183, 195, 196, 212, 213, 214, 234, 236, 239
Pennsylvania Avenue, Washington, D.C. 35
Peremohy Avenue, Kyiv 140, 141
perestroika 37, 145
Piatnitskaia Street, Moscow 87
Ploshcha 21, 39, 160, 169, 170, 171, 172, 175, 180, 184, 186
Poland 36, 133
police brutality 21, 48, 87, 146, 161, 172, 186, 202
policing 48, 49, 59, 78, 86, 87, 88, 102, 116, 117, 121, 125, 155, 157, 188, 198, 200, 206, 216, 220, 223, 236. See also *repertoire of policing*
political environment 46, 47, 52, 59, 60, 72, 73, 98, 109, 110, 112, 113, 120, 123, 124, 126, 194, 196, 197, 199, 201, 206, 208, 223, 228, 229, 230, 237, 238, 239, 240

political geography 62, 63, 72
political opportunity structure 45, 46, 47, 48, 49, 59, 72, 73, 109, 124, 126, 197
political technology 56
Popovic, Srdja 51
Poroshenko, Petro 19, 42, 130, 153
Prague 37
Presidential Administration, Kyiv 130, 134, 153
Presidential Administration, Minsk 167, 174, 179, 181, 182, 183
private space 78
process tracing 84, 108, 109, 193, 194
production of space 64, 70
prospect-refuge theory 61, 68, 73
protest areas 112, 113, 200, 201, 224, 234
proxy war 58
psychology 31, 53, 57, 223
public space 17, 19, 21, 26, 27, 37, 38, 40, 44, 49, 57, 61, 62, 64, 65, 66, 67, 68, 70, 75, 76, 77, 78, 79, 80, 84, 85, 87, 88, 93, 96, 100, 101, 102, 103, 104, 107, 109, 111, 112, 113, 114, 115, 119, 120, 139, 155, 157, 158, 165, 176, 184, 187, 188, 189, 190, 192, 193, 194, 196, 198, 199, 200, 201, 202, 203, 206, 208, 211, 213, 222, 223, 224, 227, 228, 229, 230, 234, 240, 241, 243, 244
public sphere 61, 62, 100, 157, 192
Pugachev, Emelyan 208

Pushkin Square, Moscow 87, 111, 201, 206, 207, 219, 224
Putin, Vladimir 17, 38, 42, 56, 87, 97, 190, 201, 202, 203, 204, 205, 219, 243
Rabin Square, Tel Aviv 71
rational choice theory 46
Red Army 135
Red Church, Minsk 172, 173, 184. See also *Church of Saints Simon and Helena*
Red Square, Moscow 20, 26, 37, 87, 206, 207, 211, 215
religion 97
repertoire of contention 47, 48, 49, 231, 245
Repin Garden Square, Moscow 208
Repin Square, Moscow 208
Repin, Il'ia 208, 210, 215
Republic Metro Station, Paris 234
Republic Square, Paris 28, 88, 91, 93, 229, 230, 231, 232, 233, 234, 235, 236, 238, 244
Resistance (Scb. '*Otpor!*') 50, 51, 156, 191
resource mobilisation perspective 45, 46, 48, 124
Revolution on the Granite 142, 145, 146, 148, 151
Revolution Square, Moscow 87, 190, 206, 207, 219, 224
Revolution Square, Paris 224
Rice, Condoleezza 161, 243
Riga 37, 168, 190
right to the city 61, 63, 157, 192
Ring Road, Kyiv 140

riot police 25, 88, 130, 146, 162, 183, 185, 186, 191, 234
Romania 36, 106
Rome 37
Rose Revolution 39
Routledge, Paul 72
RSCPR 43
Rukh 150, 177
Russia 15, 17, 20, 21, 38, 40, 41, 42, 43, 53, 54, 56, 57, 58, 76, 83, 87, 90, 94, 95, 97, 98, 99, 100, 101, 106, 111, 125, 129, 133, 152, 161, 162, 170, 171, 197, 200, 201, 203, 204, 205, 220, 222, 223
Russian Empire 36, 40, 162, 169
Russian Federation. See *Russia*
Russian White House, Moscow 87
Saint Sophia's Cathedral, Kyiv 134, 136
Sakharov Avenue, Moscow 87, 111, 190, 206, 207, 222, 228
Scandinavia 89
Second World War 52, 106, 107, 137, 162. See also *Great Patriotic War*
Seoul 70
Serafimovich Street, Moscow 209, 212
Serbia 51, 52, 189
Sharp, Gene 50, 51, 56
Shevardnadze 39
Shevchenko Park, Kyiv 148
Shevchenko University, Kyiv 140, 142, 146
Shevchenko, Taras 148
Shushkevich, Stanislaw 158, 161, 177

Siberia 20
Slavic Triangle 40, 41
Social media 43, 44, 76, 90, 92, 205, 214
social movements 28, 36, 37, 38, 45, 46, 47, 48, 50, 72, 76, 191
sociology 27, 45, 81, 83, 101, 109, 189, 191, 223, 242
Sophia Square, Kyiv 148
South America 58
South-Ossetia 38
Soviet 17, 18, 20, 22, 25, 36, 37, 38, 39, 40, 52, 54, 56, 57, 58, 105, 106, 107, 109, 123, 129, 133, 135, 137, 139, 144, 145, 146, 150, 155, 156, 160, 161, 162, 164, 165, 166, 168, 173, 175, 177, 179, 181, 186, 188, 189, 197, 202, 204, 223, 224, 228, 229
Soviet architecture 106, 109, 137, 164, 165, 166, 173, 181
Soviet Street, Minsk 184, 186
Square of Changes, Minsk 21
St. Petersburg 20, 95
Stalin, Joseph 36, 69, 137, 160
Stalitsa Shopping Centre, Minsk 166
Standing Up All Night 232
Statkevich, Mikola 159, 161, 163, 171, 175, 177, 185, 186
Stephan, Maria J. 51, 156, 191, 200
Stonewall Riots 35
Strategy-31 203
structure-cognitive model 46
Svislach river, Minsk 165, 175, 176

Swamp Island Embankment Road, Moscow 209, 211, 212, 213, 220
Swamp Island Street, Moscow 209, 215, 220
Swamp Island, Moscow 87, 208, 211, 213, 220
Swamp Region, Moscow 208, 209
Swamp Square Road, Moscow 209, 212, 218
Swamp Square, Moscow 28, 50, 79, 87, 90, 111, 112, 119, 126, 189, 190, 193, 196, 201, 202, 207, 208, 209, 210, 211, 212, 213, 214, 215, 216, 217, 218, 219, 220, 222, 223, 228
Swedberg, Richard 81, 82, 83, 84, 103
Sweden 83
Tahrir Square, Cairo 68, 70, 71, 158
Tajikistan 54
Taksim Square, Istanbul 70, 157
Tallinn 37
Taras Shevchenko Alley, Kyiv 134
Taras Shevchenko Boulevard, Kyiv 141
Tax Maidan 148, 151
Tbilisi 39
Tel Aviv 71
Theater Square, Moscow 87
thing (popular assembly) 33, 34, 99, 107, 117, 150, 151, 155, 245
Tiananmen Square, Beijing 35, 70, 117, 133, 156, 157, 158
Tilly, Charles 47

Trade Unions Building, Kyiv 136, 137, 138, 139, 145, 153
Transnistria 38, 106
Treaty of the Creation of the USSR 40
Triumph Square, Moscow 111, 126, 190, 206, 207, 219
Tromsø 84
Tsardom of Russia 40
Tucker, Joshua 38, 54, 157, 163, 191, 223
Tulip Revolution 39
Turkmenistan 54
Tverskaia Street, Moscow 87, 127, 201, 206, 207, 222
Twitter Revolution 39
Tymoshenko, Iuliia 147, 148, 151. See also *Freedom for Iuliia demonstrations*
UDAR (Ukrainian political party) 98
Ukraine 15, 17, 19, 25, 37, 38, 39, 40, 41, 42, 43, 49, 52, 53, 54, 56, 57, 59, 76, 83, 95, 97, 98, 99, 100, 101, 102, 105, 106, 107, 108, 125, 129, 130, 133, 136, 142, 143, 144, 145, 146, 147, 148, 151, 152, 153, 156, 160, 162, 189, 200, 203, 219
Ukraine Without Kuchma 146
urban planning 27, 61, 65, 66, 67, 72, 79, 100, 101, 192, 195
urbanism 27, 63, 65, 67, 83, 101, 118, 192, 194, 223, 242
USSR 36, 37, 40. See also *Soviet Union*
Uzbekistan 54
vecha 155. See also *viche, veche*

veche 32, 34, 150. See also *viche*, *vecha*
Verkhni horad, Minsk 169, 176
Verkhovna Rada, Kyiv 134, 136, 142, 145, 149
viche 99, 150. See also *veche*, *vecha*
Vilnius 37, 160, 162, 168, 176
Vladivostok 20
Voronin, Vladimir 39, 203
Vradiivka 148, 151
War in Donbas 129, 130, 203
War in Vietnam 35
Warsaw Pact countries 36, 37, 189
Washington for Jesus 36

Water Bypass Canal, Moscow 190, 208, 209
West, the 16, 37, 42, 50, 53, 54, 55, 56, 58, 59, 61, 88, 98, 133, 156, 160, 169, 203
West Berlin 37
Western Europe 61
Yanukovych, Viktor 98
Yellow Vests 28, 43, 88, 229, 230, 234, 236, 237, 242, 245
Yeltsin, Boris 16, 42, 203
Yerevan 39, 189
Yugoslavia 38, 51, 58
Zamkova Hill, Kyiv 134, 145
Zelenskyi, Volodymyr 15, 42
Zybitskaia Street 167, 176, 179

SOVIET AND POST-SOVIET POLITICS AND SOCIETY
Edited by Dr. Andreas Umland | ISSN 1614-3515

1   Андреас Умланд (ред.) | Воплощение Европейской конвенции по правам человека в России. Философские, юридические и эмпирические исследования | ISBN 3-89821-387-0

2   Christian Wipperfürth | Russland – ein vertrauenswürdiger Partner? Grundlagen, Hintergründe und Praxis gegenwärtiger russischer Außenpolitik | Mit einem Vorwort von Heinz Timmermann | ISBN 3-89821-401-X

3   Manja Hussner | Die Übernahme internationalen Rechts in die russische und deutsche Rechtsordnung. Eine vergleichende Analyse zur Völkerrechtsfreundlichkeit der Verfassungen der Russländischen Föderation und der Bundesrepublik Deutschland | Mit einem Vorwort von Rainer Arnold | ISBN 3-89821-438-9

4   Matthew Tejada | Bulgaria's Democratic Consolidation and the Kozloduy Nuclear Power Plant (KNPP). The Unattainability of Closure | With a foreword by Richard J. Crampton | ISBN 3-89821-439-7

5   Марк Григорьевич Меерович | Квадратные метры, определяющие сознание. Государственная жилищная политика в СССР. 1921 – 1941 гг | ISBN 3-89821-474-5

6   Andrei P. Tsygankov, Pavel A. Tsygankov (Eds.) | New Directions in Russian International Studies | ISBN 3-89821-422-2

7   Марк Григорьевич Меерович | Как власть народ к труду приучала. Жилище в СССР – средство управления людьми. 1917 – 1941 гг. | С предисловием Елены Осокиной | ISBN 3-89821-495-8

8   David J. Galbreath | Nation-Building and Minority Politics in Post-Socialist States. Interests, Influence and Identities in Estonia and Latvia | With a foreword by David J. Smith | ISBN 3-89821-467-2

9   Алексей Юрьевич Безугольный | Народы Кавказа в Вооружённых силах СССР в годы Великой Отечественной войны 1941-1945 гг. | С предисловием Николая Бугая | ISBN 3-89821-475-3

10 Вячеслав Лихачев и Владимир Прибыловский (ред.) | Русское Национальное Единство, 1990-2000. В 2-х томах | ISBN 3-89821-523-7

11 Николай Бугай (ред.) | Народы стран Балтии в условиях сталинизма (1940-е – 1950-е годы). Документированная история | ISBN 3-89821-525-3

12 Ingmar Bredies (Hrsg.) | Zur Anatomie der Orange Revolution in der Ukraine. Wechsel des Elitenregimes oder Triumph des Parlamentarismus? | ISBN 3-89821-524-5

13 Anastasia V. Mitrofanova | The Politicization of Russian Orthodoxy. Actors and Ideas | With a foreword by William C. Gay | ISBN 3-89821-481-8

14 Nathan D. Larson | Alexander Solzhenitsyn and the Russo-Jewish Question | ISBN 3-89821-483-4

15 Guido Houben | Kulturpolitik und Ethnizität. Staatliche Kunstförderung im Russland der neunziger Jahre | Mit einem Vorwort von Gert Weisskirchen | ISBN 3-89821-542-3

16 Leonid Luks | Der russische „Sonderweg"? Aufsätze zur neuesten Geschichte Russlands im europäischen Kontext | ISBN 3-89821-496-6

17 Евгений Мороз | История «Мёртвой воды» – от страшной сказки к большой политике. Политическое неоязычество в постсоветской России | ISBN 3-89821-551-2

18 Александр Верховский и Галина Кожевникова (ред.) | Этническая и религиозная интолерантность в российских СМИ. Результаты мониторинга 2001-2004 гг. | ISBN 3-89821-569-5

19 Christian Ganzer | Sowjetisches Erbe und ukrainische Nation. Das Museum der Geschichte des Zaporoger Kosakentums auf der Insel Chortycja | Mit einem Vorwort von Frank Golczewski | ISBN 3-89821-504-0

20 Эльза-Баир Гучинова | Помнить нельзя забыть. Антропология депортационной травмы калмыков | С предисловием Кэролайн Хамфри | ISBN 3-89821-506-7

21 Юлия Лидерман | Мотивы «проверки» и «испытания» в постсоветской культуре. Советское прошлое в российском кинематографе 1990-х годов | С предисловием Евгения Марголита | ISBN 3-89821-511-3

22 Tanya Lokshina, Ray Thomas, Mary Mayer (Eds.) | The Imposition of a Fake Political Settlement in the Northern Caucasus. The 2003 Chechen Presidential Election | ISBN 3-89821-436-2

23 Timothy McCajor Hall, Rosie Read (Eds.) | Changes in the Heart of Europe. Recent Ethnographies of Czechs, Slovaks, Roma, and Sorbs | With an afterword by Zdeněk Salzmann | ISBN 3-89821-606-3

24　*Christian Autengruber* | Die politischen Parteien in Bulgarien und Rumänien. Eine vergleichende Analyse seit Beginn der 90er Jahre | Mit einem Vorwort von Dorothée de Nève | ISBN 3-89821-476-1

25　*Annette Freyberg-Inan with Radu Cristescu* | The Ghosts in Our Classrooms, or: John Dewey Meets Ceauşescu. The Promise and the Failures of Civic Education in Romania | ISBN 3-89821-416-8

26　*John B. Dunlop* | The 2002 Dubrovka and 2004 Beslan Hostage Crises. A Critique of Russian Counter-Terrorism | With a foreword by Donald N. Jensen | ISBN 3-89821-608-X

27　*Peter Koller* | Das touristische Potenzial von Kam"janec'–Podil's'kyj. Eine fremdenverkehrsgeographische Untersuchung der Zukunftsperspektiven und Maßnahmenplanung zur Destinationsentwicklung des „ukrainischen Rothenburg" | Mit einem Vorwort von Kristiane Klemm | ISBN 3-89821-640-3

28　*Françoise Daucé, Elisabeth Sieca-Kozlowski (Eds.)* | Dedovshchina in the Post-Soviet Military. Hazing of Russian Army Conscripts in a Comparative Perspective | With a foreword by Dale Herspring | ISBN 3-89821-616-0

29　*Florian Strasser* | Zivilgesellschaftliche Einflüsse auf die Orange Revolution. Die gewaltlose Massenbewegung und die ukrainische Wahlkrise 2004 | Mit einem Vorwort von Egbert Jahn | ISBN 3-89821-648-9

30　*Rebecca S. Katz* | The Georgian Regime Crisis of 2003-2004. A Case Study in Post-Soviet Media Representation of Politics, Crime and Corruption | ISBN 3-89821-413-3

31　*Vladimir Kantor* | Willkür oder Freiheit. Beiträge zur russischen Geschichtsphilosophie | Ediert von Dagmar Herrmann sowie mit einem Vorwort versehen von Leonid Luks | ISBN 3-89821-589-X

32　*Laura A. Victoir* | The Russian Land Estate Today. A Case Study of Cultural Politics in Post-Soviet Russia | With a foreword by Priscilla Roosevelt | ISBN 3-89821-426-5

33　*Ivan Katchanovski* | Cleft Countries. Regional Political Divisions and Cultures in Post-Soviet Ukraine and Moldova | With a foreword by Francis Fukuyama | ISBN 3-89821-558-X

34　*Florian Mühlfried* | Postsowjetische Feiern. Das Georgische Bankett im Wandel | Mit einem Vorwort von Kevin Tuite | ISBN 3-89821-601-2

35　*Roger Griffin, Werner Loh, Andreas Umland (Eds.)* | Fascism Past and Present, West and East. An International Debate on Concepts and Cases in the Comparative Study of the Extreme Right | With an afterword by Walter Laqueur | ISBN 3-89821-674-8

36　*Sebastian Schlegel* | Der „Weiße Archipel". Sowjetische Atomstädte 1945-1991 | Mit einem Geleitwort von Thomas Bohn | ISBN 3-89821-679-9

37　*Vyacheslav Likhachev* | Political Anti-Semitism in Post-Soviet Russia. Actors and Ideas in 1991-2003 | Edited and translated from Russian by Eugene Veklerov | ISBN 3-89821-529-6

38　*Josette Baer (Ed.)* | Preparing Liberty in Central Europe. Political Texts from the Spring of Nations 1848 to the Spring of Prague 1968 | With a foreword by Zdeněk V. David | ISBN 3-89821-546-6

39　*Михаил Лукьянов* | Российский консерватизм и реформа, 1907-1914 | С предисловием Марка Д. Стейнберга | ISBN 3-89821-503-2

40　*Nicola Melloni* | Market Without Economy. The 1998 Russian Financial Crisis | With a foreword by Eiji Furukawa | ISBN 3-89821-407-9

41　*Dmitrij Chmelnizki* | Die Architektur Stalins | Bd. 1: Studien zu Ideologie und Stil | Bd. 2: Bilddokumentation | Mit einem Vorwort von Bruno Flierl | ISBN 3-89821-515-6

42　*Katja Yafimava* | Post-Soviet Russian-Belarussian Relationships. The Role of Gas Transit Pipelines | With a foreword by Jonathan P. Stern | ISBN 3-89821-655-1

43　*Boris Chavkin* | Verflechtungen der deutschen und russischen Zeitgeschichte. Aufsätze und Archivfunde zu den Beziehungen Deutschlands und der Sowjetunion von 1917 bis 1991 | Ediert von Markus Edlinger sowie mit einem Vorwort versehen von Leonid Luks | ISBN 3-89821-756-6

44　*Anastasija Grynenko in Zusammenarbeit mit Claudia Dathe* | Die Terminologie des Gerichtswesens der Ukraine und Deutschlands im Vergleich. Eine übersetzungswissenschaftliche Analyse juristischer Fachbegriffe im Deutschen, Ukrainischen und Russischen | Mit einem Vorwort von Ulrich Hartmann | ISBN 3-89821-691-8

45　*Anton Burkov* | The Impact of the European Convention on Human Rights on Russian Law. Legislation and Application in 1996-2006 | With a foreword by Françoise Hampson | ISBN 978-3-89821-639-5

46　*Stina Torjesen, Indra Overland (Eds.)* | International Election Observers in Post-Soviet Azerbaijan. Geopolitical Pawns or Agents of Change? | ISBN 978-3-89821-743-9

47　*Taras Kuzio* | Ukraine – Crimea – Russia. Triangle of Conflict | ISBN 978-3-89821-761-3

48　*Claudia Šabić* | „Ich erinnere mich nicht, aber L'viv!" Zur Funktion kultureller Faktoren für die Institutionalisierung und Entwicklung einer ukrainischen Region | Mit einem Vorwort von Melanie Tatur | ISBN 978-3-89821-752-1

49 *Marlies Bilz* | Tatarstan in der Transformation. Nationaler Diskurs und Politische Praxis 1988-1994 | Mit einem Vorwort von Frank Golczewski | ISBN 978-3-89821-722-4

50 *Марлен Ларюэль (ред.)* | Современные интерпретации русского национализма | ISBN 978-3-89821-795-8

51 *Sonja Schüler* | Die ethnische Dimension der Armut. Roma im postsozialistischen Rumänien | Mit einem Vorwort von Anton Sterbling | ISBN 978-3-89821-776-7

52 *Галина Кожевникова* | Радикальный национализм в России и противодействие ему. Сборник докладов Центра «Сова» за 2004-2007 гг. | С предисловием Александра Верховского | ISBN 978-3-89821-721-7

53 *Галина Кожевникова и Владимир Прибыловский* | Российская власть в биографиях I. Высшие должностные лица РФ в 2004 г. | ISBN 978-3-89821-796-5

54 *Галина Кожевникова и Владимир Прибыловский* | Российская власть в биографиях II. Члены Правительства РФ в 2004 г. | ISBN 978-3-89821-797-2

55 *Галина Кожевникова и Владимир Прибыловский* | Российская власть в биографиях III. Руководители федеральных служб и агентств РФ в 2004 г.| ISBN 978-3-89821-798-9

56 *Ileana Petroniu* | Privatisierung in Transformationsökonomien. Determinanten der Restrukturierungs-Bereitschaft am Beispiel Polens, Rumäniens und der Ukraine | Mit einem Vorwort von Rainer W. Schäfer | ISBN 978-3-89821-790-3

57 *Christian Wipperfürth* | Russland und seine GUS-Nachbarn. Hintergründe, aktuelle Entwicklungen und Konflikte in einer ressourcenreichen Region| ISBN 978-3-89821-801-6

58 *Togzhan Kassenova* | From Antagonism to Partnership. The Uneasy Path of the U.S.-Russian Cooperative Threat Reduction | With a foreword by Christoph Bluth | ISBN 978-3-89821-707-1

59 *Alexander Höllwerth* | Das sakrale eurasische Imperium des Aleksandr Dugin. Eine Diskursanalyse zum postsowjetischen russischen Rechtsextremismus | Mit einem Vorwort von Dirk Uffelmann | ISBN 978-3-89821-813-9

60 *Олег Рябов* | «Россия-Матушка». Национализм, гендер и война в России XX века | С предисловием Елены Гощило | ISBN 978-3-89821-487-2

61 *Ivan Maistrenko* | Borot'bism. A Chapter in the History of the Ukrainian Revolution | With a new Introduction by Chris Ford | Translated by George S. N. Luckyj with the assistance of Ivan L. Rudnytsky | Second, Revised and Expanded Edition ISBN 978-3-8382-1107-7

62 *Maryna Romanets* | Anamorphosic Texts and Reconfigured Visions. Improvised Traditions in Contemporary Ukrainian and Irish Literature | ISBN 978-3-89821-576-3

63 *Paul D'Anieri and Taras Kuzio (Eds.)* | Aspects of the Orange Revolution I. Democratization and Elections in Post-Communist Ukraine | ISBN 978-3-89821-698-2

64 *Bohdan Harasymiw in collaboration with Oleh S. Ilnytzkyj (Eds.)* | Aspects of the Orange Revolution II. Information and Manipulation Strategies in the 2004 Ukrainian Presidential Elections | ISBN 978-3-89821-699-9

65 *Ingmar Bredies, Andreas Umland and Valentin Yakushik (Eds.)* | Aspects of the Orange Revolution III. The Context and Dynamics of the 2004 Ukrainian Presidential Elections | ISBN 978-3-89821-803-0

66 *Ingmar Bredies, Andreas Umland and Valentin Yakushik (Eds.)* | Aspects of the Orange Revolution IV. Foreign Assistance and Civic Action in the 2004 Ukrainian Presidential Elections | ISBN 978-3-89821-808-5

67 *Ingmar Bredies, Andreas Umland and Valentin Yakushik (Eds.)* | Aspects of the Orange Revolution V. Institutional Observation Reports on the 2004 Ukrainian Presidential Elections | ISBN 978-3-89821-809-2

68 *Taras Kuzio (Ed.)* | Aspects of the Orange Revolution VI. Post-Communist Democratic Revolutions in Comparative Perspective | ISBN 978-3-89821-820-7

69 *Tim Bohse* | Autoritarismus statt Selbstverwaltung. Die Transformation der kommunalen Politik in der Stadt Kaliningrad 1990-2005 | Mit einem Geleitwort von Stefan Troebst | ISBN 978-3-89821-782-8

70 *David Rupp* | Die Rußländische Föderation und die russischsprachige Minderheit in Lettland. Eine Fallstudie zur Anwaltspolitik Moskaus gegenüber den russophonen Minderheiten im „Nahen Ausland" von 1991 bis 2002 | Mit einem Vorwort von Helmut Wagner | ISBN 978-3-89821-778-1

71 *Taras Kuzio* | Theoretical and Comparative Perspectives on Nationalism. New Directions in Cross-Cultural and Post-Communist Studies | With a foreword by Paul Robert Magocsi | ISBN 978-3-89821-815-3

72 *Christine Teichmann* | Die Hochschultransformation im heutigen Osteuropa. Kontinuität und Wandel bei der Entwicklung des postkommunistischen Universitätswesens | Mit einem Vorwort von Oskar Anweiler | ISBN 978-3-89821-842-9

73 *Julia Kusznir* | Der politische Einfluss von Wirtschaftseliten in russischen Regionen. Eine Analyse am Beispiel der Erdöl- und Erdgasindustrie, 1992-2005 | Mit einem Vorwort von Wolfgang Eichwede | ISBN 978-3-89821-821-4

74 Alena Vysotskaya | Russland, Belarus und die EU-Osterweiterung. Zur Minderheitenfrage und zum Problem der Freizügigkeit des Personenverkehrs | Mit einem Vorwort von Katlijn Malfliet | ISBN 978-3-89821-822-1

75 Heiko Pleines (Hrsg.) | Corporate Governance in post-sozialistischen Volkswirtschaften | ISBN 978-3-89821-766-8

76 Stefan Ihrig | Wer sind die Moldawier? Rumänismus versus Moldowanismus in Historiographie und Schulbüchern der Republik Moldova, 1991-2006 | Mit einem Vorwort von Holm Sundhaussen | ISBN 978-3-89821-466-7

77 Galina Kozhevnikova in collaboration with Alexander Verkhovsky and Eugene Veklerov | Ultra-Nationalism and Hate Crimes in Contemporary Russia. The 2004-2006 Annual Reports of Moscow's SOVA Center | With a foreword by Stephen D. Shenfield | ISBN 978-3-89821-868-9

78 Florian Küchler | The Role of the European Union in Moldova's Transnistria Conflict | With a foreword by Christopher Hill | ISBN 978-3-89821-850-4

79 Bernd Rechel | The Long Way Back to Europe. Minority Protection in Bulgaria | With a foreword by Richard Crampton | ISBN 978-3-89821-863-4

80 Peter W. Rodgers | Nation, Region and History in Post-Communist Transitions. Identity Politics in Ukraine, 1991-2006 | With a foreword by Vera Tolz | ISBN 978-3-89821-903-7

81 Stephanie Solywoda | The Life and Work of Semen L. Frank. A Study of Russian Religious Philosophy | With a foreword by Philip Walters | ISBN 978-3-89821-457-5

82 Vera Sokolova | Cultural Politics of Ethnicity. Discourses on Roma in Communist Czechoslovakia | ISBN 978-3-89821-864-1

83 Natalya Shevchik Ketenci | Kazakhstani Enterprises in Transition. The Role of Historical Regional Development in Kazakhstan's Post-Soviet Economic Transformation | ISBN 978-3-89821-831-3

84 Martin Malek, Anna Schor-Tschudnowskaja (Hgg.) | Europa im Tschetschenienkrieg. Zwischen politischer Ohnmacht und Gleichgültigkeit | Mit einem Vorwort von Lipchan Basajewa | ISBN 978-3-89821-676-0

85 Stefan Meister | Das postsowjetische Universitätswesen zwischen nationalem und internationalem Wandel. Die Entwicklung der regionalen Hochschule in Russland als Gradmesser der Systemtransformation | Mit einem Vorwort von Joan DeBardeleben | ISBN 978-3-89821-891-7

86 Konstantin Sheiko in collaboration with Stephen Brown | Nationalist Imaginings of the Russian Past. Anatolii Fomenko and the Rise of Alternative History in Post-Communist Russia | With a foreword by Donald Ostrowski | ISBN 978-3-89821-915-0

87 Sabine Jenni | Wie stark ist das „Einige Russland"? Zur Parteibindung der Eliten und zum Wahlerfolg der Machtpartei im Dezember 2007 | Mit einem Vorwort von Klaus Armingeon | ISBN 978-3-89821-961-7

88 Thomas Borén | Meeting-Places of Transformation. Urban Identity, Spatial Representations and Local Politics in Post-Soviet St Petersburg | ISBN 978-3-89821-739-2

89 Aygul Ashirova | Stalinismus und Stalin-Kult in Zentralasien. Turkmenistan 1924-1953 | Mit einem Vorwort von Leonid Luks | ISBN 978-3-89821-987-7

90 Leonid Luks | Freiheit oder imperiale Größe? Essays zu einem russischen Dilemma | ISBN 978-3-8382-0011-8

91 Christopher Gilley | The 'Change of Signposts' in the Ukrainian Emigration. A Contribution to the History of Sovietophilism in the 1920s | With a foreword by Frank Golczewski | ISBN 978-3-89821-965-5

92 Philipp Casula, Jeronim Perovic (Eds.) | Identities and Politics During the Putin Presidency. The Discursive Foundations of Russia's Stability | With a foreword by Heiko Haumann | ISBN 978-3-8382-0015-6

93 Marcel Viëtor | Europa und die Frage nach seinen Grenzen im Osten. Zur Konstruktion ‚europäischer Identität' in Geschichte und Gegenwart | Mit einem Vorwort von Albrecht Lehmann | ISBN 978-3-8382-0045-3

94 Ben Hellman, Andrei Rogachevskii | Filming the Unfilmable. Casper Wrede's 'One Day in the Life of Ivan Denisovich' | Second, Revised and Expanded Edition | ISBN 978-3-8382-0044-6

95 Eva Fuchslocher | Vaterland, Sprache, Glaube. Orthodoxie und Nationenbildung am Beispiel Georgiens | Mit einem Vorwort von Christina von Braun | ISBN 978-3-89821-884-9

96 Vladimir Kantor | Das Westlertum und der Weg Russlands. Zur Entwicklung der russischen Literatur und Philosophie | Ediert von Dagmar Herrmann | Mit einem Beitrag von Nikolaus Lobkowicz | ISBN 978-3-8382-0102-3

97 Kamran Musayev | Die postsowjetische Transformation im Baltikum und Südkaukasus. Eine vergleichende Untersuchung der politischen Entwicklung Lettlands und Aserbaidschans 1985-2009 | Mit einem Vorwort von Leonid Luks | Ediert von Sandro Henschel | ISBN 978-3-8382-0103-0

98 Tatiana Zhurzhenko | Borderlands into Bordered Lands. Geopolitics of Identity in Post-Soviet Ukraine | With a foreword by Dieter Segert | ISBN 978-3-8382-0042-2

99 *Кирилл Галушко, Лидия Смола (ред.)* | Пределы падения – варианты украинского будущего. Аналитико-прогностические исследования | ISBN 978-3-8382-0148-1

100 *Michael Minkenberg (Ed.)* | Historical Legacies and the Radical Right in Post-Cold War Central and Eastern Europe | With an afterword by Sabrina P. Ramet | ISBN 978-3-8382-0124-5

101 *David-Emil Wickström* | Rocking St. Petersburg. Transcultural Flows and Identity Politics in the St. Petersburg Popular Music Scene | With a foreword by Yngvar B. Steinholt | Second, Revised and Expanded Edition | ISBN 978-3-8382-0100-9

102 *Eva Zabka* | Eine neue „Zeit der Wirren"? Der spät- und postsowjetische Systemwandel 1985-2000 im Spiegel russischer gesellschaftspolitischer Diskurse | Mit einem Vorwort von Margareta Mommsen | ISBN 978-3-8382-0161-0

103 *Ulrike Ziemer* | Ethnic Belonging, Gender and Cultural Practices. Youth Identitites in Contemporary Russia | With a foreword by Anoop Nayak | ISBN 978-3-8382-0152-8

104 *Ksenia Chepikova* | ‚Einiges Russland' - eine zweite KPdSU? Aspekte der Identitätskonstruktion einer postsowjetischen „Partei der Macht" | Mit einem Vorwort von Torsten Oppelland | ISBN 978-3-8382-0311-9

105 *Леонид Люкс* | Западничество или евразийство? Демократия или идеократия? Сборник статей об исторических дилеммах России | С предисловием Владимира Кантора | ISBN 978-3-8382-0211-2

106 *Anna Dost* | Das russische Verfassungsrecht auf dem Weg zum Föderalismus und zurück. Zum Konflikt von Rechtsnormen und -wirklichkeit in der Russländischen Föderation von 1991 bis 2009 | Mit einem Vorwort von Alexander Blankenagel | ISBN 978-3-8382-0292-1

107 *Philipp Herzog* | Sozialistische Völkerfreundschaft, nationaler Widerstand oder harmloser Zeitvertreib? Zur politischen Funktion der Volkskunst im sowjetischen Estland | Mit einem Vorwort von Andreas Kappeler | ISBN 978-3-8382-0216-7

108 *Marlène Laruelle (Ed.)* | Russian Nationalism, Foreign Policy, and Identity Debates in Putin's Russia. New Ideological Patterns after the Orange Revolution | ISBN 978-3-8382-0325-6

109 *Michail Logvinov* | Russlands Kampf gegen den internationalen Terrorismus. Eine kritische Bestandsaufnahme des Bekämpfungsansatzes | Mit einem Geleitwort von Hans-Henning Schröder und einem Vorwort von Eckhard Jesse | ISBN 978-3-8382-0329-4

110 *John B. Dunlop* | The Moscow Bombings of September 1999. Examinations of Russian Terrorist Attacks at the Onset of Vladimir Putin's Rule | Second, Revised and Expanded Edition | ISBN 978-3-8382-0388-1

111 *Андрей А. Ковалёв* | Свидетельство из-за кулис российской политики I. Можно ли делать добро из зла? (Воспоминания и размышления о последних советских и первых послесоветских годах) | With a foreword by Peter Reddaway | ISBN 978-3-8382-0302-7

112 *Андрей А. Ковалёв* | Свидетельство из-за кулис российской политики II. Угроза для себя и окружающих (Наблюдения и предостережения относительно происходящего после 2000 г.) | ISBN 978-3-8382-0303-4

113 *Bernd Kappenberg* | Zeichen setzen für Europa. Der Gebrauch europäischer lateinischer Sonderzeichen in der deutschen Öffentlichkeit | Mit einem Vorwort von Peter Schlobinski | ISBN 978-3-89821-749-1

114 *Ivo Mijnssen* | The Quest for an Ideal Youth in Putin's Russia I. Back to Our Future! History, Modernity, and Patriotism according to Nashi, 2005-2013 | With a foreword by Jeronim Perović | Second, Revised and Expanded Edition | ISBN 978-3-8382-0368-3

115 *Jussi Lassila* | The Quest for an Ideal Youth in Putin's Russia II. The Search for Distinctive Conformism in the Political Communication of Nashi, 2005-2009 | With a foreword by Kirill Postoutenko | Second, Revised and Expanded Edition | ISBN 978-3-8382-0415-4

116 *Valerio Trabandt* | Neue Nachbarn, gute Nachbarschaft? Die EU als internationaler Akteur am Beispiel ihrer Demokratieförderung in Belarus und der Ukraine 2004-2009 | Mit einem Vorwort von Jutta Joachim | ISBN 978-3-8382-0437-6

117 *Fabian Pfeiffer* | Estlands Außen- und Sicherheitspolitik I. Der estnische Atlantizismus nach der wiedererlangten Unabhängigkeit 1991-2004 | Mit einem Vorwort von Helmut Hubel | ISBN 978-3-8382-0127-6

118 *Jana Podßuweit* | Estlands Außen- und Sicherheitspolitik II. Handlungsoptionen eines Kleinstaates im Rahmen seiner EU-Mitgliedschaft (2004-2008) | Mit einem Vorwort von Helmut Hubel | ISBN 978-3-8382-0440-6

119 *Karin Pointner* | Estlands Außen- und Sicherheitspolitik III. Eine gedächtnispolitische Analyse estnischer Entwicklungskooperation 2006-2010 | Mit einem Vorwort von Karin Liebhart | ISBN 978-3-8382-0435-2

120 *Ruslana Vovk* | Die Offenheit der ukrainischen Verfassung für das Völkerrecht und die europäische Integration | Mit einem Vorwort von Alexander Blankenagel | ISBN 978-3-8382-0481-9

121 *Mykhaylo Banakh* | Die Relevanz der Zivilgesellschaft bei den postkommunistischen Transformationsprozessen in mittel- und osteuropäischen Ländern. Das Beispiel der spät- und postsowjetischen Ukraine 1986-2009 | Mit einem Vorwort von Gerhard Simon | ISBN 978-3-8382-0499-4

122 *Michael Moser* | Language Policy and the Discourse on Languages in Ukraine under President Viktor Yanukovych (25 February 2010–28 October 2012) | ISBN 978-3-8382-0497-0 (Paperback edition) | ISBN 978-3-8382-0507-6 (Hardcover edition)

123 *Nicole Krome* | Russischer Netzwerkkapitalismus Restrukturierungsprozesse in der Russischen Föderation am Beispiel des Luftfahrtunternehmens „Aviastar" | Mit einem Vorwort von Petra Stykow | ISBN 978-3-8382-0534-2

124 *David R. Marples* | 'Our Glorious Past'. Lukashenka's Belarus and the Great Patriotic War | ISBN 978-3-8382-0574-8 (Paperback edition) | ISBN 978-3-8382-0675-2 (Hardcover edition)

125 *Ulf Walther* | Russlands „neuer Adel". Die Macht des Geheimdienstes von Gorbatschow bis Putin | Mit einem Vorwort von Hans-Georg Wieck | ISBN 978-3-8382-0584-7

126 *Simon Geissbühler (Hrsg.)* | Kiew – Revolution 3.0. Der Euromaidan 2013/14 und die Zukunftsperspektiven der Ukraine | ISBN 978-3-8382-0581-6 (Paperback edition) | ISBN 978-3-8382-0681-3 (Hardcover edition)

127 *Andrey Makarychev* | Russia and the EU in a Multipolar World. Discourses, Identities, Norms | With a foreword by Klaus Segbers | ISBN 978-3-8382-0629-5

128 *Roland Scharff* | Kasachstan als postsowjetischer Wohlfahrtsstaat. Die Transformation des sozialen Schutzsystems | Mit einem Vorwort von Joachim Ahrens | ISBN 978-3-8382-0622-6

129 *Katja Grupp* | Bild Lücke Deutschland. Kaliningrader Studierende sprechen über Deutschland | Mit einem Vorwort von Martin Schulz | ISBN 978-3-8382-0552-6

130 *Konstantin Sheiko, Stephen Brown* | History as Therapy. Alternative History and Nationalist Imaginings in Russia, 1991-2014 | ISBN 978-3-8382-0665-3

131 *Elisa Kriza* | Alexander Solzhenitsyn: Cold War Icon, Gulag Author, Russian Nationalist? A Study of the Western Reception of his Literary Writings, Historical Interpretations, and Political Ideas | With a foreword by Andrei Rogatchevski | ISBN 978-3-8382-0589-2 (Paperback edition) | ISBN 978-3-8382-0690-5 (Hardcover edition)

132 *Serghei Golunov* | The Elephant in the Room. Corruption and Cheating in Russian Universities | ISBN 978-3-8382-0570-0

133 *Manja Hussner, Rainer Arnold (Hgg.)* | Verfassungsgerichtsbarkeit in Zentralasien I. Sammlung von Verfassungstexten | ISBN 978-3-8382-0595-3

134 *Nikolay Mitrokhin* | Die „Russische Partei". Die Bewegung der russischen Nationalisten in der UdSSR 1953-1985 | Aus dem Russischen übertragen von einem Übersetzerteam unter der Leitung von Larisa Schippel | ISBN 978-3-8382-0024-8

135 *Manja Hussner, Rainer Arnold (Hgg.)* | Verfassungsgerichtsbarkeit in Zentralasien II. Sammlung von Verfassungstexten | ISBN 978-3-8382-0597-7

136 *Manfred Zeller* | Das sowjetische Fieber. Fußballfans im poststalinistischen Vielvölkerreich | Mit einem Vorwort von Nikolaus Katzer | ISBN 978-3-8382-0757-5

137 *Kristin Schreiter* | Stellung und Entwicklungspotential zivilgesellschaftlicher Gruppen in Russland. Menschenrechtsorganisationen im Vergleich | ISBN 978-3-8382-0673-8

138 *David R. Marples, Frederick V. Mills (Eds.)* | Ukraine's Euromaidan. Analyses of a Civil Revolution | ISBN 978-3-8382-0660-8

139 *Bernd Kappenberg* | Setting Signs for Europe. Why Diacritics Matter for European Integration | With a foreword by Peter Schlobinski | ISBN 978-3-8382-0663-9

140 *René Lenz* | Internationalisierung, Kooperation und Transfer. Externe bildungspolitische Akteure in der Russischen Föderation | Mit einem Vorwort von Frank Ettrich | ISBN 978-3-8382-0751-3

141 *Juri Plusnin, Yana Zausaeva, Natalia Zhidkevich, Artemy Pozanenko* | Wandering Workers. Mores, Behavior, Way of Life, and Political Status of Domestic Russian Labor Migrants | Translated by Julia Kazantseva | ISBN 978-3-8382-0653-0

142 *David J. Smith (Eds.)* | Latvia – A Work in Progress? 100 Years of State- and Nation-Building | ISBN 978-3-8382-0648-6

143 *Инна Чувычкина (ред.)* | Экспортные нефте- и газопроводы на постсоветском пространстве. Анализ трубопроводной политики в свете теории международных отношений | ISBN 978-3-8382-0822-0

144 *Johann Zajaczkowski* | Russland – eine pragmatische Großmacht? Eine rollentheoretische Untersuchung russischer Außenpolitik am Beispiel der Zusammenarbeit mit den USA nach 9/11 und des Georgienkrieges von 2008 | Mit einem Vorwort von Siegfried Schieder | ISBN 978-3-8382-0837-4

145 *Boris Popivanov* | Changing Images of the Left in Bulgaria. The Challenge of Post-Communism in the Early 21st Century | ISBN 978-3-8382-0667-7

146 *Lenka Krátká* | A History of the Czechoslovak Ocean Shipping Company 1948-1989. How a Small, Landlocked Country Ran Maritime Business During the Cold War | ISBN 978-3-8382-0666-0

147 *Alexander Sergunin* | Explaining Russian Foreign Policy Behavior. Theory and Practice | ISBN 978-3-8382-0752-0

148 *Darya Malyutina* | Migrant Friendships in a Super-Diverse City. Russian-Speakers and their Social Relationships in London in the 21st Century | With a foreword by Claire Dwyer | ISBN 978-3-8382-0652-3

149 *Alexander Sergunin, Valery Konyshev* | Russia in the Arctic. Hard or Soft Power? | ISBN 978-3-8382-0753-7

150 *John J. Maresca* | Helsinki Revisited. A Key U.S. Negotiator's Memoirs on the Development of the CSCE into the OSCE | With a foreword by Hafiz Pashayev | ISBN 978-3-8382-0852-7

151 *Jardar Østbø* | The New Third Rome. Readings of a Russian Nationalist Myth | With a foreword by Pål Kolstø | ISBN 978-3-8382-0870-1

152 *Simon Kordonsky* | Socio-Economic Foundations of the Russian Post-Soviet Regime. The Resource-Based Economy and Estate-Based Social Structure of Contemporary Russia | With a foreword by Svetlana Barsukova | ISBN 978-3-8382-0775-9

153 *Duncan Leitch* | Assisting Reform in Post-Communist Ukraine 2000–2012. The Illusions of Donors and the Disillusion of Beneficiaries | With a foreword by Kataryna Wolczuk | ISBN 978-3-8382-0844-2

154 *Abel Polese* | Limits of a Post-Soviet State. How Informality Replaces, Renegotiates, and Reshapes Governance in Contemporary Ukraine | With a foreword by Colin Williams | ISBN 978-3-8382-0845-9

155 *Mikhail Suslov (Ed.)* | Digital Orthodoxy in the Post-Soviet World. The Russian Orthodox Church and Web 2.0 | With a foreword by Father Cyril Hovorun | ISBN 978-3-8382-0871-8

156 *Leonid Luks* | Zwei „Sonderwege"? Russisch-deutsche Parallelen und Kontraste (1917-2014). Vergleichende Essays | ISBN 978-3-8382-0823-7

157 *Vladimir V. Karacharovskiy, Ovsey I. Shkaratan, Gordey A. Yastrebov* | Towards a New Russian Work Culture. Can Western Companies and Expatriates Change Russian Society? | With a foreword by Elena N. Danilova | Translated by Julia Kazantseva | ISBN 978-3-8382-0902-9

158 *Edmund Griffiths* | Aleksandr Prokhanov and Post-Soviet Esotericism | ISBN 978-3-8382-0903-6

159 *Timm Beichelt, Susann Worschech (Eds.)* | Transnational Ukraine? Networks and Ties that Influence(d) Contemporary Ukraine | ISBN 978-3-8382-0944-9

160 *Mieste Hotopp-Riecke* | Die Tataren der Krim zwischen Assimilation und Selbstbehauptung. Der Aufbau des krimtatarischen Bildungswesens nach Deportation und Heimkehr (1990-2005) | Mit einem Vorwort von Swetlana Czerwonnaja | ISBN 978-3-89821-940-2

161 *Olga Bertelsen (Ed.)* | Revolution and War in Contemporary Ukraine. The Challenge of Change | ISBN 978-3-8382-1016-2

162 *Natalya Ryabinska* | Ukraine's Post-Communist Mass Media. Between Capture and Commercialization | With a foreword by Marta Dyczok | ISBN 978-3-8382-1011-7

163 *Alexandra Cotofana, James M. Nyce (Eds.)* | Religion and Magic in Socialist and Post-Socialist Contexts. Historic and Ethnographic Case Studies of Orthodoxy, Heterodoxy, and Alternative Spirituality | With a foreword by Patrick L. Michelson | ISBN 978-3-8382-0989-0

164 *Nozima Akhrarkhodjaeva* | The Instrumentalisation of Mass Media in Electoral Authoritarian Regimes. Evidence from Russia's Presidential Election Campaigns of 2000 and 2008 | ISBN 978-3-8382-1013-1

165 *Yulia Krasheninnikova* | Informal Healthcare in Contemporary Russia. Sociographic Essays on the Post-Soviet Infrastructure for Alternative Healing Practices | ISBN 978-3-8382-0970-8

166 *Peter Kaiser* | Das Schachbrett der Macht. Die Handlungsspielräume eines sowjetischen Funktionärs unter Stalin am Beispiel des Generalsekretärs des Komsomol Aleksandr Kosarev (1929-1938) | Mit einem Vorwort von Dietmar Neutatz | ISBN 978-3-8382-1052-0

167 *Oksana Kim* | The Effects and Implications of Kazakhstan's Adoption of International Financial Reporting Standards. A Resource Dependence Perspective | With a foreword by Svetlana Vlady | ISBN 978-3-8382-0987-6

168 *Anna Sanina* | Patriotic Education in Contemporary Russia. Sociological Studies in the Making of the Post-Soviet Citizen | With a foreword by Anna Oldfield | ISBN 978-3-8382-0993-7

169 *Rudolf Wolters* | Spezialist in Sibirien Faksimile der 1933 erschienenen ersten Ausgabe | Mit einem Vorwort von Dmitrij Chmelnizki | ISBN 978-3-8382-0515-1

170 *Michal Vít, Magdalena M. Baran (Eds.)* | Transregional versus National Perspectives on Contemporary Central European History. Studies on the Building of Nation-States and Their Cooperation in the 20th and 21st Century | With a foreword by Petr Vágner | ISBN 978-3-8382-1015-5

171 *Philip Gamaghelyan* | Conflict Resolution Beyond the International Relations Paradigm. Evolving Designs as a Transformative Practice in Nagorno-Karabakh and Syria | With a foreword by Susan Allen | ISBN 978-3-8382-1057-5

172 *Maria Shagina* | Joining a Prestigious Club. Cooperation with Europarties and Its Impact on Party Development in Georgia, Moldova, and Ukraine 2004–2015 | With a foreword by Kataryna Wolczuk | ISBN 978-3-8382-1084-1

173 *Alexandra Cotofana, James M. Nyce (Eds.)* | Religion and Magic in Socialist and Post-Socialist Contexts II. Baltic, Eastern European, and Post-USSR Case Studies | With a foreword by Anita Stasulane | ISBN 978-3-8382-0990-6

174 *Barbara Kunz* | Kind Words, Cruise Missiles, and Everything in Between. The Use of Power Resources in U.S. Policies towards Poland, Ukraine, and Belarus 1989–2008 | With a foreword by William Hill | ISBN 978-3-8382-1065-0

175 *Eduard Klein* | Bildungskorruption in Russland und der Ukraine. Eine komparative Analyse der Performanz staatlicher Antikorruptionsmaßnahmen im Hochschulsektor am Beispiel universitärer Aufnahmeprüfungen | Mit einem Vorwort von Heiko Pleines | ISBN 978-3-8382-0995-1

176 *Markus Soldner* | Politischer Kapitalismus im postsowjetischen Russland. Die politische, wirtschaftliche und mediale Transformation in den 1990er Jahren | Mit einem Vorwort von Wolfgang Ismayr | ISBN 978-3-8382-1222-7

177 *Anton Oleinik* | Building Ukraine from Within. A Sociological, Institutional, and Economic Analysis of a Nation-State in the Making | ISBN 978-3-8382-1150-3

178 *Peter Rollberg, Marlene Laruelle (Eds.)* | Mass Media in the Post-Soviet World. Market Forces, State Actors, and Political Manipulation in the Informational Environment after Communism | ISBN 978-3-8382-1116-9

179 *Mikhail Minakov* | Development and Dystopia. Studies in Post-Soviet Ukraine and Eastern Europe | With a foreword by Alexander Etkind | ISBN 978-3-8382-1112-1

180 *Aijan Sharshenova* | The European Union's Democracy Promotion in Central Asia. A Study of Political Interests, Influence, and Development in Kazakhstan and Kyrgyzstan in 2007–2013 | With a foreword by Gordon Crawford | ISBN 978-3-8382-1151-0

181 *Andrey Makarychev, Alexandra Yatsyk (Eds.)* | Boris Nemtsov and Russian Politics. Power and Resistance | With a foreword by Zhanna Nemtsova | ISBN 978-3-8382-1122-0

182 *Sophie Falsini* | The Euromaidan's Effect on Civil Society. Why and How Ukrainian Social Capital Increased after the Revolution of Dignity | With a foreword by Susann Worschech | ISBN 978-3-8382-1131-2

183 *Valentyna Romanova, Andreas Umland (Eds.)* | Ukraine's Decentralization. Challenges and Implications of the Local Governance Reform after the Euromaidan Revolution | ISBN 978-3-8382-1162-6

184 *Leonid Luks* | A Fateful Triangle. Essays on Contemporary Russian, German and Polish History | ISBN 978-3-8382-1143-5

185 *John B. Dunlop* | The February 2015 Assassination of Boris Nemtsov and the Flawed Trial of his Alleged Killers. An Exploration of Russia's "Crime of the 21st Century" | ISBN 978-3-8382-1188-6

186 *Vasile Rotaru* | Russia, the EU, and the Eastern Partnership. Building Bridges or Digging Trenches? | ISBN 978-3-8382-1134-3

187 *Marina Lebedeva* | Russian Studies of International Relations. From the Soviet Past to the Post-Cold-War Present | With a foreword by Andrei P. Tsygankov | ISBN 978-3-8382-0851-0

188 *Tomasz Stępniewski, George Soroka (Eds.)* | Ukraine after Maidan. Revisiting Domestic and Regional Security | ISBN 978-3-8382-1075-9

189 *Petar Cholakov* | Ethnic Entrepreneurs Unmasked. Political Institutions and Ethnic Conflicts in Contemporary Bulgaria | ISBN 978-3-8382-1189-3

190 *A. Salem, G. Hazeldine, D. Morgan (Eds.)* | Higher Education in Post-Communist States. Comparative and Sociological Perspectives | ISBN 978-3-8382-1183-1

191 *Igor Torbakov* | After Empire. Nationalist Imagination and Symbolic Politics in Russia and Eurasia in the Twentieth and Twenty-First Century | With a foreword by Serhii Plokhy | ISBN 978-3-8382-1217-3

192 *Aleksandr Burakovskiy* | Jewish-Ukrainian Relations in Late and Post-Soviet Ukraine. Articles, Lectures and Essays from 1986 to 2016 | ISBN 978-3-8382-1210-4

193 *Natalia Shapovalova, Olga Burlyuk (Eds.)* | Civil Society in Post-Euromaidan Ukraine. From Revolution to Consolidation | With a foreword by Richard Youngs | ISBN 978-3-8382-1216-6

194 *Franz Preissler* | Positionsverteidigung, Imperialismus oder Irredentismus? Russland und die „Russischsprachigen", 1991–2015 | ISBN 978-3-8382-1262-3

195 *Marian Madeła* | Der Reformprozess in der Ukraine 2014-2017. Eine Fallstudie zur Reform der öffentlichen Verwaltung | Mit einem Vorwort von Martin Malek | ISBN 978-3-8382-1266-1

196 *Anke Giesen* | „Wie kann denn der Sieger ein Verbrecher sein?" Eine diskursanalytische Untersuchung der russlandweiten Debatte über Konzept und Verstaatlichungsprozess der Lagergedenkstätte „Perm'-36" im Ural | ISBN 978-3-8382-1284-5

197 *Alla Leukavets* | The Integration Policies of Belarus and Ukraine vis-à-vis the EU and Russia. A Comparative Case Study Through the Prism of a Two-Level Game Approach | ISBN 978-3-8382-1247-0

198 *Oksana Kim* | The Development and Challenges of Russian Corporate Governance I. The Roles and Functions of Boards of Directors | With a foreword by Sheila M. Puffer | ISBN 978-3-8382-1287-6

199 *Thomas D. Grant* | International Law and the Post-Soviet Space I. Essays on Chechnya and the Baltic States | With a foreword by Stephen M. Schwebel | ISBN 978-3-8382-1279-1

200 *Thomas D. Grant* | International Law and the Post-Soviet Space II. Essays on Ukraine, Intervention, and Non-Proliferation | ISBN 978-3-8382-1280-7

201 *Slavomír Michálek, Michal Štefansky* | The Age of Fear. The Cold War and Its Influence on Czechoslovakia 1945–1968 | ISBN 978-3-8382-1285-2

202 *Iulia-Sabina Joja* | Romania's Strategic Culture 1990–2014. Continuity and Change in a Post-Communist Country's Evolution of National Interests and Security Policies | With a foreword by Heiko Biehl | ISBN 978-3-8382-1286-9

203 *Andrei Rogatchevski, Yngvar B. Steinholt, Arve Hansen, David-Emil Wickström* | War of Songs. Popular Music and Recent Russia-Ukraine Relations | With a foreword by Artemy Troitsky | ISBN 978-3-8382-1173-2

204 *Maria Lipman (Ed.)* | Russian Voices on Post-Crimea Russia. An Almanac of Counterpoint Essays from 2015–2018 | ISBN 978-3-8382-1251-7

205 *Ksenia Maksimovtsova* | Language Conflicts in Contemporary Estonia, Latvia, and Ukraine. A Comparative Exploration of Discourses in Post-Soviet Russian-Language Digital Media | With a foreword by Ammon Cheskin | ISBN 978-3-8382-1282-1

206 *Michal Vít* | The EU's Impact on Identity Formation in East-Central Europe between 2004 and 2013. Perceptions of the Nation and Europe in Political Parties of the Czech Republic, Poland, and Slovakia | With a foreword by Andrea Pető | ISBN 978-3-8382-1275-3

207 *Per A. Rudling* | Tarnished Heroes. The Organization of Ukrainian Nationalists in the Memory Politics of Post-Soviet Ukraine | ISBN 978-3-8382-0999-9

208 *Kaja Gadowska, Peter Solomon (Eds.)* | Legal Change in Post-Communist States. Progress, Reversions, Explanations | ISBN 978-3-8382-1312-5

209 *Paweł Kowal, Georges Mink, Iwona Reichardt (Eds.)* | Three Revolutions: Mobilization and Change in Contemporary Ukraine I. Theoretical Aspects and Analyses on Religion, Memory, and Identity | ISBN 978-3-8382-1321-7

210 *Paweł Kowal, Georges Mink, Adam Reichardt, Iwona Reichardt (Eds.)* | Three Revolutions: Mobilization and Change in Contemporary Ukraine II. An Oral History of the Revolution on Granite, Orange Revolution, and Revolution of Dignity | ISBN 978-3-8382-1323-1

211 *Li Bennich-Björkman, Sergiy Kurbatov (Eds.)* | When the Future Came. The Collapse of the USSR and the Emergence of National Memory in Post-Soviet History Textbooks | ISBN 978-3-8382-1335-4

212 *Olga R. Gulina* | Migration as a (Geo-)Political Challenge in the Post-Soviet Space. Border Regimes, Policy Choices, Visa Agendas | With a foreword by Nils Muižnieks | ISBN 978-3-8382-1338-5

213 *Sanna Turoma, Kaarina Aitamurto, Slobodanka Vladiv-Glover (Eds.)* | Religion, Expression, and Patriotism in Russia. Essays on Post-Soviet Society and the State. ISBN 978-3-8382-1346-0

214 *Vasif Huseynov* | Geopolitical Rivalries in the "Common Neighborhood". Russia's Conflict with the West, Soft Power, and Neoclassical Realism | With a foreword by Nicholas Ross Smith | ISBN 978-3-8382-1277-7

215 *Mikhail Suslov* | Geopolitical Imagination. Ideology and Utopia in Post-Soviet Russia | With a foreword by Mark Bassin | ISBN 978-3-8382-1361-3

216 *Alexander Etkind, Mikhail Minakov (Eds.)* | Ideology after Union. Political Doctrines, Discourses, and Debates in Post-Soviet Societies | ISBN 978-3-8382-1388-0

217 *Jakob Mischke, Oleksandr Zabirko (Hgg.)* | Protestbewegungen im langen Schatten des Kreml. Aufbruch und Resignation in Russland und der Ukraine | ISBN 978-3-8382-0926-5

218 *Oksana Huss* | How Corruption and Anti-Corruption Policies Sustain Hybrid Regimes. Strategies of Political Domination under Ukraine's Presidents in 1994-2014 | With a foreword by Tobias Debiel and Andrea Gawrich | ISBN 978-3-8382-1430-6

219 *Dmitry Travin, Vladimir Gel'man, Otar Marganiya* | The Russian Path. Ideas, Interests, Institutions, Illusions | With a foreword by Vladimir Ryzhkov | ISBN 978-3-8382-1421-4

220 *Gergana Dimova* | Political Uncertainty. A Comparative Exploration | With a foreword by Todor Yalamov and Rumena Filipova | ISBN 978-3-8382-1385-9

221 *Torben Waschke* | Russland in Transition. Geopolitik zwischen Raum, Identität und Machtinteressen | Mit einem Vorwort von Andreas Dittmann | ISBN 978-3-8382-1480-1

222 *Steven Jobbitt, Zsolt Bottlik, Marton Berki (Eds.)* | Power and Identity in the Post-Soviet Realm. Geographies of Ethnicity and Nationality after 1991 | ISBN 978-3-8382-1399-6

223 *Daria Buteiko* | Erinnerungsort. Ort des Gedenkens, der Erholung oder der Einkehr? Kommunismus-Erinnerung am Beispiel der Gedenkstätte Berliner Mauer sowie des Soloveckij-Klosters und -Museumsparks | ISBN 978-3-8382-1367-5

224 *Olga Bertelsen (Ed.)* | Russian Active Measures. Yesterday, Today, Tomorrow | With a foreword by Jan Goldman | ISBN 978-3-8382-1529-7

225 *David Mandel* | "Optimizing" Higher Education in Russia. University Teachers and their Union "Universitetskaya solidarnost'" | ISBN 978-3-8382-1519-8

226 *Mikhail Minakov, Gwendolyn Sasse, Daria Isachenko (Eds.)* | Post-Soviet Secessionism. Nation-Building and State-Failure after Communism | ISBN 978-3-8382-1538-9

227 *Jakob Hauter (Ed.)* | Civil War? Interstate War? Hybrid War? Dimensions and Interpretations of the Donbas Conflict in 2014–2020 | With a foreword by Andrew Wilson | ISBN 978-3-8382-1383-5

228 *Tima T. Moldogaziev, Gene A. Brewer, J. Edward Kellough (Eds.)* | Public Policy and Politics in Georgia. Lessons from Post-Soviet Transition | With a foreword by Dan Durning | ISBN 978-3-8382-1535-8

229 *Oxana Schmies (Ed.)* | NATO's Enlargement and Russia. A Strategic Challenge in the Past and Future | With a foreword by Vladimir Kara-Murza | ISBN 978-3-8382-1478-8

230 *Christopher Ford* | Ukapisme – Une Gauche perdue. Le marxisme anti-colonial dans la révolution ukrainienne 1917-1925 | Avec une préface de Vincent Présumey | ISBN 978-3-8382-0899-2

231 *Anna Kutkina* | Between Lenin and Bandera. Decommunization and Multivocality in Post-Euromaidan Ukraine | With a foreword by Juri Mykkänen | ISBN 978-3-8382-1506-8

232 *Lincoln E. Flake* | Defending the Faith. The Russian Orthodox Church and the Demise of Religious Pluralism | With a foreword by Peter Martland | ISBN 978-3-8382-1378-1

233 *Nikoloz Samkharadze* | Russia's Recognition of the Independence of Abkhazia and South Ossetia. Analysis of a Deviant Case in Moscow's Foreign Policy | With a foreword by Neil MacFarlane | ISBN 978-3-8382-1414-6

234 *Arve Hansen* | Urban Protest. A Spatial Perspective on Kyiv, Minsk, and Moscow | With a foreword by Julie Wilhelmsen | ISBN 978-3-8382-1495-5

235 *Julie Fedor, Eleonora Narvselius (Eds.)* | Diversity in the East-Central European Borderlands. Memories, Cityscapes, People | ISBN 978-3-8382-1523-5

236 *Regina Elsner* | The Russian Orthodox Church and Modernity. A Historical and Theological Investigation into Eastern Christianity between Unity and Plurality | ISBN 978-3-8382-1568-6

237 *Bo Petersson* | The Putin Predicament. Problems of Legitimacy and Succession in Russia | With a foreword by J. Paul Goode | ISBN 978-3-8382-1050-6

ibidem.eu